TECHNIQUES OF ECONOMIC FORECASTING

An Account of the Methods of
Short-term Economic Forecasting
used by the Governments of
Canada France *the* Netherlands
Sweden *the* United Kingdom
and the United States
with an introduction by
C W McMAHON

ORGANISATION FOR ECONOMIC
CO-OPERATION AND DEVELOPMENT
PARIS 1965

The Organisation for Economic Co-operation and Development was set up under a Convention signed in Paris on 14th December 1960 by the Member countries of the Organisation for European Economic Co-operation and by Canada and the United States. This Convention provides that the OECD shall promote policies designed:

- to achieve the highest sustainable economic growth and employment and a rising standard of living in Member countries, while maintaining financial stability, and thus to contribute to the development of the world economy;
- to contribute to sound economic expansion in Member as well as non-member countries in the process of economic development;
- to contribute to the expansion of world trade on a multilateral, non-discriminatory basis in accordance with international obligations.

The legal personality possessed by the Organisation for European Economic Co-operation continues in the OECD which came into being on 30th September 1961.

The members of OECD are Austria, Belgium, Canada, Denmark, France, the Federal Republic of Germany, Greece, Iceland, Ireland, Italy, Japan, Luxembourg, the Netherlands, Norway, Portugal, Spain, Sweden, Switzerland, Turkey, the United Kingdom and the United States.

CONTENTS

Foreword 7

I A GENERAL SURVEY OF THE PROCEDURES AND PROBLEMS OF OFFICIAL SHORT-TERM ECONOMIC FORECASTING *by C. W. McMahon* . 9
1 Introduction 9
2 Procedures for Official Forecasting 11
3 The General Method Used in Official Forecasting 14
4 Some Major Conceptual and Methodological Issues 23
5 How Useful Are the Forecasts? 28
6 Concluding Remarks 34

II CANADA: SHORT-TERM FORECASTING IN THE FEDERAL SERVICE ... 37
1 Introduction 37
2 The General Application and the Timing Pattern of Forecasts .. 41
3 Basic Factors Determining the Outlook in Canada 44
4 The Materials for Forecasting 46
5 Assembling and Checking the Forecast 58
6 Summary and Conclusions 61

III FRANCE: THE PREPARATION OF ECONOMIC BUDGETS 63
1 Introduction 63
2 The First Stage of Forecasts 63
3 The Second Stage of Forecasts 65
4 The Third Stage of Forecasts 66
5 Shorter-term Forecasts 67

IV THE NETHERLANDS: SHORT-TERM ECONOMIC PLANNING AND FORECASTING 69
1 Introduction 69
2 Characteristics of Short-term Planning in the Netherlands 70
3 Forecasting Techniques 73
4 Evaluation of Forecasts 76

V SWEDEN: SHORT-TERM FORECASTING 83
1 General Principles for Economic Forecasts 83
2 Production 88
3 Exports 92
4 Imports 99
5 Investment 103

	6	Household Incomes and Expenditures	114
	7	Public Consumption	119
	8	The Credit Market	121
VI		THE UNITED KINGDOM: SHORT-TERM ECONOMIC FORECASTING	127
	1	Forecasting Domestic Activity	127
	2	Forecasting the Balance of Payments	141
VII		THE UNITED STATES: SHORT-TERM FORECASTING BY THE PRESIDENT'S COUNCIL OF ECONOMIC ADVISERS	147
	1	Organization of Economic Forecasting	147
	2	The Strategy of the Forecast	149
	3	Methods of Forecasting the Main Expenditure Categories	153
	4	Conclusion	167
		BIBLIOGRAPHY	169
	1	Canada	169
	2	France	169
	3	The Netherlands	169
	4	Sweden	170
	5	The United Kingdom	171
	6	The United States	172

FOREWORD

Much of the success achieved in promoting economic progress in the post war period has been due to the way in which policies have been directed to the avoidance of sudden and erratic fluctuations in the level of economic activity. In formulating and implementing appropriate economic policies, a necessary first step is the careful and accurate assessment of a country's economic prospects. The preparation of short-term economic forecasts has, therefore, become an increasingly important aspect of economic policy, and there has been considerable development and improvement in the procedures and techniques used.

Since systematic forecasting is a relatively recent development and since the close connection between the assessment of prospects and the formulation of policies inevitably raises political issues at the time, little has been published about the procedures used in official economic forecasting. It is my conviction that the publication of this study, containing accounts of the methods used in six important countries—Canada, France, the Netherlands, Sweden, the United Kingdom and the United States—will prove to be a valuable and timely contribution to the understanding and development of this important task of government policy.

The study is a result of a discussion arranged by the OECD, at the request of some of the countries concerned, so that government economists might compare their respective methods and procedures of forecasting. Though primarily arranged for the benefit of the technical experts themselves, it is the belief both of the OECD and of the authorities concerned that this account has much wider public interest. The pursuit of sound policies by governments requires that there should be a body of informed opinion that understands the problems with which governments are faced. For this reason it is desirable that there should be fairly wide understanding both of the possibilities and the limitations of economic forecasting.

It is also desirable that, on a more technical plane, there should be a close interchange of ideas between economists in government service and those in universities and research institutes working on similar problems. Economic forecasting, and hence economic policy, should be based on a detailed knowledge of the working of the economy, which only much detailed research can provide. This interchange has been hindered by the paucity of publication, which this study may do something to remedy.

The accounts here published of the methods used in the different countries were discussed at a meeting of experts at the OECD. Mr. C. W. McMahon, then of Magdalen College, Oxford, and now at the Bank of England, was commissioned by the Secretariat to prepare a general survey, summarising the results of this discussion and comparing the techniques used in different countries. His survey which prefaces the present volume, is published on the responsibility of the Secretariat.

In the conclusion to this survey, Mr. McMahon states it as his view that, since the potential benefits in the way of better economic policies might be very large in relation to the cost, " it would seem no more than prudent for governments to invest more resources in the further development of forecasting "—in particular by the improvement of national statistics, by providing more facilities for official work on forecasting, and by encouraging and financing more academic research in this field.

There is also scope for more international collaboration in the field of economic forecasting; and this lies close to the OECD's general role in facilitating consultation on economic policies. The Member countries of the OECD include most of the major industrial countries outside the Sino-Soviet area; and developments within the OECD countries collectively go far to determine the course of trade in the world as a whole, and therefore go far to determine also the course of each country's exports. For most countries, however, fluctuations in exports have been an important element in fluctuations in total demand; and such fluctuations have proved especially difficult to predict. It may therefore be, as Mr. McMahon suggests, that a more systematic " pooling or confronting " of the forecasts of industrial countries would help each in making its own forecasts. The meetings of the various committees of the OECD provide many opportunities for the exchange of views between the official economists of Member countries; and it is our hope that, with the development of such exchanges, the Organisation can render a useful service to its Member governments in the formulation of their policies.

Thorkil KRISTENSEN,
Secretary General
Organisation for Economic Co-operation
and Development, Paris

CHAPTER I

A GENERAL SURVEY OF THE PROCEDURES AND PROBLEMS OF OFFICIAL SHORT-TERM ECONOMIC FORECASTING

by

C. W. McMahon

1 INTRODUCTION

Most governments now accept formal responsibility for the level of economic activity. This implies that they have to take a view about the appropriate pressure of demand, i.e. the relationship between aggregate demand and aggregate supply in the economy. It also implies that they have to take whatever measures they think necessary—fiscal or monetary measures, direct controls, or perhaps merely persuasion—to achieve this relationship. There has been much discussion in all countries about both the pressure of demand to be aimed at, and the best weapons to use to achieve it. These two questions are, however, only the second and third stages of stabilisation policy-making. There has been much less discussion of the first stage: assessing what will happen to aggregate demand and supply if nothing is done.

The necessity of making a short-term forecast and the difficulties in doing so, are indeed sometimes practically assumed away in debates on economic policy. Governments are taken to know what the situation they are confronted with is like, and are criticised either in political terms for being too deflationary or too inflationary, or in more technical terms for having used one policy weapon rather than another. In fact, a government is never dealing with a perfectly known past or present situation; it is dealing with the future. There are three time-lags, any one of which would ensure that this was so. First there is a lag between the event and the appearance of the statistics before the policy-makers in assimilable, processed form—so that the policy-maker never sees " today ", only " yesterday ". Secondly, there is a lag between receiving information and taking action on it; this is partly because there is a minimum time in which wise and deliberated decisions can be made, partly because there is often institutional inflexibility about decision-taking, e.g. an annual Budget. Thirdly, there is a lag between the implementation of a policy and its full direct and indirect effects on the economy.

In spite of these facts two arguments against the necessity or desirability of forecasting are sometimes advanced. Some people believe that making quantitative forecasts for the whole economy is inextricably linked with "planning" in some sense unacceptable to them. Others believe that the whole activity is so difficult, and that forecasts are so likely to be wildly wrong, that they are bound on average positively to mislead the policy-maker so that he would be better without them. These arguments are examined further below.[1] Here it is sufficient to say that most governments do in fact believe in the importance of making quantitative short-term forecasts of the economy as an integral step in stabilisation policy; and testify to this belief by devoting some of the scarce resources of official economists and statisticians to this task. Nevertheless there are two reasons why the activity is less discussed than other aspects of policy making: only some of the countries which make official forecasts publish them; and even fewer countries have published full accounts of the way they assess prospects and of their particular difficulties.

The accounts given in this book of how the governments of six major countries go about their short-term forecasting should, therefore, have considerable interest for those concerned with the possibilities and difficulties of stabilisation policy. At a more technical and academic level, they may have some bearing on the important and fascinating subject of the practical usefulness of economic theory. Professional economists will be able to see, for example, what view the official experts take of the consumption function; to what extent they are able to avoid having a theory of investment; and which analytic problems relatively little covered in the academic literature (such as the short-run relationship between output and unemployment) particularly occupy them.

The book is a result of an exchange of views among government economists meant primarily for their own mutual benefit. At the request of some Member countries of OECD, seven countries (Canada, France, Germany, the Netherlands, Sweden, the United Kingdom, the United States) were invited to submit accounts of their forecasting procedures. In September 1963 a meeting was held at OECD attended by experts from the seven countries. Subsequently all of these countries except Germany agreed that their accounts might be published, after some revisions and amplifications had been made in the light of the discussion; and it is these six countries which are discussed here. Their separate accounts do not record all that emerged in discussion; and one object of this introductory chapter is to bring out some of the points that were raised. This is deferred to Sections 4 and 5.

The plan of the remainder of this chapter is as follows. Section 2 is concerned with some general questions of forecasting procedure—where is the forecasting done? how often? etc.—on which the positions in the six countries are brought out and compared. Section 3 describes in a simplified way the basic method of forecasting followed in all the countries. Some individual differences are noted in passing here, but it is believed that as a matter of fact differences are not great enough to make one general account seriously misleading. Section 4, directed somewhat more specifically to the professional reader, is devoted to a discussion of a number of relatively controversial conceptual and methodological issues, some of which are

---

1. See page 28.

A general survey

not fully broached in the country papers but most of which were discussed at the meeting. Section 5 is concerned with the problems of testing and evaluating forecasts and with the directions in which they may best be improved. Here too the questions are not all fully set out in the country papers but were discussed. Section 6 gives briefly some of my own conclusions. In all the earlier sections I have attempted to do no more than report and interpret agreements and disagreements among the official experts.

2 PROCEDURES FOR OFFICIAL FORECASTING

Purposes of forecasts

In all cases the short-term forecasts are, as has been said already, made primarily for budgetary and monetary policy; but there are often subsidiary aims. In the Netherlands the forecasts play a role in the process of wage determination. In the United States, government agencies such as the Post Office make use of forecasts of developments in, say, personal income or particular kinds of expenditure and output, as a guide to their management and operating decisions. Similarly in the Netherlands a number of firms in the private sector make use of the macro-economic forecasts. In countries engaged in medium-term planning (such as France) one of the main purposes of a short-term forecast may be to provide information on the progress of the economy towards longer-term objectives.

The institutional frame-work

In all countries many individual departments and institutions contribute their specialised knowledge of particular areas to the forecast. But there is some divergence in the degree of centralisation of the forecasting process. It appears to be relatively highly centralised in France, the Netherlands and Sweden; rather less so in the United Kingdom, the United States and Canada. In France the work is carried out in SEEF (Service d'Etudes Economiques et Financières du Ministère des Finances); in the Netherlands by the Central Planning Bureau (which belongs formally to the Ministry of Economic Affairs) and in Sweden by the Economic Division of the Ministry of Finance and the National Institute of Economic Research (Konjunkturinstitutet). In the United Kingdom various departments co-operate in the preparation of the forecasts under the leadership of the Treasury. In the United States the forecast which is described in this book and which underlies the Budget is made by a small group representing three agencies: the Bureau of the Budget, the Treasury, and the Council of Economic Advisers. Other official forecasts are also made, however, in the Departments of Agriculture, Commerce, and Labor, and the Board of Governors of the Federal Reserve System, and those making the "three-agency" forecast draw on expert advice in these and other departments as well as outside the official machine altogether. In Canada responsibility for making the forecast is relatively widely diffused though closely co-ordinated; the economic branches of the Department of Trade and Commerce, the Department of Finance, the Department of Labour, and the Research Branch of the Bank of Canada

A general survey

all contribute to the forecasting process, with the Dominion Bureau of Statistics providing the statistical national accounts frame-work.

Timing of forecasts

There is a marked similarity in the timing and frequency of forecasts in all the six countries. In all cases, the most important forecasting exercises are geared to the Budget and the most common pattern is for there to be three of them for each year:
- *a)* A first forecast made three to six months before the Budget is presented;
- *b)* A second forecast made as a basis for (and in some cases published with) the Budget;
- *c)* A third forecast made three to six months after the Budget, and incorporating the effects of the Budget measures.

This pattern is precisely followed in France, the Netherlands[1], Sweden and the United Kingdom. The United States omit the first forecast; Canada omits the third. But in the case of Canada and the United States forecasting is a relatively continuous business: the United States three-agency group makes full forecasts every quarter, and the Canadians re-appraise the position continuously though not in such a formal way. Thus for these two countries the omission of one of the three main forecasts is more apparent than real.

Period forecast

The period of time which is forecast is not, of course, in any way necessarily connected with the frequency with which, or the particular times at which, forecasts are made. In respect of the period forecast, there is a sharp and important divergence among the countries represented. The forecasts made in Canada, France, the Netherlands and Sweden all refer to a full year—either a calendar or a Budget year. In these countries some assessment of current and expected developments in quarterly terms may be made from time to time during the year[2]. But these are distinctly subsidiary exercises and largely take the form of interpolations into the main year-to-year forecasts. On the other hand the United Kingdom and the United States forecasts are made entirely in quarterly terms. In the United States the number of quarters forecast varies from two to four, in the United Kingdom from four to six, depending on the time of year.

This difference between the United Kingdom and the United States on the one hand and the remaining countries on the other is more than technical. It is discussed in Section 4.

Assumptions of forecasts

In all countries at least one forecast a year is made on the assumption of unchanged policies. That is, a picture is drawn of what appears likely to

---
1. In the case of the Netherlands the first forecast is not published; the second incorporates the effects of the Budget proposals.
2. See, for example, the Dutch paper, page 75.

A general survey

happen if the government does nothing, so facilitating a decision on what, if anything, should be done. " Unchanged policies " is in principle ambiguous: it could mean the same levels, or the same rates of change, of government expenditures or government receipts; the same budget surplus or deficit; the same wage and salary rates for government employees or the same rate of increase as in the previous year; etc. In practice the meaning is that those policies which the government is able or willing to change in the interests of economic stabilisation are assumed unchanged. Easily the most important of these is the structure of tax rates. But if, for example, controls on consumer credit, building or imports were in existence at the time of the forecast, these too would be explicitly assumed to continue. Trends in government expenditure, however, are usually forecast from existing information just as other types of expenditure are forecast. Government credit policies are also usually assumed constant; but in the United States, where the three-agency group does not include the Board of Governors of the Federal Reserve System, whose actions are independent of the Administration, developments in monetary policy may be explicitly forecast.

The forecast made after the Budget will in all countries incorporate whatever measures have been taken and will, therefore, more closely represent an outcome expected and desired by the authorities. (This is less true in the United States than in the other countries, because the independence of the legislature from the executive in the United States means that the Budget proposals may not have been implemented; or at least that such action as has been taken may diverge more widely from the Administration's wishes than will normally be the case in other countries).

If this after-Budget or " second-stage " forecast is published it may take the form of, or be thought of, as a plan (e.g. in the Netherlands)—in a way that the pre-Budget or " first-stage " forecast could not be so considered.[1]

Publication of forecasts

The participating countries show the full possible range of attitudes to publication of their forecasts. Sweden publishes all three of her yearly forecasts; France and the Netherlands publish two forecasts a year; the United States regularly publishes one forecast in the Budget, with modified revenue estimates in the Mid-year Budget Review if one is published; Canada and the United Kingdom publish nothing.[2] Publication of a forecast raises some theoretical and practical issues which are discussed in Section 4.

---

1. See Section 4, page 25, for elaboration of this point.
2. Some quantitative forecasts were published annually, just before the Budget, by the United Kingdom Government in the *Economic Survey* from 1947 to 1951. From 1952 to 1962 the *Economic Survey* was primarily an account of the previous year with no more than a page or two on the prospects, written largely in qualitative terms. Since 1963 the *Economic Survey* has been replaced by the *Economic Report*, which provides simply an account of the previous year.

3 THE GENERAL METHOD USED IN OFFICIAL FORECASTING

One of the most striking points which emerged from the discussion was the degree of similarity among the methods of forecasting employed in the various countries. There are certainly differences, some of which are discussed in the next section but these do not seem to be great enough to render an account of a basic common method either impossible or seriously misleading.

All forecasters are attempting to estimate (on the basis of certain assumptions) the future relationship between total demand in the economy and the economy's capacity to meet demands made on it. In all cases some of the items to be forecast are regarded as given, or autonomous; others as functionally derived from known data for the economy or from the autonomous items. An example may make the distinction clearer to the non-professional reader. Fixed investment in a succeeding period might in principle be forecast by asking all businessmen what they intended to invest, adding up the answers, and accepting the total, say an increase of x per cent. This would be regarding investment as entirely autonomous from the forecaster's point of view. Of course, the businessmen would all have had reasons for their decisions: they would be making them on the basis of present and past trends in the economy. But the forecaster would not himself be trying to establish what these reasons were, how investment was in fact being determined. On the other hand, the forecaster might have established to his own satisfaction, from examining the data for previous years, that (to take a deliberately over-simple possibility) investment in any year was always precisely linked to the level of undistributed profits in the previous year. In this case he could forecast investment as a derived variable, needing only to know the previous year's profits.

All countries, then, regard some items as autonomous, some as functionally determined. Moreover, there is a substantial measure of agreement in practice as to which items are regarded in each way. When it comes to constructing a full forecast from the autonomous and the derived variables, there is a difference in approach which has often been emphasised in general comments on forecasting methods: some countries (notably the Netherlands) " solve " their forecast, i.e. find the equilibrium level of expected demand and supply, by solving a set of simultaneous equations; other countries (notably the United Kingdom) solve the forecast by a method of successive approximation. This difference in method though interesting and important, does not represent a fundamental difference in approach, as will be seen.

We may now proceed to describe the general method of forecasting common to all the participating countries.

We begin with the five main components of demand or expenditure—consumers' expenditure, public expenditure, private fixed investment, investment in stocks, and exports. Of these, public expenditure, private fixed investment, and exports are in practice regarded in most countries as at least largely autonomous from the forecaster's point of view; consumers' expenditure and investment in stocks are regarded as derived or " endogenous " variables.

A general survey

Public expenditure

The forecast of public expenditure (i.e. both current and capital expenditure on goods and services by all public authorities) is based on known plans and programmes. In practice a good deal of work is usually necessary: in translating programmes from budgetary to national income terms, in estimating the rate of realisation of programmes, in estimating the relationship between contract placements, cash payments and work done, and sometimes in translating current value figures into constant prices.

Exports

The forecast of exports is usually derived largely from forecasts of activity abroad (which is universally taken as autonomous or " exogenous " to the economy under consideration) together with plausible or established relationships between foreign activity and foreign demand for the country's goods. Export order positions and the views of industrialists, trade associations, commercial attachés abroad, etc. are also taken into account. There are two ways in which export forecasts may be partly determined " endogenously, " i.e. derived from the rest of the forecast for the economy. Allowance may be made for expected changes in domestic prices (relative to expected price movements abroad); and for the expected degree of over or under-utilisation of capacity in the economy. All countries are prepared to modify their export forecasts in the light of expected supply limitations or change in competitiveness. In most cases this is done qualitatively; in the case of the Netherlands it is done quantitatively. But in all cases, the exogenous element in the export forecast dominates.

Business fixed investment

All six countries except the United Kingdom make some use of functional relationships to derive an estimate of business fixed investment. Both financial variables—profits, company taxes and depreciation allowances, indicators of general liquidity—and non-financial variables—capacity utilisation[1], and movements of sales and output—are used. However, in practice most countries do not lay major stress on these relationships and it is only in the Netherlands' first two forecasts that business investment is forecast endogenously from these relationships. For the final Netherlands forecast information on investment intentions is available and is sometimes used to " disturb " the equations. In some countries estimates of cash flow and liquidities play an important part in " consistency checks " on the plausibility of their forecasts. With the exception of the Netherlands, countries are agreed in relying almost entirely on non-causal or " pre-flow " anticipations data for forecasting business fixed investment. Thus this item is, in practice, regarded as very largely autonomous. Many types of " pre-flow" data are drawn upon. Some countries, especially the United Kingdom and the United States, make use of series of orders for capital goods, building contractors' orders, work on architects' drawing boards, etc. But by far

---

1. The inadequacy of measures of capacity utilisation is discussed further on page 27.

the most important type of pre-flow data is investment intentions. All countries carry out surveys of the intentions of a sample of firms several times a year. These must usually be processed and adjusted in many ingenious and sophisticated ways (so that the longer the survey has been in existence the better results it can be made to give), but the final result is normally the most important piece of evidence in coming to a forecast of business fixed investment. The period of the economic forecast, however, frequently exceeds the horizon of the intentions surveys and " causal " relationships are necessary for longer run forecasts of business fixed investment.

Housebuilding

Countries vary a good deal in their approach to forecasting housebuilding, but in general it too is regarded as largely autonomous. With knowledge of the average length of time taken to build a house, fairly good forecasts for up to three quarters ahead may often be derived from information on the number of starts and, even better, where they apply, on the number of permits or licences granted. This evidence is usually supplemented by qualitative expectations of the effects of changes in interest rates and the financial position of building societies, etc. Some work has been done, especially in the United States, on trying to find a way of deriving housebuilding functionally from other data. Thus an aggregate demand-supply model might be built up, the demand for housing being estimated from trends in family formation rates and being compared with the growth in the stock of houses. So far such approaches do not appear to have been very successful, perhaps, as the United States paper suggests, because the concept of a national housing market is inappropriate: there is, rather, a host of small local markets, developments in which are difficult to assess.

Investment in stocks

All countries treat investment in stocks and consumers' expenditure as endogenous, i.e. as functionally determined by known or autonomous items. In attempting to forecast investment in stocks, use is generally made of the concept of some " normal " relationship between stocks and total sales towards which businesses constantly try to move; although some countries (e.g. the United Kingdom) take account of the phasing of stockbuilding in past cycles, in general little is known about what governs the speed at which stocks move towards the normal or equilibrium ratio and this hypothesis has therefore as yet been of only limited help in practice. All countries would try to take account of speculative influences in any particular situation (e.g. rapidly rising prices for a commodity or the expectation of a strike), but apart from the Netherlands none uses any systematic relationship with price changes. There is unanimous agreement that forecasting investment in stocks is the most difficult part of the whole operation. The rate of stockbuilding is everywhere highly volatile; changes in it may be very large in proportion to changes in other items in the short period; and it is common experience to have large errors—even to have the direction of change wrong—in forecasts of stockbuilding. Sweden's latest forecasts, however, include some equations for stockbuilding.

A general survey

Consumers' expenditure

Consumers' expenditure is in all countries treated as being primarily a function of personal disposable income. In none of them has the ratio between disposable income and consumption, or between changes in disposable income and changes in consumption proved stable; but all use modifications of some simple ratio with some success. Most countries find that in the short run consumption is relatively insensitive to changes in income either up or down, adjusting to them only with a lag; but in most countries the fluctuations in the marginal propensity to consume from quarter to quarter are only partly explained on the hypothesis of a lag. In France a rule of thumb which has been used is that in the face of a change in real income households attempt first to maintain the volume of their consumption and the value of their savings, dividing any balance (either plus or minus) in fixed proportions between consumption and savings. Many countries (in particular the United States) find it important to consider expenditure on consumer durables separately from the rest of consumption. Expenditure on non-durables and services tends to exhibit insensitivity to both rises and falls in income while expenditure on durables is highly sensitive to such changes.

A number of countries have tried in different ways to take account of factors other than disposable income which may influence consumption, in particular, consumers' asset/liability and liquidity positions. The Dutch equation for consumption contains, as explanatory variables, time and demand deposits as an index of liquidity as well as price changes and movements of consumption in the recent past. The United Kingdom attempts to take account of movements in outstanding consumer debt and bank loans and changes in controls over consumer credit. The United States also takes changes in liquidity and consumer credit terms into consideration but emphasises their fundamentally permissive nature which makes it, in United States experience, impossible to derive stable relationships between them and consumption.

If consumption is primarily dependent on personal disposable income, then before it can be added to the other elements of demand to give a forecast of total demand, it is necessary to have an estimate of disposable income. This in turn is regarded as largely dependent on total final demand. There are two ways of proceeding. Either a relationship between total expenditure and disposable income is forecast, and then the resulting equations are solved to give the values of both total demand and the two endogenous components; this is basically what the United States and (in a more complex way) the Netherlands do . Or, on the other hand, one can begin by taking what looks a plausible figure for consumption or personal income (having regard to the forecasts of the non-consumption items and past relationships between non-consumption and consumption) and then derive from the corresponding estimate of total demand a forecast for personal disposable income which will yield in turn a forecast of consumption. If this differs from the estimate first taken, this estimate will have to be altered and the process worked through again, and so on, until a self-consistent forecast is reached. This method of successive approximation is the method followed by Canada, Sweden and the United Kingdom. It is

A general survey

clear, however, that in either case it is necessary to have a view about the relationship between total final demand and disposable income.

Total output estimated by the " successive approximation " method

Consider first the successive approximation procedure, as this perhaps shows the reasoning behind the forecasting more easily. A plausible first approximation to the value of consumers' expenditure enables a total of final expenditure to be assumed. This must equal the value of home output produced together with the value of indirect taxes and imports. The value of indirect taxes for any particular total expenditure is fairly easy to determine with reasonable accuracy from a knowledge of the tax rates and some idea of the broad pattern of expenditure. Forecasting imports is more difficult. In general, the method is to assume that imports are determined by movements in total demand after a time-lag. Most countries have found that they can improve their estimates by disaggregating total imports and making separate forecasts for particular commodity groups by relating them to expected trends in particular variables: e.g. food imports may be related to personal incomes, raw materials imports to industrial production. Sweden, in particular, appears to have been quite successful with import equations of this kind. In general, countries seem reasonably satisfied with their ability to estimate imports—certainly more satisfied than they are about exports—though at times when there are big movements in stockbuilding or when domestic capacity comes under strain substantial errors can easily be made.

Once indirect taxes and imports have been forecast and subtracted from the forecast of total final expenditure we have an estimate of total output or gross national product (GNP). The next stage is to see what this implies for incomes, prices, employment and unemployment. For this it is necessary to estimate the growth in the capacity of the economy, i.e., in potential GNP. This can in principle be thought of as derived from forecasts of the employable labour force and the increase in labour productivity. Most countries can make use of well-established demographic trends for short-term forecasts of the labour force, combined with ad hoc adjustments, for e.g., a change in the school-leaving age, immigration or emigration, a move out of civil employment into the army (as in 1956 in France) or the reverse (as in 1963 in France).

Given a forecast of the employable labour force, a forecast of actual employment, and hence of unemployment, necessarily implies a forecast of productivity; in each country the latter is in effect regarded as having both a trend and a cyclical component. The trend increase in productivity is largely derived from extrapolation of past trends. Often[1] the aggregate estimate will be built up from a number of estimates for individual industries. Some attempt may be made to allow for the effects of investment in previous periods, but this is usually only where the effects of the investment on productive capacity are relatively easy to see and to measure (e.g. electricity generation). Again, both France and the United Kingdom have found that the change in output attributable to an autonomous change in the labour

---

1. See particularly the Swedish paper, pages 88 ff.

force (due to conscription or immigration, for example) may have to be estimated on the basis of a different productivity from the average of the economy. But in general such modifications of the trend are likely to be small.

The cyclical element in productivity is another matter. Countries find that when the pressure of demand changes, employment is relatively insensitive—or, as suggested in the United Kingdom paper, adjusts to the new level of demand only after a time-lag—largely perhaps because certain types of labour are " hoarded " by employers, or regarded as overhead. The resultant fluctuations in the ratio of output to employment (i.e. productivity) are often large in relation to the underlying trend and must be carefully forecast on the basis of a judgement about where the economy is in the business cycle and past performance.

In all countries, it is found that as demand rises in relation to supply, not merely does unemployment fall, but the average number of hours worked and the " participation rate " both normally increase. That is, there will be increased overtime working and a number of marginal workers —such as house-wives and retired people—will be drawn into employment. These trends must be estimated before any forecast of GNP can be translated into a forecast of unemployment. Several countries—in particular the United Kingdom and the United States—have formulated numerical relationships between changes in GNP and changes in unemployment.

Having forecast employment, the next step is to forecast the increase in average earnings. This is usually regarded as partly autonomous—the forecaster uses any knowledge he may have about pending wage negotiations, etc.—but partly endogenous: the increase in negotiated rates is likely to depend, at least to some extent, on the prevailing pressure of demand, and this may have a further influence on the degree to which actual earnings exceed negotiated rates. Combining employment and average earnings yields the total of wages, the largest component of personal income. The other components are forecast in a relatively routine way: salaries, rent and self-employed incomes may be estimated partly from extrapolation of past trends, partly by keeping them in some relationship with wages. Government transfers, except for unemployment benefits, are taken as autonomous. Dividend payments may be regarded as a function of profits and hence endogenous to the forecast. An income tax function can then be applied to the total of personal incomes to give disposable income.

When prices are changing rapidly it might be thought that a relationship between consumers' expenditure and disposable income adjusted for price changes would yield better results than a relationship based on nominal values. Only the United Kingdom, however, appears to make the deflation an integral part of their forecast process; the Netherlands and Sweden use a relationship in current prices while the United States and Canada, although making a forecast of consumers' prices, have not stressed this aspect of their forecasting in recent years. If prices are changing significantly, however, it would seem desirable to make explicit allowance for the effects on consumption.

Consumer prices will depend on a number of factors such as import prices, the supply and demand position in the food sector, and movements in unit labour costs. The United Kingdom has developed an interesting theory of price determination in which the important variable is not actual labour costs at any particular time, but *trend* labour costs, derived from the trend in hourly earnings and the trend increase in productivity.

Once consumer prices have been forecast, expected personal disposable income can be deflated to yield a forecast of real personal disposable income. From this may be derived, as has already been discussed, a forecast for consumption. If this derived estimate of consumption differs from the figure assumed at the beginning of the forecasting process[1], then the whole forecast is obviously inconsistent. A new value for consumption must be assumed and the procedure worked through again to yield a second derived estimate. If assumed and derived estimates still differ, a third estimate must be made, and so on until a value is found which provides a self-consistent forecast.

Though it seems convenient to treat the forecast of potential economic capacity as a separate element in the forecast, it could be argued that this is already implicit in the forecasts of employment, unemployment and productivity[2]. Thus, an increase in demand greater than the " trend " increase in productivity implies an increase in the pressure of demand, and of " cyclical " productivity, and a decline in unemployment; and vice versa. In practice therefore, the effect of changes in the pressure of demand on the forecasts of demand have to be allowed for. Two other possible interactions between demand and supply should be mentioned. According as the forecast implies a particularly high or low pressure of demand, the " successive approximation " countries may shade their original forecasts of wage increases up or down. The short term effect of an increase in demand may be considerable and therefore in the case of a forecast over the very short period (e.g. a quarter) any change in wages might call for a revision of the demand forecast. In a longer term forecast, however, a change in wages is likely to have much less effect on the overall demand forecast since the forecast of prices would also have to be altered. The theories of price determination held by the official forecasters mean that the combined effect of changing wage and price forecasts on expected real personal disposable income and hence on expected real consumption will be small. Again, a particularly high or low pressure of demand is likely to affect the relationship between home supplies and imports and may also affect exports. (Or to put this another way, a forecast " gap " may be reflected in the balance of payments as well as in the level of unemployment). Thus in some circumstances, forecasters may have to recast their estimate of total demand slightly as a result of taking a higher or lower value for exports. Unless exports are very large in relation to national product, however, such adjustment will tend to be small.

Total output estimated by other methods

It may finally be helpful to compare the " successive approximation " method, which has just been described, with the methods of the United States and the Netherlands. This comparison may help to illuminate the

---

1. See page 17.
2. See pages 18 and 19.

successive approximation method, revealing a basically simple rationale beneath its seeming complexity.

In discussing the relationship of disposable personal income to GNP, the United States paper emphasizes the estimation of gross corporate saving and net government receipts—items to be subtracted from GNP to get disposable personal income—rather than the summation of components of personal income. Practice in this regard is subject to change from time to time, depending on the development of improved relationships and the preferences of the particular individuals preparing the forecast. Whether disposable personal income is derived by building up or subtracting off, the procedure involves the development of a functional relationship between GNP and disposable personal income.

By developing an explicit relationship between personal disposable income and GNP as well as an explicit relationship between consumption and disposable income, the United States forecasters are able to derive a simultaneous forecast of consumption expenditure and personal disposable income from the forecast of total nonconsumption. Using these relationships, they are in a position to solve a simple system of simultaneous equations of the following form:

$$Y = N + C$$
$$C = f(Y_d)$$
$$Y_d = g(Y)$$

where Y = gross national product; N = Nonconsumption expenditure, net of imports; C = Consumption expenditure; and Y_d = personal disposable income. To take a simple imaginary example, suppose N were forecast to be 400, while C is believed to be four-fifths of Y_d and Y_d is predicted as three-fourths of Y, then,

$$Y = 400 + 0.8 Y_d = 400 + 0.8 (0.75 Y)$$
$$= 400 + 0.6 Y$$
$$\therefore Y = 1000$$
$$Y_d = 750$$
$$C = 600$$

The development of an explicit relationship between GNP and disposable personal income permits this simultaneous calculation. It provides a first approximation to GNP, consumption, and disposable income, which is subsequently modified and adjusted by "successive approximation," taking account of the detailed components of personal income.

How does this compare with the methods of the "successive approximation" countries? The latter usually do not attempt to forecast profits directly, but in common with the United States they do in fact believe in and use a determinate relationship between non-consumption expenditure and personal disposable income. Briefly, their underlying assumptions are: any change in total expenditure at constant prices generates changes in imports, indirect taxes and domestic output; any change in domestic output will be associated with a change in labour income made up of a change in the number of man-hours worked and a change in earnings per hour; to the change in labour income must be added changes in transfer incomes both from the government and from companies (as dividends and interest) to yield the change in personal income; deduction of taxes yields the change in personal disposable income in money terms; and this may be deflated by the expected change in prices to yield the change in real personal disposable income. But changes in man-hours worked and hourly earnings in combination with changes in productivity (all of which are forecast) imply the change in unit labour costs; and this together with the forecast change in the price of final output, implies a forecast change in profits. The " successive approximators " do, therefore, implicitly forecast the distribution of the national product between profits and labour, just as the United States do explicitly. Moreover, in all the countries the forecasters believe that the distribution of income shows marked cyclical fluctuations which it is important to assess.

The reason why despite this underlying similarity of assumptions about the working of their economies a number of the countries do not use a single " portmanteau " relationship between non-consumption expenditure and personal disposable income and so " solve " the forecast in one step is not of course because of any inherent clumsiness of approach or unwillingness to use simple algebra. It is rather that because there are so many intermediate relationships linking non-consumption and personal disposable income, because many of these relationships are difficult to predict and tend to vary greatly over the business cycle, and because so much of the data is inadequate, inaccurate and conflicting, the " successive approximators " prefer to spell the process out, scrutinising each step for plausibility, " tinkering " with the individual relationships whenever they believe that the particular circumstances warrant it.

This completes the account of the underlying approach to forecasting both aggregate demand and aggregate supply in Canada, France, Sweden, the United Kingdom and the United States. There remains the Netherlands. It has already been emphasised that in the Netherlands as in the other countries some elements of both supply and demand are treated as autonomous and some as functionally determined; moreover, there is a good deal of uniformity as to which elements are treated in which way. What distinguishes the Netherlands method is that all the functional relationships are specified precisely in the form of equations. All the links between non-consumption expenditure and consumption which have been discussed above are given precise quantitative form by the Dutch, as are the interactions between demand and supply. As a result, once the values of the autonomous variables have been decided on, the whole forecast can in principle be mathematically solved in one operation. In comparing the Dutch methods with those of other countries, two points should be borne in mind. Firstly the beliefs about the way the different elements in the economy interact on each other are broadly similar in all the countries. While the Dutch equations sometimes contain variables to which the other countries do not appear to give much emphasis, it will often be found that these have very small weight in the equations. Secondly it also seems probable that when the limitations in the accuracy of the data are taken into account it is often the case that the Dutch equations are little more sensitive to the complex interactions which they alone take formal account of than the more crudely and qualitatively expressed relationships used by the other countries. The relative advantages and disadvantages of the econometric method compared with the more eclectic method of the other countries are discussed below[1].

4 SOME MAJOR CONCEPTUAL AND METHODOLOGICAL ISSUES

Period forecast

As stated earlier, the United Kingdom and the United States forecasts are made in terms of projected developments quarter by quarter over the following six to eighteen months. The forecasts of the other participating countries, however, are made for a full year—either a calendar or a budget year—so that they yield simply year-to-year comparisons. This difference is not merely technical; it represents an important difference in approach. The main arguments on both sides, advanced in the country papers and more fully in the discussion, are as follows:

— In favour of quarterly forecasting:

a) it enables one to see the path the economy is expected to take, and the point it is expected to reach, on certain assumptions. By contrast, a comparison of the estimates for one full year with those of another may conceal more than it reveals. Not merely may there be a change of direction within the coming year, which will not show up; the change may have already taken place and the forecast indicate the opposite. If for example the GNP rises steadily from 100 at the beginning of year 1 to 106 at the end of the year and then declines steadily to 104 at the end of year 2, a correct forecast of the GNP for year 2 would show it as 2 per cent *higher* than in year 1. Such a forecast would give no idea of the movement from the time when the forecast is to be presumed to have been made, i.e. a decline through year 2; and without careful and explicit interpretation in terms of the level already reached at the end of year 1, it would be positively misleading. The forecasters might well have some idea of what was going to happen *during* year 2 but they would not be giving a quantified description of the most significant aspect of their forecast.

b) The effects of any measure taken will be distributed over time. To make a sensible decision about a particular measure it is necessary to be able to assess its effects on the path taken by the economy. It is not meaningful to speak of the effects of a given measure in, say, a calendar year except by adding together the estimated effects in each particular quarter—and to do this properly one needs estimates of what would happen in the absence of the measure in each particular quarter.

c) The quarter is a more meaningful or logical unit of time for the economy than a year. Most of the important time-lags in economic decision-making are (except in the case of very big investment

---

1. See page 26.

projects) shorter than a year. For seeing and understanding what happens in an economy a breakdown into quarters is the most helpful approach.

Those who do not make quarterly forecasts generally accept the force of these arguments. They would all be prepared to agree that in an ideal world forecasting by quarters would be better than forecasting by full years. However, in the world as it is, they argue:

a) Their data are not good enough to give quarterly figures any meaning. Both France and the Netherlands, for example, are prepared for certain purposes to split their annual forecast into four quarters in a more or less arbitrary way (interpolation); they do not think that in making quarterly forecasts they could or would be doing anything very different from this. Obviously, it is relevant whether one has quarterly figures for the past, which is the case for only half of the countries concerned, Canada, the United Kingdom, and the United States. However, although Canada's quarterly series is well established, she does not make quarterly forecasts, while the United Kingdom made quarterly forecasts before she had quarterly data for the past.

b) Some countries (France in particular) envisage bigger returns in terms of improved forecasts from devoting the scarce resources of their forecasting staff to developing new statistical series or tools—e.g. input-output tables—or to improving their econometric equations than from putting their forecasting in a quarterly framework. On the other hand the Netherlands is at present engaged in developing a quarterly econometric model.

Publication of forecasts

As stated earlier, Canada and the United Kingdom publish no forecasts, while most of the other countries publish most of the forecasts they make. The main arguments advanced against publication are:

a) A government may not wish to expose itself to the risk of embarrassment if its forecast proves seriously wrong.

b) Difficulties may be caused by the " announcement " effect, i.e., the publication of a government expectation of a certain change may thereby influence that very change. If the government forecasts a large deficit in the balance of payments or a large increase in wage rates or a large fall in private investment, private decision makers may be influenced to act in ways which will exacerbate these developments.

Those countries which publish fully urge against these arguments that:

a) Publication facilitates informed discussion of policy making and contributes to raising the general level of thinking about the economy by putting the issues in quantitative terms and making it easier to see where there is agreement and where disagreement.

b) The dangers of embarrassment to the authorities can easily be overestimated. The growth in the sophistication of the interested public, which publication fosters, lessens the degree to which a government will be attacked for having made a mistake in its forecast. Moreover, it becomes easier to distinguish between policies which proved inappropriate because they were based on a bad forecast and those which turned out not to have the effect required.

c) Most of the difficulties about embarrassment and announcement effects apply only to " second stage " forecasts (i.e. those which incorporate government policies[1]). They do not apply (or apply much less strongly) to a set of forecasts produced on the assumption of *unchanged* policies, as a basis for discussion and understanding of what the government proposes to do.

The use of non-national-income-accounts material

Because their purpose is to facilitate the management of the economy all forecasts considered in this exercise are couched in quantitative terms in a national accounts framework. However, the forecaster can draw upon various kinds of qualitative data, and several frameworks other than that of the national accounts for analysing quantitative data. How much help are these?

First, there is the whole apparatus of questionnaires and surveys of intentions and expectations. Even when these are couched in quantitative terms they may be used by the forecaster in indirect rather than direct ways. Thus in the United States some industries are asked to state, in addition to their quantitative investment intentions (which as we have seen are very important in all countries for the official forecast of investment), their sales expectations for the same period, also expressed in quantitative terms. In the words of the United States paper: " The sales expectations themselves do not have predictive value, but they are useful in adjusting the investment anticipations. For manufacturing industry since 1948, the errors in the sales forecast explain most of the revision in the annual investment plans; for each one percent excess of actual over expected sales, investment has exceeded anticipations, on the average by 1.1 per cent. The forecaster can replace the manufacturers' sales forecast by his own and then revise the investment anticipation. "[2] Canada uses her unique survey of employment expectations in a similar fashion as a check on independently derived employment forecasts.

When the surveys and questionnaires are purely qualitative, involving questions such as whether things are, or are expected to be, better or worse, higher or lower, than at a previous time, they can naturally only be used indirectly in a national accounts forecast. There is some disagreement between countries about the use which can be made of this kind of material. In their favour it is argued that the answers can be very quickly processed so that any picture which does emerge is likely to be more up-to-date than most other forms of data. Further, the fact that they are couched in qualitative terms means that they may often be answered by very senior people in industry—those who will actually be making decisions— while detailed quantitative questions may often have to be answered at a

---

1. See page 13.
2. See page 155.

lower level in the firm. It is also possible to ask conditional, hypothetical questions in such surveys, the answers to which might provide important clues to how business reacts to policy changes; against this, however, one must always be uncertain what weight to attach to the answer to a purely hypothetical question. Of the six countries, France appears to pin the greatest faith on the ultimate potentiality of qualitative surveys. Most of the other countries are sceptical of their use in improving a national accounts forecast; but they would add that most of the surveys are still very new. It may be too soon to judge their ultimate uses.

Another example of a possible non-quantitative tool for forecasters is the so-called business cycle leading indicators. These are statistical series which have historically shown a tendency to " turn " some months ahead of the business cycle. Sometimes several may be combined together to yield a " diffusion index." The movement of such an index is some kind of average of the movements of the component indicators. Canada is the only participating country whose official forecasters use these devices. They use them as part of a wide general apparatus of business cycle analysis and have found this helpful. Canada, of course, has been in a special position in that she has been subject to strong exogenous cyclical influences from the United States economy.

Some countries make use of quantitative estimates of the economy made in a framework other than that of the national income accounts. The two main examples are flow-of-funds and input-output estimates. No one has established a fully satisfactory flow-of-funds set of accounts with useful predictive power of its own. But a number of countries use a more or less sophisticated framework of financial flows as a check on the plausibility and consistency of their basic national income forecast. France makes a good deal of use of an input-output matrix and is devoting considerable effort to improving it. No other countries make use of this kind of analysis at an aggregate level for short-term forecasting. Many feel that their data are not good enough to construct a good table; and that they could not rely enough on the stability of the coefficients to use a table relating to a period some years previously. Sweden, the Netherlands and the United Kingdom make some use of the general technique, however, for making forecasts for individual strategic industries (e.g. construction).

Econometrics and eclecticism

There has been much argument over whether forecasting is better done econometrically or eclectically. On behalf of econometrics it is urged that any rational forecast of a variable must be based on at least qualitative and implicit functional relationships; but that so long as the relationships remain qualitative and implicit there is no way of testing and improving them; only if assumptions about the causal chains in the economy are set out quantitatively will it be possible to see the full implications of these beliefs and to test them against reality. On behalf of an eclectic approach it is urged that there will constantly be special factors in a situation of which the forecaster will want to take account, which he will be unable to do without making arbitrary changes in his equations; that quantification is always liable to lead one to underweight factors that cannot be satisfactorily quantified, and to seduce one away from a close study of the always limited and unsatisfactory data towards the intellectual pleasures of model-building.

In discussions on these matters the Dutch are normally pointed to as representing the econometric approach while most of the other countries are castigated or congratulated for their eclecticism.

In fact, the distinction between the different countries' methods is less sharp than it appears. All the participating countries except the United Kingdom use an econometric model; but except for the Netherlands it is used primarily as a consistency check, rather than as the primary method of making the forecast itself.[1] Moreover, as has already been emphasised and as will appear from a study of the country papers themselves, all countries think and work in terms of exogenous variables and endogenous or functionally related variables; all use equations for at least some parts of their forecast. On the other hand, the Netherlands forecasters who rely most on econometric methods, attempt to allow for information which is not contained in the equations of the model, and are in practice prepared to "disturb" their equations to take account of particular factors or to replace them by non-causal estimates (e.g. forecasts of investment from intentions surveys). It should be added, however, that in practice, the Netherlands forecasters rarely take account of special influences not incorporated in the model, since such influences seldom seem sufficiently important; in fact the earlier forecasts which are most important from the point of view of economic policy rely chiefly on the econometric model.

It is clear then there remains a substantial difference between the approach of the Netherlands and that of, say, the United Kingdom. Nevertheless, the difference is not so great as may appear at first sight; the contrast often drawn between a precise, rigorous, scientific, but inflexible and mechanical approach, ascribed to the Netherlands, and an imprecise, subjective, amateur but flexible and judgmental approach, ascribed to the United Kingdom, is misleading and false. Reference to the Netherlands' paper[2], will confirm this.

The concept of capacity

There was a good deal of discussion at the meeting about the concept and measurement of capacity and capacity utilisation—both of the economy and at the level of the firm—and about its usefulness in explaining or predicting investment, productivity and unemployment. It seems worth saying something about this here.

The value of the stock of capital plays important roles in economic theory. In combination with a capital/output ratio, it determines the productivity and productive capacity of the economy. Similarly, in a number of "acceleration" theories of investment, the stock of capital together with a concept of a desired degree of utilisation and with changes in demand is treated as partly determinant of the rate of new investment. In view of this it is perhaps striking that the concepts of the capital stock or of physical capacity are seldom used.

---

1. See the comments in the United States paper on the use of a model to fortify the forecaster's courage, page 150.
2. See especially pages 75 and 76.

It has always been recognised that the measurement of the capital stock poses difficult practical and theoretical problems; these difficulties are partly responsible for the fact that the concept is not used. Only the United States has any measures of capacity utilisation, although this in itself has not proved very useful for predicting investments. It does, however, constitute additional information for assessing the intentions surveys. The other countries are not actively interested in developing such measures, on the grounds that they would not be likely to yield returns, in terms of improved investment forecasts, commensurate with the effort involved in compiling them. As has been emphasised, most rely heavily on intentions surveys and would prefer to devote statistical resources to improving these.

It will be clear, however, that in view of its vital role in the forecasts, the difficulty of measuring and of forecasting the growth of potential GNP (or what has previously been called the underlying non-cyclical increase in productivity) remains serious. A number of countries have emphasized that the unemployment of labour provides the best means of measuring the extent of the spare capacity in the economy and hence of gauging potential GNP. This may be either because labour is the limiting factor or because labour capacity and physical capacity are kept closely in step by investment. Nevertheless, since the estimates of potential GNP in past years remain shaky, little has been done to explore the reasons for changes in the rate of growth of economic capacity. In forecasting the growth of capacity most countries, therefore, rely on some kind of extrapolation, which is clearly satisfactory only so long as changes in trends do not occur.

5 HOW USEFUL ARE THE FORECASTS?

The nature of the exercise was such that little space is given in the papers to defending the practice of making any forecasts at all. However, some things on this subject were said in the discussion, and it seems appropriate that this introductory chapter should comment on the case that can be and has been made against all forecasting. Except where particular differences of view are explicitly referred to, the following can probably be taken as representing broadly the view of all six countries.

As was mentioned at the outset, there are two kinds of basic objection to forecasting: first, that because it is so difficult, the inevitable errors are likely to be so large that forecasts will tend to mislead rather than help; and secondly, that forecasting is bound up with " planning "—i.e. either that it is not necessary unless the authorities believe in planning, or that to engage in forecasting is in some way bound to involve the authorities in planning the economy. These two objections will be considered in turn.

There is no doubt that it is difficult to forecast accurately. In all the countries one could point to forecasts which proved to be badly wrong. A simple comparison of forecast with outcome is by no means a fully satisfactory test of a forecast's adequacy[1]. But even on the more pragmatic test of " did the forecast help the policy maker? " it would be easy to find examples of forecasts which have positively misled policy. However, the

---

1. See pages 31 and 32.

important question is not whether forecasts are always right, or even whether they are right more often than they are wrong, but whether there is a better alternative to framing economic policy on the basis of quantitative national income forecasts.

One might argue that an economy is inherently stable and self-righting, so that the best policy is to do nothing: fluctuations will iron themselves out and attempting to hasten or augment the self-correcting process involves the risk (through mistakes in the forecasts or in estimating the time-lags involved) of making the situation worse, aggravating the fluctuations instead of ironing them out. This argument has some force as a caution against too great a reliance on forecasts, excessive concentration on stability in the very short-term and excessive use of policy measures in the attempt to achieve this. But in its extreme form, i.e. that economies are inherently so stable that it is wiser not to try to manage them at all, the argument is unconvincing. The weight of historical and comparative evidence suggests that, on the whole, entirely " unmanaged " economies have done less well than those where governments have assumed the responsibility of managing them, though of course it is possible to find exceptions to this rule in particular countries at particular times.

There is a further point that where government expenditure comprises a significant proportion of total expenditure and government receipts a significant proportion of total incomes, as is the case in any modern state, it is very difficult for a government to have no policies towards the economy. Whatever decisions a government takes about its expenditures and receipts will react on the rest of the economy, and it would be implausible to suggest that the self-correcting powers of the economy will be unaffected whatever the government does.

This leads to the consideration of a second argument against the wisdom of stabilisation policy based on forecasting. It is sometimes urged that while a modern government cannot, strictly speaking, have *no* policies towards the economy, it will be best advised to frame all its stabilisation policy in an automatic, mechanical, rule of thumb way, taking no specific decisions in the light of the position and prospects of the economy at any particular time. To some extent all countries follow this practice: unemployment benefits and a progressive tax system are both examples of automatic stabilisers. On the other hand, a traditional rule of thumb for policy—balancing the budget at all times—is now generally agreed to be more likely to destabilise than to stabilise the economy. Some economists argue that a standard automatic increase in the volume of money each year would be sufficient to keep an economy on a stable growth path. Discussion of such theories is outside the scope of this book. It may simply be said here that a substantial majority of professional economists would disagree with the view that stabilisation policy can be entirely automatic: certainly none of the official forecasters concerned in this exercise would accept it.

Even if it were agreed that governments must take specific measures from time to time in the interests of stabilising the economy, it might be argued that this could best be done without taking any view about the future, or at least by reducing the predictive element in policy to a minimum. On this view governments would wait until the situation clearly demanded action before taking any, and then take relatively small steps, observing the effects of each and stopping when enough had been done. The answer to this is that because of the three time-lags mentioned at the beginning of this chapter,—the informational lag, the decision-making lag and the policy-effect lag—a government is necessarily dealing with the " future " in taking any measures; i.e., it is dealing with developments after the period to which the latest information it possesses relates. The practical consequence of this is that attempting to operate only on the current situation is likely to involve very big zig-zags for the economy; and for many economies the freedom of manoeuvre is so small that such a procedure would be impossible: if one waited until the situation demonstrably already needed corrective action one would often be forced to take very drastic action to put it right— action necessary for the short-term but against the long-term interest.

There remains the argument that though it is necessary to have a view about the future in framing economic policies, nevertheless quantitative national income forecasts are not the best way to reach such a view. What are the possible alternatives? There would seem to be two, in principle: extrapolation, or assuming that things will go on as they have been doing; and " intuitive " judgments on how things will develop. Extrapolation of present trends sounds fairly simple, and might in fact be so if we were only concerned with a single magnitude (though even here when there are seasonal, cyclical, and trend elements superimposed on one another, there will be many possible simple extrapolations depending on the particular past period chosen to establish the movement which is to be extrapolated). When there are a great many items moving in quite different ways and with many interrelationships, to project existing trends becomes a complicated operation. It begins indeed to approximate to short-term forecasting as understood in this study. Much of what the official forecasters in the six countries do is, in fact, elaborate and sophisticated extrapolation, with allowances made for any particular changes in trend which there is reason to expect.

Finally, there is the " intuitive " approach based on " feel " of the situation. Certainly, forecasting is so inexact a business that judgment must play a very important part in it. Some people will be found to have a better " feel " of the economic situation than others in the same position. But any such qualitative judgments must depend on facts or intentions, just as quantitative forecasts do; what distinguishes good judgment from bad is the weight given to different pieces of evidence, not the privileged access to some special kind of evidence. A preference for qualitative judgments over quantitative forecasts, as such, is misplaced. If a judgment is rational it must benefit by taking into account all the numerical magnitudes used in a quantitative forecast and the best views that can be reached on all the relationships that hold good in the economy. However, to the extent that a judgment is not expressed quantitatively, it will be harder to be sure exactly what is being taken into account and whether all the implications have been fully assessed; and it will be much more difficult for fruitful discussion and argument between different individuals concerned in the policy-making process to take place.

A real argument against quantitative forecasts is that they have a spurious air of precision: there is always a danger that they will mislead by appearing to give certainty where even probability is hard to achieve. There is much force in this point; and everyone concerned with forecasts—

makers, users, outside observers—needs to be constantly on guard against slipping into an acceptance of sets of figures at more than their true value. Once this is admitted, however, it might fairly be claimed that certainly all the working forecasters, and in most cases the official policy-makers, are aware of the dangers. It is the outside observers—and in particular the most sceptical commentators—who most frequently tend to attach exaggerated importance to the precise numerical magnitudes in any forecast, and, as a result, tend to criticise the forecasts with inappropriate severity when the actual outcome diverges markedly from them.

The upshot of the foregoing arguments would appear to be that however imperfect our ability to predict, some kind of forecasting is necessary in framing economic policies; and that this is better done systematically and quantitatively than by hunch. There is a danger that the spurious air of accuracy may mislead but it would be defeatist to abdicate making quantitative forecasts for this reason. There may be some need to educate those unfamiliar with the methods, possibilities, and limitations of forecasting—which this present study may help to meet—but it will always be necessary for anyone concerned with forecasts to be consciously on his guard.

We may now turn briefly to the other kind of objection sometimes raised to forecasting, namely, that it is inextricably connected with " planning " in some pejorative sense. This is a misapprehension, fostered perhaps partly by the undoubted, but not necessarily relevant, fact that the more a government wishes to engage in detailed planning the greater will its need for detailed forecasts be.

A distinction was drawn earlier between first and second stage forecasts: those based on unchanged policies and those incorporating any changes in policy deemed appropriate by the authorities. Clearly a first stage forecast has no necessary connection of any kind with planning; and to make a second stage forecast implies no more than that the government has certain general objectives and is prepared to influence aggregate demand and supply to attain them. This applies to every modern government—those which believe in various forms of " planning " and those which do not. Nor is there any observable correlation between the degree of detail of forecast and the " interventionism " of the government making it. The United States has perhaps the most elaborate and fully developed forecasting-procedure but could not be said to engage in " planning " in any meaningful sense of the term.

Improving the forecasts

Much has been said on the limitations and inaccuracy of forecasting as it is done at present. How may it be improved? The problem may be divided into two: improving the understanding of how an economy works—getting better relationships or equations; and getting better data.

In improving the functional relationships or hypotheses about the way the economy works, the most obvious procedure is the normal scientific one of testing the hypotheses for their predictive value. Carrying out postmortems on past forecasts would seem a basic step in obtaining better ones. All the countries do attempt to carry out some kinds of post-mortems but there is general agreement on the extreme difficulty of extracting helpful information from them. Since some of the difficulties may not be immediately obvious to those not concerned in the operation it seems worth briefly listing those stressed by the forecasters themselves.

First there is the obvious point that the purpose of official forecasts is not to predict the future but to guide policy. Thus if a forecast made on the assumption of unchanged policies shows, for example, the development of a serious deficit in the balance of payments, and as a result certain measures are taken to improve the balance of payments, then the actual outcome will, of course, differ completely from the picture shown by the forecast. In such a case, the falsification of the forecast provides its entire raison d'être: it is successful; but testing the quantitative accuracy of any of its component parts is likely to be extremely difficult.

Secondly, suppose the first difficulty does not exist. The forecast on the basis of unchanged policies shows a reasonably satisfactory position and, as a result, policies are not changed; but an imbalance between supply and demand in fact appears. In this case, we can certainly judge the forecast to have been a bad one on the crucial test that it led to bad policies. But even now there will be many problems in making a meaningful test of its predictive accuracy. Does one measure the accuracy of each individual item in relation to absolute magnitudes or to percentage changes? How does one weight accuracy in one item against inaccuracy in another? A forecast can be wrong for the "right" reasons or right for the "wrong" reasons, i.e. there may be compensating errors; the exogenous variables may be correctly estimated while wrong functional relationships are assumed; or the functional relationships may be right and the exogenous variables wrong.

The inaccuracy of the data and their subsequent revision provide further difficulties in practice. If, as is usually the case, when the time comes to carry out a post-mortem, many of the statistics that the forecasters were using have been revised, it may be difficult to know how the forecast would have differed if the revised data had been available when it was made. Moreover, the revising process never ends. Post-mortems done a year or five years later might show that the forecast was better or worse than was first thought.

Finally, there is the question of what one is testing a forecast against. What is the appropriate alternative procedure compared with which one wants to find whether the actual forecast is better or worse? A common approach is to compare the forecast with a so-called "naïve model"—i.e. some kind of extrapolation of recent trends. But, as has already been suggested[1], there is room for argument about the form this should take. "A simple extrapolation of current trends" is an ambiguous concept, and according to the particular "naïve" model chosen, the actual forecast may look good or bad.

None of the foregoing should be taken to suggest that it is impossible to test forecasts scientifically against reality. With much care and statistical expertise, most of the difficulties can be partly or wholly surmounted. One of the major advantages of a fully econometric model is that testing it is easier than is the case with the more eclectic approaches. The points to be

---

1. See page 30.

emphasised are simply, first, the inappropriateness of any simple "Were you right or wrong?" approach; and secondly, the limitations still placed on the development of an understanding of how any economy works by the inadequacies of the data.

At many points all the papers refer to inadequacies of the statistics. There are a number of references to improvements in the forecasts that have been made possible as a result of improvements in the statistics: see, for example, the great stress that Canada lays on the development of seasonal adjustments and quarterly data.[1] Much of the argument about the possibility of forecasting by quarters, the use of a more econometric approach or input-output data and the difficulty of forecasting stock movements, turns largely on the strength or weakness of the statistical material.

Most forecasters would probably agree that the most difficult and important part of their job is not estimating by means of established relationships what is going to happen "tomorrow" but really understanding where the economy is and what is happening in it "today". This is not a matter simply of the amount of detail available on the economy, or even of its up-to-dateness. It is a matter of how good the figures actually are—what meaning can be given to them, how likely they are to be revised, how they may best be reconciled when (as continually happens) they yield conflicting implications and so on. Thus the most important source of further improvements in all the countries concerned is probably the improvement and development of statistics. The importance of the range, frequency, speed of production, liability to revision and accuracy of the statistics available to a forecaster is obvious and may seem to need no labouring. But the over-riding nature of the limitations imposed by the data is often underestimated by both administrators and politicians on the one hand and academic economists on the other.

There is some measure of agreement over which items are relatively easy to forecast adequately and which relatively difficult. Most countries appear to be reasonably satisfied with their ability to handle increases in wage rates and prices, the trend rate of productivity growth and, somewhat less confidently, public expenditure and imports. Private fixed investment still presents difficulties but in most cases intentions surveys are being steadily improved and yielding steadily improving results. Consumers' expenditure presents a special case. Most countries appear to feel relatively happy about their ability to explain and predict its movement in broad terms; but it is such a large item that a proportionate error which would be unimportant in estimating many other items can have serious consequences.

Performance is probably worst in all countries in estimating movements in stock-building and in exports. Stock-building presents difficulties both of data (the statistics are everywhere among the weakest) and of relationship: though it seems clear that stock movements probably must ultimately be explained in terms of stock/sales ratios, the precise way to use such ratios is as yet not found. Movements in stockbuilding are so erratic and volatile that one might be pessimistic about ever predicting short-term movements very satisfactorily. However, some comfort may perhaps be taken from the fact that in the slightly longer term most stock movements are self-correcting.

---

1. See pages 40 and 44.

The difficulty with forecasting exports consists both of the difficulty of forecasting the exogenous variables, i.e. the movements of income and output in other countries, and of saying how they then will affect particular countries' exports, i.e. of establishing the relationships. Given the importance of the first factor, the export forecasts would probably be greatly improved if countries had an opportunity of pooling or confronting their individual forecasts at regular intervals.

6 CONCLUDING REMARKS

It may be worth ending this chapter with some brief conclusions of my own on some of the questions which the study raises. The overwhelming impression is of the high degree of sophistication which characterises official short-term forecasting in all the six countries. It is striking how complex and advanced the methodology already is when it is borne in mind how recently it is in most of the countries that some of the most basic statistics were available at all, and how very unsatisfactory and inadequate many important statistical series still are in all the countries, and how relatively few resources have been devoted to the activity. It seems to me beyond question that forecasting is of the first importance in good policy making. Most sceptics would be convinced, I think, if not from reading the attached papers, then certainly from discussion with official forecasters themselves, that the people who actually prepare the forecasts are more aware of their limitations than anyone else is likely to be. Any picture of them as blandly quantifying the unquantifiable or, through obsession with theoretical models, making errors about the future that someone with common sense could avoid, is very wide of the mark. It would be difficult, in the present state of knowledge, to provide more useful guidance as to how the economy was likely to devlop than the official forecasting procedures would reveal.

However, the official forecasters would be the first to emphasise the room that exists for improvement. In view of the very high returns available in this field it would seem no more than prudent for governments to invest more resources in the further development of forecasting. The three main ways in which this might best be done are:

a) Much greater development of statistics: improvement of frequency and accuracy of current series; development of seasonal adjustments and, very important, of national income data on a quarterly basis where this does not at present exist; development of new series; expansion and improvement of sample surveys, especially the investment intentions surveys.

b) Expansion of the number of officials engaged in forecasting. To improve forecasts it is necessary to establish and improve the knowledge of the behaviour of the economy and of the relationships among its different parts; and to do this it is necessary that the officials engaged in the job do not have to spend all their time preparing particular forecasts—or doing other more or less unrelated jobs—but have some time available for research to improve their methods. Other countries might find it profitable to follow the Netherlands and Sweden in having a research unit virtually within the official machine.

c) Wider use of universities and research institutes. The most fruitful research in this field will probably always be done by those actually engaged in the operation, but there is a limit to how much official forecasters can do. There are two promising lines of approach. Independent research centres specifically devoted to or concentrating on problems of business cycle research and of forecasting could profitably be encouraged in those countries which lack them. And more use might be made of academic economists by the official commissioning of specific projects related to the working of the economy. To be successful, however, this last would entail giving the research worker full access to the raw material as it comes to the official forecaster. For progress to be made it is essential to bridge the gap between the simplifying theorist on the one hand, and the working forecaster immersed in a mass of unsatisfactory and unprocessed data on the other.

The achievement of the last of these aims would be greatly facilitated by full publication of government forecasts. In any case, the arguments in favour of publication advanced by those countries which do publish[1] appear to me overwhelming. The apparent difficulties are of the kind that seem serious to governments before they take a step but quickly disappear once the step is taken.

The arguments for forecasting a quarterly path rather than a year-to-year change also seem to me overwhelming. I can think of no better use of the scarce resources of statisticians and other officials in those countries which do not analyse or forecast in a quarterly frame-work than to put themselves in a position to do so.

All the official forecasters agree that it is helpful or even necessary to consider consumption of durables separately from the rest of consumption. Expenditure on durable goods, or at least on motor cars, is often not determined by current income, and when such expenditure is by firms it is called fixed investment; these goods have a relatively long life; there is often a well-established resale market; they may be partial substitutes or complements to house-building; and they are often produced by firms predominantly engaged in making producer goods. For all these reasons, it seems to me long overdue that expenditure on motor cars at least, and perhaps on some other consumer durables, should be classified together with house-building as personal investment, not as consumption. The classifications used in official national accounts is a question beyond the scope of this study, but in the construction of forecasts, I believe that this change would be of some real, though necessarily small, help.

Finally, it may be worth remarking, in view of the great importance attached to monetary policy in many countries and to its undoubted effects in many cases, that it is somewhat disappointing that the models used in most countries take so little systematic account of the effects of monetary policy. In my view, attention should be concentrated not so much in developing complete flows of funds accounts as on intensive study of those sectors where the importance of monetary policy might on *a priori* grounds be expected to be greatest. The most important such areas probably

---

1. See pages 24 and 25.

A general survey

include the effect of changes in the availability in consumer credit on the demand for durables, the effect of changes in the cost or availability of mortgage finance on house-building, and the effect of changes in the availability of bank loans on private investment. Many countries attempt to allow for some or all of these effects, but there is room for much more systematic study.

CHAPTER II

CANADA: SHORT-TERM FORECASTING IN THE FEDERAL SERVICE

1 INTRODUCTION

The work on short-term forecasting in Canada has its origins in the 1945 White Paper on Employment and Income[1], published just one month before the end of the war in Europe. In this paper the Government set out in broad outline the policies which it intended to follow during the period of reconstruction which would begin with the cessation of hostilities. The major theme of this paper was that the adoption of high and stable levels of employment and income, and higher standards of living, would be a primary aim of Government policy in the post-war period. These objectives were partly rooted in the experience of the 1930's. The great depression which preceded the war had demonstrated that industrialized economies were not self-regulating mechanisms which would necessarily or automatically adjust to a level of full employment. The experience of depression had forced theoreticians and Government policy-makers alike to re-examine their positions and to probe more deeply for an understanding of economic processes. The problems of a controlled wartime economy drew attention to the need for a broader range of economic information to assist the central Government in managing the affairs of the nation. And the post-war reconstruction period now presented new and difficult problems of adjustment in which the Government would necessarily be expected to play a major role. Against this background the 1945 White Paper placed on record the key objectives which the Government intended to pursue in carrying forward its reconstruction programme in the post-war years.

In line with these objectives, the Government acted to establish a more comprehensive and fully integrated system of economic reporting. The initial task was to improve and extend the statistical tools available for charting the course of current and prospective economic developments, and to establish a framework for measuring the level and outcome of the nation's economic performance. In 1945, a Central Research and Development Staff was established at the Dominion Bureau of Statistics, charged with the task of coordinating the Bureau's work in the field of economic statistics and of developing a set of national income accounts for Canada. A quarterly labour force survey was begun at about the same time, and steps were taken to establish a survey of the capital investment intentions of businesses and governments. Concurrently, the Economic Research Branch of the

---

1. *Employment and Income, With Special Reference to the Initial Period of Reconstruction* (King's Printer, Ottawa, April 1945).

then Reconstruction Department was assigned responsibility for preparing on a regular basis short-term forecasts of the level of economic activity[1].

A statement of objectives with respect to the statistical programme then getting under way and the nature and purpose of the forecasting work as it was envisaged at the time, is contained in the following paragraphs; these general objectives have provided the broad guide-lines for the work up to the present day:

> "The process of ascertaining the facts of economic development is now being accelerated in Ottawa and several Departments are co-operating towards this end. But equally, if not more, important is the need for constant awareness of these facts in all the Federal Departments. It is not a matter of providing them with detailed knowledge that may be interesting or useful. The purpose is much more specific and vital. It is to provide a basis for common thinking on a wide range of government activities in order that they may be integrated into a consistent whole in relation to the end toward which the Government is now striving. Departmental policies have to be aimed at more than Departmental responsibilities; they have to be considered also in relation to their effect on the general level of economic activity, which by itself has become one of the Government's principal concerns. In time the problems associated with this new Government responsibility may call for new administrative techniques, but meanwhile it is desirable to develop a wider understanding and recognition of the broad national objectives against which individual Departmental policies have to be considered and developed.
>
> "Among the new duties dictated to the Federal Service by the Government's policy, is that of forecasting as carefully as possible, the future course of employment and income in Canada. The development and application of successful Government policies will depend largely on its ability to foresee in time, the need for certain types of action. . . .
>
> "Its aim is to foresee broad movements sufficiently in advance to give the Government time to prepare compensatory or remedial action. The initial forecast will not, in fact, be fulfilled if such action is prompt and effective. The importance of timing cannot be too strongly emphasized. The forces that generate booms and depressions are cumulative in their operation. A slight modification of existing Government policy may suffice to arrest adverse developments in their early stages. But when business confidence has been badly shaken and when unemployment and the fear of unemployment have made inroads in consumer spending, then the task of restoring confidence and checking the downward movement is immensely more difficult. The scope and scale of remedial action is correspondingly increased. The earlier action is taken, the less action will be required and the more effective it will be. . . ."

---

1. With the completion of the principal tasks of reconstruction, this forecasting function was transferred, together with the economic staff, to the Department of Trade and Commerce in 1948.

Canada

Two main features of the forecasting work as it subsequently evolved in Canada were foreshadowed in this statement, and merit special attention. The first is that the broad approach to the work was essentially interdepartmental. The Economics Branch of the Department of Trade and Commerce maintains a continuous review of the developing economic situation in Canada and provides an advisory service in this respect within the federal service in the form of circulated reports and special briefing material as required for particular purposes. This specialized service carried out in the Branch is separate from the policy work of the Department. In addition, other Departments or Agencies concerned with broad economic matters maintain within their own organizations an expert knowledge of the developing economic situation in order to provide the interpretative background necessary for the discharge of their responsibilities. Accordingly, the economic outlook is kept under close scrutiny in the Financial Affairs and Economic Analysis Division of the Department of Finance, the Economics and Research Branch of the Department of Labour and the Research Department of the Bank of Canada. While the kind of interpretative assessment prepared in each of these groups is tailored to the particular needs of their respective Departments, the necessity of having to arrive at reasonable working conclusions on the general outlook is common to all four groups. In working out the basis for such conclusions there is frequent consultation among the analysts concerned. Also, with respect to the detailed analysis within particular segments of the overall outlook, there is considerable specialization among the foregoing groups together with other agencies having a specialized knowledge of particular fields. For example, forecasts of capital expenditures are based to a large extent upon surveys of investment intentions, carried out by the Dominion Bureau of Statistics in collaboration with the Economics Branch of the Department of Trade and Commerce[1]. The Central Mortgage and Housing Corporation, which administers the National Housing Act, prepares forecasts of housing expenditures. Forecasts of government spending are based on an analysis of budgetary estimates compiled by the federal Department of Finance together with such information as may be available with respect to the spending plans of the provincial and municipal authorities. Agricultural experts at the Dominion Bureau of Statistics and in the Department of Agriculture provide assessments on the outlook for farm markets and production. Balance of payments forecasts are prepared by an interdepartmental group including representatives from the Department of Trade and Commerce, the Bank of Canada, the Dominion Bureau of Statistics, and the Department of Finance. Regular short-term forecasts of employment and unemployment are made by the Department of Labour in connection with its responsibilities for the analysis of developments in the labour market. The basic national accounts reference framework to which all of these projections are anchored is prepared at the Dominion Bureau of Statistics. Such a diversity of sources, while it permits a high degree of specialization and expertise, necessitates frequent consultation and discussion among Departments to

---

1. See *Private and Public Investment in Canada, Outlook 1964* (and earlier years), (Queen's Printer, Ottawa).

coordinate programmes and to ensure consistency with respect to definition and the basic assumptions regarding the outlook.

A second feature of the forecast is that improvements in forecasting techniques and methods have gone forward in step with the development and elaboration of the country's system of economic statistics. Thus, in its early stages, forecasting was essentially a crude projection from a relatively primitive and incomplete set of annual national accounts figures. As gaps were filled and a more complete framework of annual data became available, the forecasting work benefitted both from the resulting improvement in knowledge and from the development of more eleborate techniques which this more complete material made possible. One such technique was the development of an econometric model based on annual data. At a later date, about the middle of the 1950's, the development of quarterly seasonally-adjusted data permitted much more precise study of business cycle fluctuations in Canada, with a consequent improvement in forecasting capability. In an economy where cyclical forces are in evidence, a crucial consideration in any short-term forecast is the present position of the economy in relation to the previous cyclical peak or trough. The work on seasonal adjustment has in fact had a most important and pervasive influence on economic studies in Ottawa; and no single development in the past seven or eight years has done more to improve the statistical basis of the forecasting work than the bringing into use of a wide range of seasonally-adjusted economic statistics, including quarterly national accounts data. More recently, considerable work has been done in Canada to develop and test a set of economic indicators with leading, coincident and lagging properties, along the lines of the business cycle research pioneered by the National Bureau of Economic Research in the United States. This work and the techniques associated with it have had a major influence on forecasting in Canada as experience has been accumulated on their applications to business cycle analysis.

It will be evident from the foregoing discussion that the approach to forecasting in Canada is eclectic in nature and that no single "school" or method predominates. The final product represents a fusion of several approaches. Quantitative analysis goes hand-in-hand with "informed judgment" of subject matter experts. Surveys of spending plans or intentions play an important part in the procedures. Knowledge accumulated on the behaviour of business cycles in Canada and in the United States is used in conjunction with the indicator approach, to judge the timing and composition of cyclical swings in economic activity and to check on the "reasonableness" of the forecast. Aggregative projections based on cyclical trends are supported and checked by reconciliations at the commodity, industry, or market level. An econometric model, given the assumptions of the forecast, provides a test of its consistency with respect to underlying relationships[1]. To a considerable extent each one of these approaches serves as a check upon the other; where different conclusions are suggested,

---

1. See Brown, T. M., "A Forecast Determination of National Product, Employment, and Price Level in Canada from an Econometric Model", *Studies in Income and Wealth*, Volume 28 (National Bureau of Economic Research, Princeton University Press, Princeton, N.J., 1964), pp.59-96.

the forecaster is forced to enquire into the reasons. Taken all together, they comprise a working system of forecasting which has stood up well under the test of experience.

2 THE GENERAL APPLICATION AND THE TIMING PATTERN OF FORECASTS

In broad terms the objective of short-term forecasting is to maintain on a continuing basis the fullest possible understanding of the forces shaping the course of the economy over the ensuing year or so. Such understanding permits the formation of realistic assumptions concerning the probable levels of the more comprehensive measures of general activity in the period ahead.

Within the field of federal government operations, such forecasts form a necessary part of the background needed for the formulation of annual government programmes, and for various aspects of the legislative programme including the federal Budget. Planning of departmental programmes for the forthcoming fiscal year (April to March) usually reaches its culmination in the preceding October to December period. Parliamentary sessions in Canada have customarily commenced early in the calendar year, but on occasion, begin in the fall.

As regards the timing of forecasts for the foregoing purpose, the usual approach has been to prepare projections for the forthcoming calendar year. Preliminary thinking on the significant features of the outlook for next year begins in about August. Papers providing some quantitative indication of key elements of the outlook such as capital expenditure and foreign trade are customarily in hand by October or November. These in turn provide the basis for preliminary assessments of the probable level of general activity in the year ahead. Such preliminary assessments are usually made during the last quarter of the year, the actual timing depending upon relevant government programmes. Further elaboration and refinement of these preliminary assessments takes place during the first quarter of the calendar year as more up-to-date information becomes available. The principal need for quantitative forecasts as a support in the planning of legislative and other government programmes usually culminates with the introduction of the federal Budget. Thereafter, up-dated assessments of the progress of the economy are made as required for informational and other purposes.

The government's Budget proposals are presented to Parliament each year against the background of a statement on the country's current economic position, and the government's view of the outlook in the year ahead. At the same time, in the presentation of the financial plan in the Budget, it is customary to table a forecast of revenues to be expected in the coming year based on the anticipated level of gross national product. These revenue estimates are calculated in some detail from expected levels of profits, labour income, imports, and the other flows which underlie the main GNP forecast.

The working papers on the economic outlook thus provide a part of the interpretative background against which the formulation of the government's budgetary programme takes place, as well as a part of the background for the government's assessment of the general economic situation and outlook

Chart 1. NATIONAL ACCOUNTS: CANADA AND U.S.A.
QUARTERLY SEASONALLY ADJUSTED — INDEX 1957-61 = 100

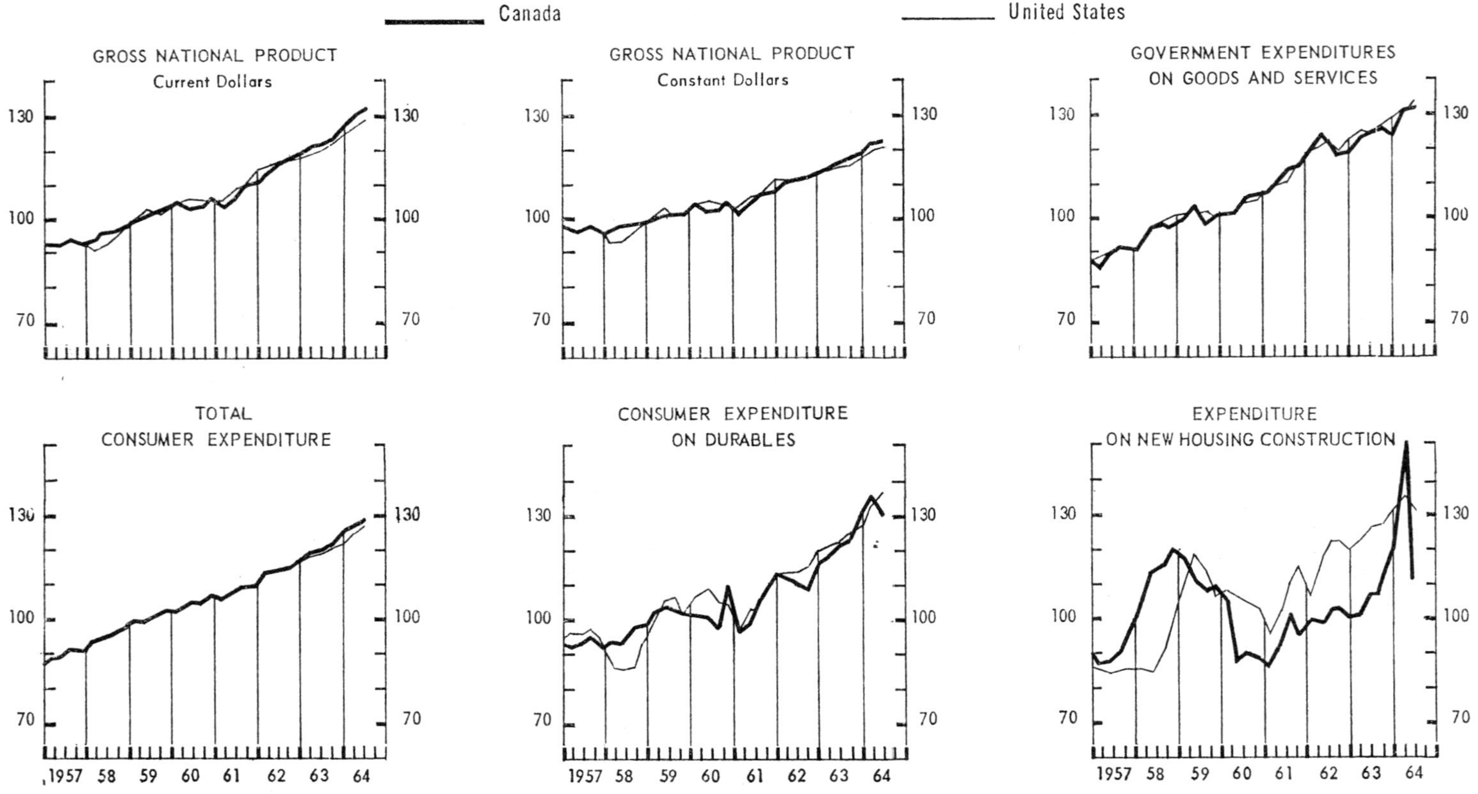

——— Canada   ——— United States

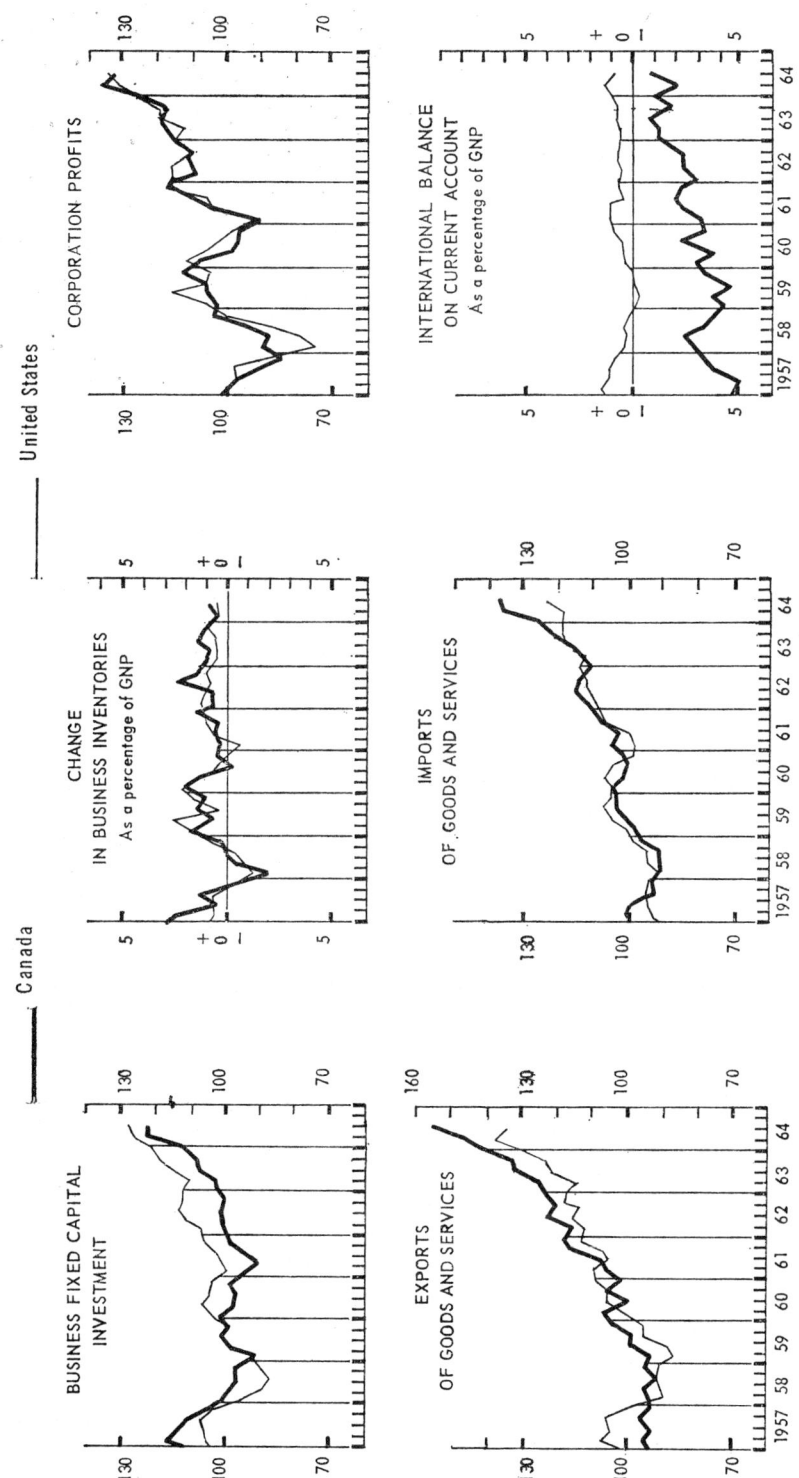

in the Budget statement. They also provide the statistical basis of the government's revenue forecast for the forthcoming fiscal year.

Quantitative calendar year forecasts are usually set out in the form of estimates for the full year, for comparison with actual figures of the previous year. Some indication of probable trends over the course of the year is also attempted to the extent that such estimates are considered meaningful.

Short-term forecasting in Canada does not form part of a general economic " plan " aimed at certain " target " objectives. Nor is there a single " official " published forecast other than such figures as the Minister of Finance may include in presenting his Annual Budget. Prior to the Budget, a common view is generally established through informal interdepartmental consultation, but at other times short-term forecasts relating either to the general outlook or to more particular sectors of the economy (e.g. the balance of payments, unemployment, government cash requirements) may be made either through interdepartmental working parties or by the individual departments and agencies primarily concerned. In this way the short-term forecasts which provide background information in connection with the formulation of government economic policy, are subject to continuous review and change rather than to periodic adjustment at specified intervals.

3 BASIC FACTORS DETERMINING THE OUTLOOK IN CANADA

Apart from government policies and programmes, two considerations are of primary importance in determining the short-term economic outlook in Canada—the current position and trend of the economy—and the situation and outlook abroad, particularly in the United States. Any forecast of conditions in Canada must be developed within the framework of these two broadly determining sets of considerations.

Turning to the first of these determining factors, it is clear that economic developments over the short-term future emerge from and are shaped by influences and tendencies which are a part of the current economic situation. For the assessment of the short-term outlook, it is thus essential to know what recent trends have been, and what the main factors are in shaping these trends. When this is known, the most crucial part of the forecast becomes a matter of judging whether these trends, and the factors underlying them, will continue or be reversed.

This point may appear self-evident, but it is one that deserves to be given special emphasis. A sound and correct appreciation of current economic conditions, and trends in the recent past, is a basic prerequisite to good forecasting. A related observation in this connection is the importance of having a wide range of statistical information on a seasonally-adjusted basis: for only when the data have been seasonally-adjusted is it possible to isolate and identify the underlying movement of the series[1].

---

1. This point is of special significance for Canada where the seasonal component of time series greatly exceeds the trend-cycle component, masking the underlying movement of the data.

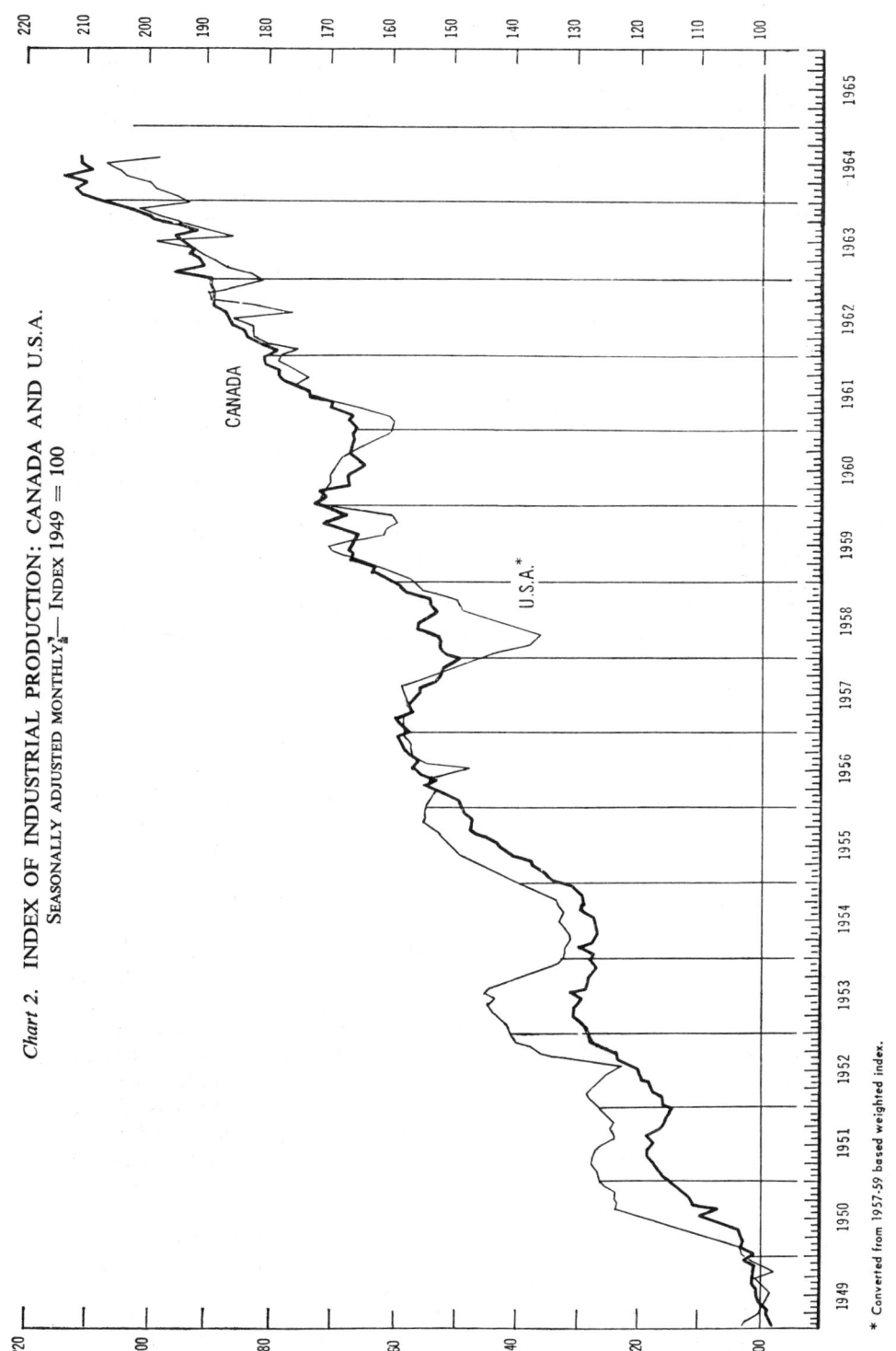

Chart 2. INDEX OF INDUSTRIAL PRODUCTION: CANADA AND U.S.A.
Seasonally adjusted monthly — Index 1949 = 100

* Converted from 1957-59 based weighted index.

Once purely seasonal influences have been eliminated, tested knowledge of business cycle behaviour based on typical relationships over previous cycles facilitates the identification of cyclical forces which can then be assessed in relation to trend and independent influences.

The second major point in this connection is the bearing on the forecast of economic conditions and prospects outside of Canada, and particularly in the United States. About 20 per cent of Canadian output of goods and services is sold in export markets. The United States economy forms the largest single market for Canadian exports, accounting for 60 per cent of total exports, and the effects of economic developments in the United States are transmitted to the Canadian economy through export markets as well as through a broad net-work of relationships which exists between the two economies. As Charts 1 and 2 show, cyclical fluctuations in Canada have tended to reflect strongly the rhythm of the United States economy. Thus, a great deal of attention in Canada is given over to following the trend of developments in the United States, and to making independent assessments of the outlook for the United States economy with particular reference to the implications for Canada.

To sum up, the basic shape of the Canadian forecast is broadly determined by current conditions and trends in the domestic economy, and by economic prospects in foreign markets. The manner in which the materials and methodology of the forecast are employed to throw light on these two central questions and on the outlook in general is indicated in the following sections.

4 THE MATERIALS FOR FORECASTING

Before turning to a discussion of operating procedures, it will be useful to describe in greater detail the basic source materials which are drawn upon in the course of preparing forecasts.

The national accounts

The national accounts possess a number of well-known features which endow them with important advantages for forecasting work. In the first place, they form a comprehensive and inter-related framework within which large masses of statistical material can be organized in a systematic way and reduced to manageable summary terms. In the second place, they are partly self-checking, to the extent that the income and expenditure sides are always in conceptual balance; if these two elements of a forecast do not yield a statistical balance, it is clearly not an internally consistent forecast. These features of the national accounts act as an important disciplinary force over the forecast in the same way that they serve to enforce consistency over the collection of historical data.

The national accounts framework therefore provides the reference base from which the principal projections are made. Statistical forecasts usually include the familiar GNP and expenditure statement, with details given for personal income and its disposition, the industrial composition of private and public investment, and a commodity and geographical breakdown of merchandise exports; a forecast of employment and unemployment is also included. No use is made of input-output relationships or flow-of-funds accounting, in preparing forecasts—indeed, the statistical basis for such an approach is almost entirely lacking, although development work in these areas is presently under way. The global estimates are not explicitly translated into industry terms, although these estimates themselves reflect the results of extensive analysis of market forces affecting particular commodities and industries. The basic framework of statistical forecasts is thus a fairly simple one, with only broad national aggregates presented. The statistical projections are accompanied by a textual statement describing the assumptions which underlie the forecast, and commenting analytically on the current position and outlook in the various markets in which the nation's output is sold, and on other factors which have been considered in developing the estimates.

Forecasts of national income and expenditure are usually drawn up in terms of annual averages only. Analysis of quarterly and monthly trends plays an important part in the calculations and in the textual comment, but quarterly forecasts are not usually explicitly set out. Trend projections which make use of the movement of quarterly seasonally-adjusted national accounts components play an important part in the estimation of many of the calendar year averages—and in checking the "reasonableness" of annual estimates derived independently. This is because quarterly estimates which measure the position as at the final quarter of the year provide a much more "up-to-date" base for projection than annual averages; and because quarterly projections can more readily take account of information concerning the stage of the business cycle which would be lost to view in the annual averages. In addition, it is often fairly easy to form a judgment about the reasonableness of quarterly rates of change which are implied in annual averages, moving from the final quarter of the current year through to the end of the forecast period; if these fall outside of the range of normal experience, a second look at the annual estimate is called for. The quarterly national accounts therefore play a vital role in preparing and checking the forecast, even though the forecast itself is not explicitly presented in quarterly terms.

The capital investment intentions survey

Capital expenditure both public and private presently amounts to about 22 per cent of Canada's GNP, while capital outlays within the business sector (excluding housing) amount to about 14 per cent.

Since capital programmes, particularly those of larger businesses and public agencies, are customarily planned in advance, the collection of information on these plans appears as a logical approach to forecasting this type of expenditure. Accordingly, the survey of investment intentions is the principal instrument used in arriving at short-term forecasts of capital outlays.

A survey of capital investment intentions was instituted in Canada just after the end of World War II. This took the form of a mail questionnaire to all the larger business establishments, and to a sample of the smaller ones, requesting dollar figures on planned outlays for plant and equipment in the year ahead, including expenditures for replacement. A trial survey was done by the Department of Reconstruction and Supply in 1945. The first published report was for the year 1946, the survey being conducted in the spring of that year. This initial survey covered about 12,000 business establishments. In the following few years the survey was expanded to cover most sectors of the Canadian economy including governments at all levels, non-profit institutions, and trade and financial enterprises. In addition, surveys were made of residential building plans. By 1948 the coverage of the survey was broadly comparable to that employed currently: some 20,000 individual establishments are now included. Until 1950 the survey was the responsibility of the Departments of Reconstruction and Supply, and Trade and Commerce, with the Dominion Bureau of Statistics doing the actual mailing and the machine tabulations of the returns. Following 1950, the Dominion Bureau of Statistics accepted prime responsibility for the survey, including sampling, collection and processing of the data. The Department of Trade and Commerce continued to be responsible for analytical textual material and the publication of the reports.

The survey is designed to provide the basic material for a report on the investment intentions of all sectors of the Canadian economy. For these purposes investment is defined as gross expenditures for durable physical assets (housing, non-residential construction, and machinery and equipment) but excluding outlays for land, used assets and consumers' durables. The totals actually reported are adjusted to allow for non-reporting and non-surveyed firms[1]. In addition, in some sectors the survey approach is not considered practical, and estimates based on other types of material are prepared for such sectors as agriculture and fishing. Estimates of outlays for residential construction are prepared by the federal housing agency, the Central Mortgage and Housing Corporation. These estimates are based on a survey by the field representatives of the Corporation, with modifications being made at Head Office in line with prospective economic trends. By these means estimates are made of the total investment intentions of all sectors of the economy. Details are also prepared by regions, cross classified by industry. About 75 per cent of total private and public investment is actually reported in the survey.

The survey is made in December for the year following, the compilation of national totals is completed by early February, and the results appear in published form about a month later. In addition to intentions, the survey asks for information on actual expenditures in the year just ended. This permits a check on the predictive performance of the survey. In general, as Chart 3 shows, the survey has performed reasonably well, but the results do suggest that businessmen tend to overestimate investment intentions in years in which economic activity turns down, and to under-estimate their expenditures over the course of the subsequent upturn. A mid-year survey with a limited coverage (4500 firms) is carried out each June to determine whether investment intentions as stated at the beginning of the year have been revised in any way; the performance of the mid-year survey is also

---

1. Surveys are not made for agriculture, fishing, independent retailers, and very small establishments. About 22 per cent of total private and public investment is represented by sectors which are not surveyed or by firms which fail to report.

and equipment outlays, consumer expenditures, and inventory stockbuilding, all of which have a high import content. Imports are highly sensitive to changes in the Canadian business cycle, rising more sharply than output and demand in the upward phase of the cycle, and declining more sharply during the downward phase. Knowledge of these relationships is used to form a judgment of the expected level of commodity imports for purposes of the forecast. Individual studies of commodity imports, classified by end-use, are also carried out as a check on the consistency of the forecast. However, unlike the export forecast where the totals tend to be built up from the detail, the import forecast is initially made at the aggregative level and commodity detail is provided mainly as a check and to give depth to the analysis.

The forecast for the non-merchandise items in the balance of payments is carried out by officials of the Dominion Bureau of Statistics who have special knowledge of developments and prospects in this area.

The preliminary forecast prepared in this way is reviewed by an interdepartmental committee to ensure that the estimates are not in conflict with the views or judgment of any one of the subject matter experts from the four Departments involved. The figures are modified where it can be shown that they do not reflect all of the information available, or where it can be argued that the emphasis has been misplaced. The forecast is thus in the nature of a compromise estimate which reflects the considered judgment of the most knowledgeable group of people in this field within the government service.

The predictive performance of the balance of payments forecast has been satisfactory, with a tendency for errors in the components to cancel out. This reflects in part the dominant position of the United States economy in Canada's foreign trade picture, and its influence on the level of domestic economic activity. Thus, an overestimate of commodity exports based on too sanguine a view of prospects for the United States economy will tend to be offset by errors in the same direction in commodity imports based upon too optimistic a view of domestic levels of activity. Despite the degree of cyclical variability in both exports and imports, there is some degree of built-in safety margin which operates in favour of the forecaster.

The balance on non-merchandise transactions tends to be much more stable than the balance on merchandise account, and the forecast error here is not usually significant.

The econometric model

Development work on the construction of econometric models for the Canadian economy was initiated in the Department of Reconstruction and Supply in 1947. Since that time the further development and use of models has been an integral part of the short-term forecasting work of the Economics Branch of the Department of Trade and Commerce.

In the earlier years model construction was hampered by lack of suitable data and much time was spent in preparing and up-dating the required historical series. As more comprehensive data became available from the Dominion Bureau of Statistics, more time could be applied to the development and testing of relationships. In recent years the use of high-speed for the federal sector which is expected to prove useful in forecasting both income and expenditure items and related financial developments within a consistent national accounts framework.

At the provincial and municipal levels, the situation is less satisfactory. Some indication of the likely changes in magnitude of the capital programmes of provincial governments and a few large municipalities is obtained at the time of the October preliminary survey of large companies. More complete information on capital expenditure programmes of provincial and municipal governments is obtained by questionnaire for the year-end survey of investment intentions. Full information on projected outlays for non-capital items becomes available only with the presentation of the annual budget early in each year. Prior to this time, forecasts of current expenditures are based on qualitative information in conjunction with projections of past trends which, for the post-war period, have followed a fairly regular upward course.

The balance of payments forecast

Responsibility for the balance of payments forecast is shared jointly by the Department of Trade and Commerce, the Bank of Canada, the Department of Finance and the Dominion Bureau of Statistics. The forecast is prepared by a working committee of representatives from these four government agencies. The balance of payments forecast forms a part of the general economic forecast developed within the framework of the national income and product accounts. However, because of the special dependence of the Canadian economy on foreign trade, it also has important uses in its own right as a guide for policy considerations in the foreign trade and payments field.

Tentative forecasts of key sectors of the balance of payments for the calendar year are made toward the end of the preceding year. These estimates are revised and up-dated in the light of new developments as the need arises.

There are three main parts to the balance of payments forecast, each of which involves a quite different approach. These consist of the forecasts for commodity exports, commodity imports, and non-merchandise transactions. The commodity export forecast is based largely upon the examination of market conditions relating to each commodity export (about one hundred items are estimated individually). These commodity assessments are in turn carried out against the background of a close examination of economic conditions in Canada's major markets—the United States, the United Kingdom and Commonwealth, Western Europe and Japan. There is thus a very large amount of supporting detail underlying the broad aggregative forecast for commodity exports. Economic conditions in the United States are, of course, the major consideration in the forecast since 60 per cent of Canadian exports are sold in that market; aggregative projections of seasonally-adjusted data based on an appraisal of the stage of the business cycle in the United States are used to cross-check the estimates of that country.

On the import side, the forecast is basically related to the outlook for domestic demand, with particular reference to prospects for new plant indicated in Chart 3. Since the mid-year survey is carried out at a time when actual capital outlays for five months are known, it is much less of a "forecast" than the December intentions survey, at which time no actual expenditures have been made. As would be expected, the results of the mid-year survey have proven to be more closely in line with realized investment expenditures than the initial survey taken at the beginning of the year.

The results of the year-end survey of investment intentions are not available in time for the preliminary outlook assessments customarily made toward the end of the calendar year. Yet to move the survey forward would impair the quality of the material collected insofar as many businesses, particularly small and medium-sized firms, seem unable to give reasonably firm estimates of capital outlays for the ensuing calendar year prior to the year-end. To meet the need for earlier information on prospective capital outlays in the business community, a preliminary survey of the investment plans of about one hundred large companies is conducted in October. Investment plans seem to be developed with a longer lead time in large companies and it has been found that such companies, by October, can usually indicate the size of their projected investment for the coming year in reasonably specific terms subject perhaps to one or two qualifications. This preliminary survey is conducted by personal interview which contributes to a better insight into the investment plans of major companies and the respective industries than would be possible by means of mail questionnaires.

The companies now covered in this preliminary October survey account for more than one-half of total capital outlays in the business community. In general, the results of this preliminary survey have provided a fairly reliable indication of the ensuing year's investment programme for the business community as a whole.

The government estimates

Forecasts of government expenditure in Canada are based on two major sets of information—the capital investment intentions of governments as obtained from the investment survey discussed above—and an analysis of the regular budgetary estimates of the various levels of government.

At the federal level, the expenditure estimates for the fiscal year (April to March) are generally available in preliminary form in December of the preceding year. Anticipated outlays for goods and services, divided between capital and current items, and for transfer payments and subsidies, are extracted from these estimates. Conversion of the estimates from a fiscal year to a calendar year is carried out on a *pro rata* basis.

Continuing reviews and analyses of budgetary revenues and expenditures and the non-budgetary and financing transactions which make up the public accounts are carried out by the Securities Department of the Bank of Canada, and in the Department of Finance, the Taxation Division and the Cash Management Division of the staff of the Comptroller of the Treasury. At the same time, a detailed forecast of federal government transactions on the national accounts basis is kept up in the Research Department of the Bank of Canada and this is reconciled frequently with the budgetary presentation. Considerable progress has also been made in the Research Department of the Bank in the development of an integrated set of accounts

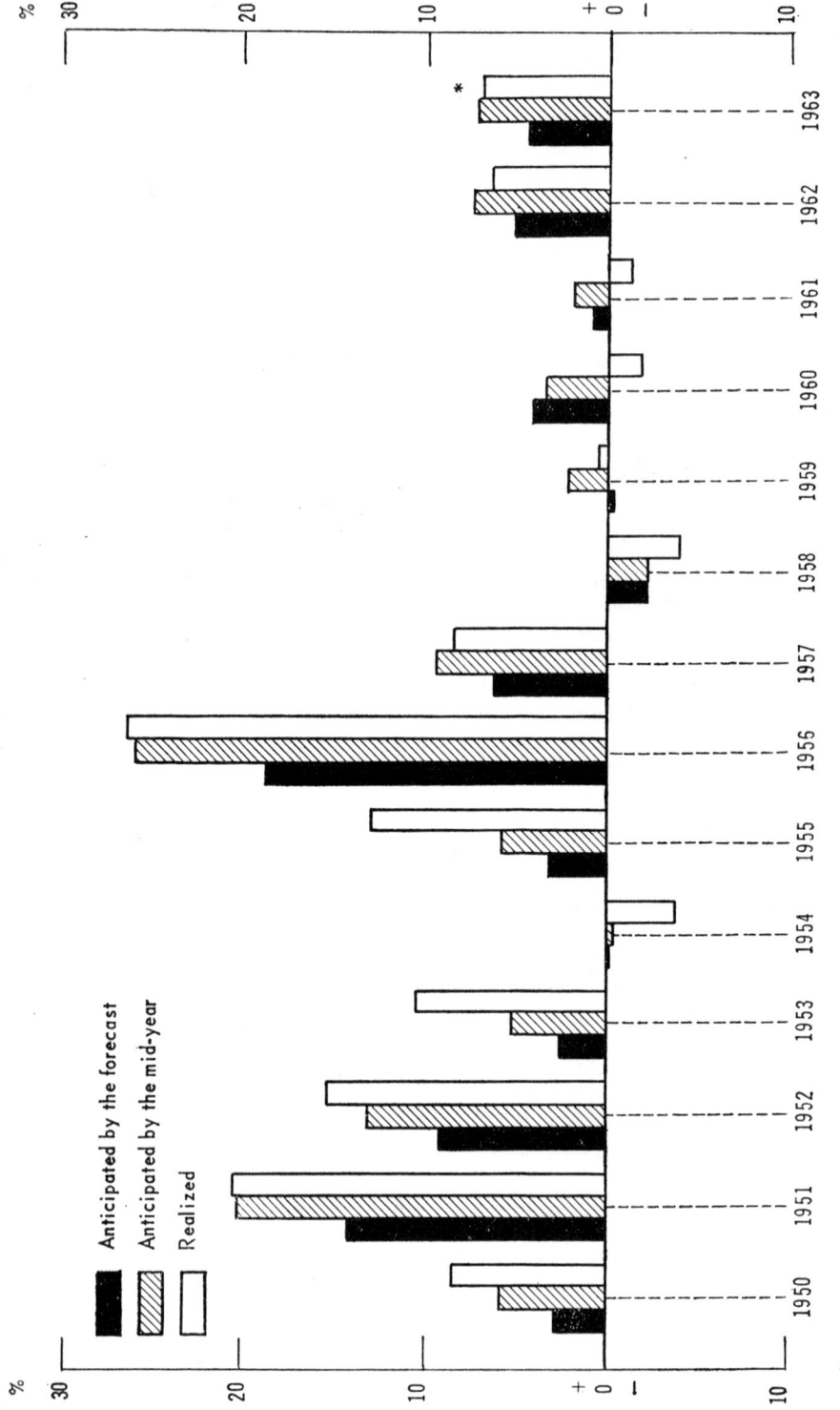

Chart 3. TOTAL CAPITAL EXPENDITURES PRIVATE AND PUBLIC
Per cent change from previous year

■ Anticipated by the forecast
▨ Anticipated by the mid-year
☐ Realized

*. Preliminary.

computers has tremendously extended the scope of model applications by facilitating additional testing and the solution of more complicated systems.

Model development since 1947 has been aimed at explaining the systematic portion of real flows, with real demand treated in somewhat more detail than real supply. The original model consisted of eleven equations; the model used in 1962 contained some sixty-odd equations. Most of the expansion has been in the direction of more detail with respect to the tax-transfer structure, but some disaggregation and refinement has been carried out with respect to behaviour and technological relationships as well.

While the models have concentrated on the explanation of the generation of real flows, they do contain certain stock variables such as consumer holdings of durables and semi-durables, consumer debt, consumer liquid assets, and business inventories. Stock variables occur usually in lagged form as explanatory variables.

The application of econometric models, as developed for the Canadian economy, does not comprise, in itself, a self-contained forecasting technique, but requires the insertion of assumed levels for exogenous variables in the forecast period. For the model now in use, the exogenous variables are exports, government expenditure and housing. In earlier models, plant and equipment expenditure was treated as exogenous but a fairly satisfactory relationship has been developed for this component of expenditure. On occasion an equation is " disturbed " in a particular way to take account of information on some non-recurring condition not provided for in the estimated structure, e.g., the investment in gas pipelines which was almost certain to follow a government decision to permit the export of natural gas.

Such a model has proven of particular use in the earlier phases of assessment of the likely pattern of economic developments in the coming year. On the basis of tentative assumption with respect to exports and other exogenous items, the model is solved to arrive at estimates for the principal dependent variables including GNP, its principal income and expenditure components, and employment and unemployment. A further adaptation of the model solution gives the repercussions on all other variables of an assumed change in any particular variable. In this way the model is of particular use in arriving at first approximations of the general pattern of trends in the coming year and in maintaining internal consistency among the principal components of the system while shifting from one set of assumptions to another.

The equations making up the model are, of course, representative of the normal relationships which have prevailed during the period covered by the basic data. Estimates derived from such a model may need adjustment to take account of new and special features of the current situation.

By and large, however, the predictive performance of the model, given the assumptions for exogenous variables, has been notably meaningful in both recessionary and expansionary periods, particularly as regards real flows in the economy. The model has been less reliable in forecasting the price components of the system and has tended to overstate the price changes. The structure dealing with the generation of the price variable is being modified to try to overcome this weakness.

For the year 1962, the model solution, on the basis of given exogenous assumptions, showed an increase in the GNP of 7.2 per cent, with an increase in the price component of 1.9 per cent, and an increase in the volume component of 5.2 per cent. The pre-budgetary estimate of GNP arrived at after further consideration of all relevant information called for an increase of 7.2 per cent in GNP, 6.0 per cent in volume terms and an implied price increase of 1.1 per cent[1].

Econometric models used to date have been applicable for annual periods. Work is now proceeding on the development of a quarterly model.

The business cycle indicator approach

Interest in business cycle indicators for Canada which would facilitate the interpretation of current and prospective economic developments was stimulated by the work of the National Bureau of Economic Research on *Statistical Indicators of Cyclical Revivals and Recessions*, published in 1950[2]. This study presented a list of United States economic time series chosen for the historical consistency of the relationship between their specific cycle turns and the turning points of the United States business cycle. The twenty-one series selected were divided into " leading ," " lagging " and " coincident " groups, depending upon whether their specific cycle turns normally displayed a tendency to lead, lag or coincide with the business cycle reference dates.

Following the development of methods of producing high quality seasonal adjustments quickly and cheaply by electronic computers, work was undertaken in Canada in 1955 and 1956 to evaluate the cyclical behaviour of Canadian series equivalent to the NBER's group of business cycle indicators. The study[3], completed in 1957, indicated that the relevant Canadian indicators performed almost identically, in relation to the Canadian cycle, to the way in which the United States indicators performed in relation to the United States business cycle. The decision was taken to maintain these series on an up-to-date basis and to compute summary measures of the dominant tendencies in the indicators (such as diffusion and general indexes) which would supplement their use for current analysis and the assessment of the short-term outlook.

In the six years that have passed since work began in this area, the Canadian economy has passed through two business cycle contractions and recoveries. Experience accumulated in the use of the indicators over this period has led to a broader understanding of the techniques of business cycle analysis developed by the National Bureau of Economic Research and a much greater appreciation of their value and application for forecasting work. But it is not simply the development of indicators with leading, lagging and coincident properties which has so strongly influenced the Canadian work. More importantly, it is the employment of the whole broad apparatus

---

1. In fact, the rise in GNP in 1962 was 7.9 per cent, with prices higher by 1.7 per cent.
2. NBER Occasional Paper No. 31, reprinted as Chapter 7 of *Business Cycle Indicators* (National Bureau of Economic Research, Princeton University Press, Princeton, 1961), p. 184.
3. "Indicators of Cyclical Recessions and Revivals in Canada", *Business Cycle Indicators*, Chapter 10, p. 294. See also " Canadian Business Cycles since 1919; a Progress Report," *Canadian Journal of Economics and Political Science,* May 1958, p. 166.

of business cycle analysis associated with their use[1] which has made such a powerful impact, including the dating of reference cycle turning points, the use of cycle-on-cycle comparisons, diffusion indexes and general amplitude adjusted indexes (which measure dominant tendencies in large numbers of series), and techniques for gauging the probable duration and amplitude of business cycle swings. There can be no doubt that this approach and the techniques associated with it have shed important light on business cycle developments in Canada, and have served as an important aid in the forecasting work.

The indicator approach to analysis and forecasting involves two major initial steps: first, the identification of the stage reached in the current business cycle; second, the placing of recent and current developments in historical perspective. These two steps permit analysis of current developments within the interpretative framework of typical cyclical behaviour over previous cycles. This analysis in turn permits judgments to be made of the probable sequence of future developments, and the general orders of magnitude of the changes which might be expected in the key variables.

It should be emphasized that the business cycle indicator approach is not, in general, used in a direct way to forecast the precise timepaths of the variables, or the exact date of turning points in advance of the event. But knowledge of the current stage of the business cycle provides a cross-check on the reasonableness of estimates derived independently; it forces the forecaster to allow for the impact of probable cyclical developments on the magnitudes being predicted. And, in addition, cycle-on-cycle comparisons impose the requirement that the estimate be reasonable from the perspective of the normal cyclical behaviour of the variable. This process thus subjects the forecast estimates to two important constraints which aid the forecaster in reaching a judgment.

Other research findings of the National Bureau of Economic Research with respect to business cycle behaviour provide additional guides to the forecasting work. These include: the finding that rates of change in the first six months of recovery following a trough tend to be greater the sharper the preceding contraction; the fact that the highest rates of change experienced in the course of the business cycle usually occur during the first few months of recovery; that thereafter the rates of increase tend gradually to decline towards the business cycle peak; the tendency for the relative severity of a recession to be indicated by the average rates of decline in certain leaders over the first four to six months following the reference peak; the tendency for strength in an expansion to be reflected in earlier strength in the leading indicators; the tendency for declines in an aggregate to be preceded by declines in rates of increase and in the diffusion or " scope " of the expansion among components. All of these findings provide useful guide-lines for the forecaster in shaping his judgments.

Seasonal influences apart, the course of economic activity in Canada, as in the North American economy generally, is strongly influenced, and often dominated by the business cycle. It follows that cyclical forces must be carefully considered in any assessment of future trends in the economy.

---

1. Described in *Business Cycle Indicators*.

Economic Forecasting

Industry and commodity analysis

Analytical studies on international commodity markets and on market conditions in particular Canadian industries, carried out in various branches of the federal service, provide spot information frequently of value in developing certain parts of a forecast of general activity. Comprehensive reviews of current and prospective trends in the major sectors of Canadian industry are prepared periodically in the Economics Branch of the Department of Trade and Commerce. While these industry assessments are not developed to the point of making aggregative output estimates, they nevertheless provide useful insight into likely trends within particular sectors of the economy.

Forecasts of employment and unemployment

Regular assessments of the current employment and unemployment situation and outlook constitute an essential part of the task of maintaining a continuing review of the economic situation in Canada. In general, the methodology underlying such forecasts centres on the relationship between changes in output, productivity, and the labour force. The question, broadly, is whether the projected levels of output and demand as anticipated in the GNP forecast are likely to be sufficient to absorb fully the expected increase in the labour supply, given certain assumptions as regards productivity in the year ahead. In reaching a judgment on this question, a forecast must be made of the anticipated increase in the labour force in the light of expectations concerning the natural increase of the population, the level of net immigration, and participation rates[1]. In addition, a key consideration is the course of productivity in the year ahead. Past trends in productivity provide the basic guide-lines for the estimate in this area, but modifications must be made in the light of the position of the economy in relation to the stage of the business cycle. Cyclical upturns have in the past been marked by sharp gains in productivity, while cyclical declines have been accompanied by a drop in productivity or a retardation in the rate of productivity growth.

Drawing all of these projections together in a consistent framework, the forecast of the change in employment levels is determined as the resultant of two inter-acting factors—the anticipated change in the physical volume of output, and the anticipated change in the production-employment ratio, i.e. productivity. The forecast of unemployment is determined as the difference between the total labour supply estimated as above, and the forecast level of employment.

While these procedures constitute the broad approach to the assessment of the outlook for employment and unemployment in the context of the general working papers on the overall economic situation, they are supplemented in an important way by more detailed work carried out in the Department of Labour. Twice each year the Department prepares a situation

---

1. In the short run, participation rates, and hence the labour force, are primarily influenced by the cyclical demand for labour. Consequently, an assessment is usually made first of labour demand by at least major industries. This information, plus the knowledge of how various groups of workers behave in the labour market over the cycle, forms the background for making necessary judgments about participation rates.

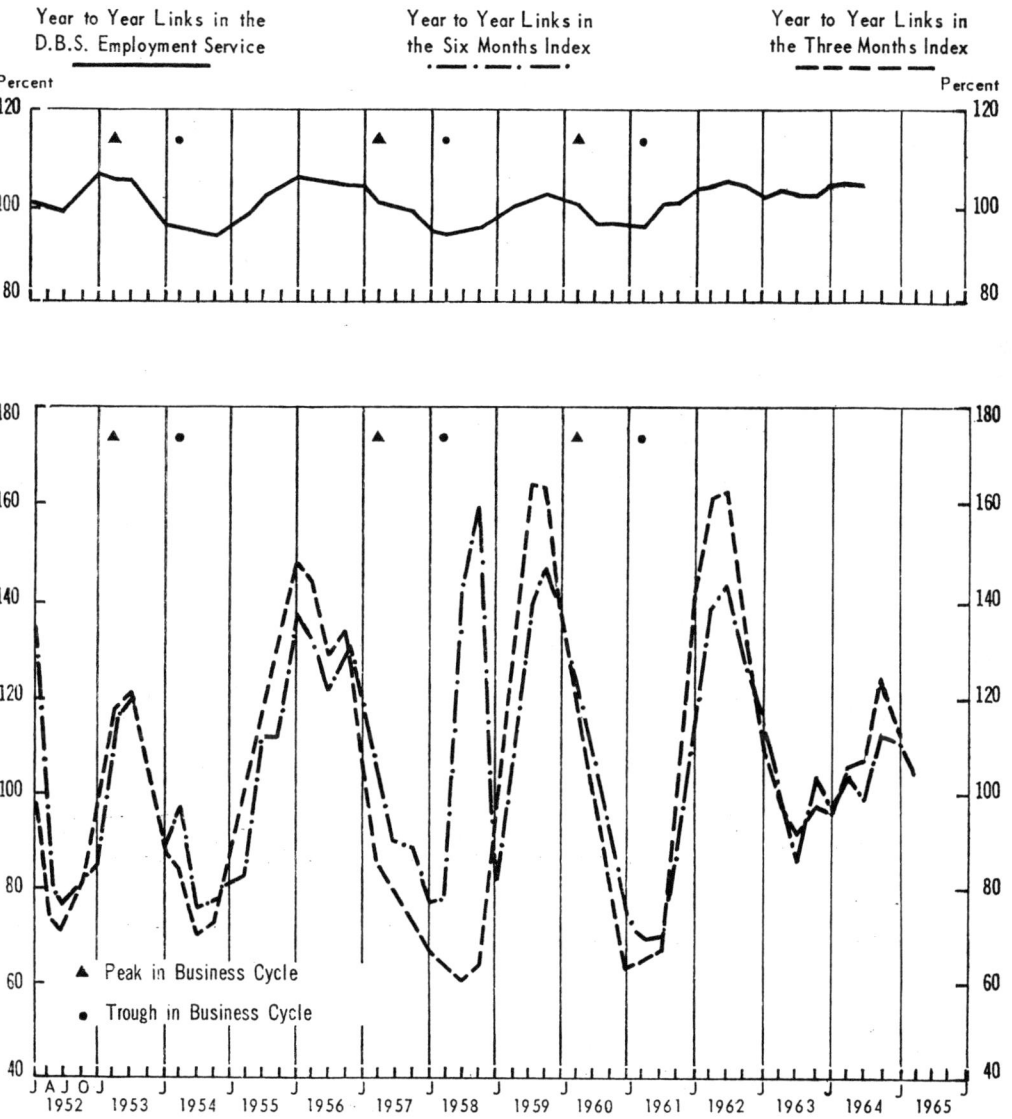

Chart 4. COMPARISON OF THE YEAR TO YEAR LINKS IN THE D.B.S. EMPLOYMENT INDEX WITH THE YEAR LINKS IN THE FORECAST DIFFUSION INDEXES FOR MANUFACTURING

NOTE· The D.B.S. data are taken from monthly machine runs provided by the Labour Division, D.B.S., and have been strike adjusted. The E.F.S. diffusion indexes have been computed from quarterly tabulations of the sample establishment data reported to the Economics and Research Branch, Department of Labour.

report, "Employment and Unemployment Outlook," which provides estimates of the labour force, employment and unemployment for the period six months ahead. These reports are circulated within the government on a confidential basis. In addition, the Department undertakes a quarterly survey of manufacturers' employment intentions for periods three and six months following the date of the survey. These are also circulated on a confidential basis under the title "Employment Forecast Survey." Originally, this survey attempted to cover many more industries besides manufacturing, but sampling difficulties led to a decision, in 1956, to discontinue the estimates for the non-manufacturing area. Since 1957, the estimates have been prepared in the form of "diffusion indexes" which show the proportion of manufacturing establishments surveyed that expect an increase in employment over the level a year earlier (see Chart 4). One index corresponds to the three month forecast, and the other to the six month forecast.

A word should be said about the nature of these diffusion indexes. The six-month forecast diffusion index simply reflects the percentage of reporting establishments which forecast, six months prior to the target date, year-to-year gains in their employment at the target date. The indexes therefore say nothing about the absolute levels of employment to be expected, but merely indicate the strength (or "widespreadness") of businessmen's expectations as to whether employment will be higher than last year at the time of the forecast date. The year-to-year links in the indexes merely indicate whether the percentage of reporting firms or establishments anticipating gains in their employment is higher or lower than for the corresponding period last year.

In addition to the interpretative material described above, the Department of Labour maintains a continuing series of field interview reports, representing summaries of interviews conducted by officers of the Department with senior officers of Canadian industry. The interviews are aimed at obtaining qualitative information on problems and conditions in particular industries as they bear on the labour market. The interviews range over a broad area touching on markets and the general business outlook for the industry, the position of inventories, whether there are shortages of particular classes of skills, training programmes, expectations with respect to employment, the effects of devaluation on the companies' sales and profit position, and so forth. These reports are highly valuable since their cumulative effect is to provide a "feel" for the business situation as it is developing in the country, and this serves as a qualitative check on analytical judgments based on the movement of broad aggregative statistics. As the reports of these interviews are highly confidential, they are distributed on a restricted basis within the federal service.

5 ASSEMBLING AND CHECKING THE FORECAST

The broad methodological basis of forecasting has been described in the preceding sections. It remains to comment briefly on the general procedures which are followed in applying this methodology to derive a comprehensive statistical forecast in the context of the national accounts framework.

The most volatile elements of the forecast are inventories, corporation profits, and imports. These show wide swings over the course of the business cycle; profits may rise by as much as 30 per cent from trough to peak, on a seasonally-adjusted basis; imports, by 25 per cent; and inventories may swing around by as much as a billion and a half dollars (at annual rates) over the course of a twelve month period. The tremendous volatility in these key components of the forecast make it imperative that the forecaster has developed a view of the stage of the business cycle at the time the forecast is made, and the prospects for cyclical changes over the year ahead. In arriving at this judgment, the whole apparatus of business cycle analysis is drawn upon, including the statistical indicators described above. Using this approach, it is possible to arrive at a view of how the main components of the forecast are likely to move over the next twelve months, based on the record of their performance over previous cycles—and also, to make a judgment as to whether the cyclical movements are likely to be mild or strong. To reach a sound judgment on these questions is a most important part of the forecast. Following this, it becomes a question of going through the components of the forecast in careful detail to test the consistency and reasonableness of the hypothesis.

As has been indicated, a number of the key elements on the expenditure side are already given: the estimates of housing, non-residential construction, and machinery and equipment, from the capital investment survey; government expenditures, from the analysis of the government estimates; exports and imports of goods and services, from the balance of payments forecast. There remain only two components to complete the expenditure side—an estimate for consumer expenditure, and an estimate of the expected change in inventories. The estimate for consumer expenditure is basically income-determined, and depends substantially upon the forecasts developed on the income side which are described later. Certain uniformities are observable in consumer behaviour patterns in relation to their income position. The recent record shows that the real volume of per capita consumption in Canada has declined only in years in which there has also been a decline in real disposable income per capita; these have all been years of recession. The record also shows that the declines in real per capita consumption have tended to be smaller than the declines in real per capita disposable income; consumers are strongly resistant to any downward shift in their standards of consumption, despite the fact that their income position may be impaired. In addition, to the extent that standards of consumption have been cut in years of economic downturn, the durable goods group—the most postponable item of consumer outlays—has been the one most heavily affected. Finally, the record shows that there has been a strong inclination for consumers to improve their standards of consumption as improvements have occurred in their real disposable income per capita. Knowledge of these income - behaviour relationships is used in arriving at the forecast estimate for consumer spending. Allowances are made for special conditions which may obtain with respect to the market for consumer durables—for example, the outlook for housing completions is directly related to the market for major appliances—and the receptiveness of consumers to the new automobile models can occasion wide variations in car sales. The econometric model solution also is available as an independent check on the estimates of consumer spending so derived.

The estimate of inventory change in the forecast year is largely determined by the present level of stocks, sales, the degree of capacity utilization, price trends, and by the forecaster's view of the likely course of the business cycle. Improbable values can be ruled out in the light of expectation with respect to the business cycle; within the range established as reasonable, the estimate becomes a matter of the forecaster's best judgment.

With the exception of corporation profits, the components of the income side exhibit a much greater degree of stability than do the components of the expenditure side of the national accounts. The estimate of corporation profits, a highly volatile item, is essentially determined by the forecaster's view of how the cycle will move over the course of the forecast period, combined with knowledge of the typical behaviour of corporation profits over previous business cycles. Expectations with regard to output, costs and prices also play a part in the figuring. The estimates of labour income are determined in the light of employment prospects (appraisals here are made in collaboration with the Department of Labour), and an evaluation of the outlook for changes in wage rates and average hours worked. Knowledge of collective bargaining agreements and the degree of labour unrest can shed a useful light on the extent to which wage rate pressures are likely to arise, while average hours worked tend to fluctuate in response to cyclical swings in the overall level of business activity. The labour income estimates are thus also affected by the forecaster's view of the present stage of the cycle and the prospects for cyclical change over the year ahead. Estimates of military pay and allowances, and a large part of the transfer payment component of personal income (not including unemployment benefits) are derived from an analysis of the government estimates. The forecast of net income of farm operators is prepared with the assistance of experts from the Dominion Bureau of Statistics and the Department of Agriculture who have a close knowledge of production and market prospects for the main agricultural commodities; the forecast of crop production, however, is based on a ten-year average, since weather conditions cannot be predicted with any degree of reliability, and acreages sown are not known until the spring of the forecast year.

Other components of the income side are built up and fitted into the overall framework of the forecast on the basis of such information and knowledge of relationships as is available. Rents, interest, and miscellaneous investment income must allow for the prospective level of interest rates, rents, the increase in the stock of dwellings, and the outlook for profits or losses in connection with the activities of a number of government business enterprises. The estimates of net income of non-farm unincorporated businesses are fashioned in the light of typical experience over previous business cycles. The estimates of indirect taxes less subsidies are estimated in several parts: the subsidy figures are derived from the government estimates; customs import duties are linked to the anticipated level of imports; excise duties and taxes are tied into the anticipated level of retail sales and factory shipments; real property taxes are projected on the basis of past trends. Estimates of direct personal taxes are derived from the forecast levels of personal income on the basis of measures of elasticities developed from previous experience. Finally, the estimates of capital consumption are constructed with an allowance for the expected change in the business cycle over the forecast period; business firms have tended to lower their capital consumption write-offs in times of declining cyclical activity in order to present a more favourable profits picture, and to raise them during the subsequent cyclical upswing in order to reduce profit levels.

In short, all relevant information is taken into account in the estimation of the likely trend of each component of the GNP. Throughout this process the econometric model provides a general check on consistency with respect to underlying relationships among the various components.

In concluding this review of the way in which a forecast is assembled, it should be emphasized that the judgment of the forecaster is the controlling element, and his skill and experience in quantitative analysis is not subordinated to mechanical techniques, but draws upon them for support. Once a forecast is assembled in this way, the results are subject to interdepartmental scrutiny. Modifications and adjustments are made where they appear to be warranted.

6 SUMMARY AND CONCLUSIONS

There have now been some sixteen years of experience with short-term economic forecasting in Canada. What can be said by way of generalizing about this experience as a concluding note to this review? Several points may be reiterated:

a) Short-term forecasting in Canada does not form a part of a general economic " plan " aimed at the achievement of certain " target " objectives, but simply serves as background information in connection with the formulation of Government programmes.

b) The approach to forecasting in Canada is typically eclectic and draws upon a wide variety of forecasting techniques which serve in large part as checks upon each other. These include surveys of intentions, business cycle indicators, analysis of government estimates, econometric models, commodity and industry analysis, and " informed judgment ".

c) Surveys of businessmen's intentions (see capital investment survey) have provided useful information with respect to changes in direction, approximate orders of magnitude, and industry and regional detail, but to some extent have underestimated the strength of investment spending on the upward side of the cycle, and the weakness of investment spending on the downward side.

d) The apparatus of business cycle analysis developed at the National Bureau of Economic Research in the United States, and adapted for Canadian use, has greatly strengthened the work on forecasting in Canada.

e) Improvements in forecasting techniques have gone forward step-in-step with the development and strengthening of the country's system of economic statistics. The framework of the forecast, and the econometric models, were made possible by the development of a detailed system of annual and quarterly national accounts. The work on business cycle analysis was made possible by the development of a wide range of seasonally-adjusted data.

f) The situation and outlook in the world at large and particularly in the United States is one of the most important determinants of trends in the Canadian economy, and much time and attention is given to following external developments.

g) The overall approach to forecasting in Canada is interdepartmental and forecasts draw heavily upon materials and expert knowledge from various Departments and Agencies of the Government.

h) By and large much of the work on forecasts within the government service is carried out by analysts not primarily involved in the policy work by their Departments.

CHAPTER III

FRANCE: THE PREPARATION OF ECONOMIC BUDGETS

1 INTRODUCTION

The methods of preparing economic budgets differ according to the type of budget. Sometimes the aim is to determine the most likely trend of the economy in the light of the decisions of the Government and the principal economic agents; other times, the aim may be to study the results of alternative policies. Budgets of the first type are most often prepared in September of one year for the following year, or right at the beginning of the year for the current year; the second are prepared at the beginning of one year for the following year. This note deals with the methods of preparing *forecast* budgets.

These methods attempt to effect a compromise between the two alternative approaches confronting the national accountants responsible for short term economic forecasts: either to use econometric relationships which are generally better verified on macro-economic variables or to use direct information which is available only for micro-economic variables.

This compromise is obtained as follows: in a first stage the department responsible for this work prepares a global projection which is subsequently disaggregated in the same framework in which the final economic budget will later be drawn up. In the second stage the various items in this account are referred to a great many external bodies so as to obtain the maximum information about the decisions already taken by the economic agents or about their intentions. In a third stage a synthesis is made of all the information obtained.

2 THE FIRST STAGE OF FORECASTS

The first forecast made by the body responsible for the preparation of the economic budgets involves the use of extremely simple models which vary from year to year. One reason for the variation is the position of the year in the period covered by the Plan. As is well known, projections covering a period of four or five years are now regularly made in France, within the framework of the national accounts, which are also used for short-term forecasts. These medium-term projections generally require a number of forecast studies to be made, some of which may be directly used for the preparation of the economic budgets, in particular during the first years of each four-year or five-year period. Moreover, the constraints imposed by economic policy vary from one year to another and the implementation of policies sometimes makes it possible to replace an econometric relationship.

Finally, it should be emphasized that the aim of this centralised work is not to have the best possible forecast—which would require the use of a far more elaborate model than those at present used by the French national accountants—but to obtain forecasts sufficiently approximate to enable the information stage to proceed under satisfactory conditions. The model used is a global one and reproduces in full the " tableau économique d'ensemble " which is the most abridged form in which the French national accounts are regularly published. This " tableau économique d'ensemble " gives an overall balance of supply and use of resources and of lending and borrowing, but also gives details on distribution and especially of income redistribution. Its preparation, therefore, already requires a fairly detailed breakdown of government expenditure projects and fairly detailed revenue estimates. As in most of the global models, the essential relationship is that between changes in consumption and changes in incomes.

The prospective " tableau économique d'ensemble "thus obtained is then broken down within the framework of the detailed national accounts. In the case of goods and services, the change in each final demand component is separated into volume and price changes. The value at constant prices is then broken down according to the classification of goods and services which is used in the French input-output table. This classification now contains 76 items. For consumption of households this breakdown uses a range of elasticity coefficients derived from family budgets studies, from study of time series and from information on developments abroad collected for the preparation of the Plan. For consumption of general government and for investment, the breakdown uses coefficients derived from the latest accounts except when there is some known reason for modifying them. Thus, from the information available about the nature of purchases by general government, and in particular defence purchases, it is sometimes possible, at this stage of the work, to have a breakdown of consumption which is closer to reality. Exports and imports are also broken down according to the detailed classification of products; this is done by teams specialising in this work.

When a breakdown of final demand by type of product is available, the production of each product is calculated by inversion of the previous year's input-output matrix.

Financial operations are also analysed by preparing, at this stage of work, a flow-of-funds forecast table which generally uses linear relationships. In particular it is usually assumed that the distribution of investment of non-financial enterprises and households among the various types of financial assets is proportional to the amounts for previous years and that there will be stability in the institutional composition of the various sources of money supply. A certain number of relationships are employed with regard to the growth tendencies of particular types of loans connected with investment and purchase operations. It often happens that the policy announced by the Government involves certain monetary or financial constraints which considerably limit the degrees of freedom for the construction of forecast flow-of-funds tables.

France

3 THE SECOND STAGE OF FORECASTS

The second stage is to improve separately each item in the accounts prepared centrally, and particularly each item in the input-output table. For this, all existing sources of information are taken into consideration.

For the balance of goods and services, these sources are numerous and vary according to the item. For consumption of households in particular a survey of consumers' intentions is used. This survey is carried out twice a year by the " Institut National de la Statistique et des Études Économiques. " It covers a random sample of approximately 8,000 households which are partly changed in each survey. It gives the intentions of households for the following six months for the purchase of motor cars, household electrical appliances, and clothing and footwear, and information on the trend of their financial situation. In addition, other forecast surveys carried out by public bodies and sometimes even private bodies may be used for comparison with the results of the calculation.

For gross fixed asset formation of public enterprises the amount and nature of the work which they anticipate carrying out in the coming year is discussed each year in the " Conseil de direction " of the " Fonds de Développement Économique et Social"; thus fairly accurate information is available about this future investment which constitutes approximately 30 per cent of the investment of non-financial enterprises.

For gross fixed asset formation of private enterprises the sources of information are naturally not so good. However, it is possible to use the survey of enterprises which is carried out by the "Institut National de la Statistique et des Études Économiques" (INSEE). This survey takes place mainly among the major industrial concerns and consequently gives direct information on projects covering a large proportion of private investment. Twice a year (in March and November) it is particularly concerned with investment questions. Business men are asked to state the amount which they anticipate with some certainty they will spend on equipment and also the amount they might spend under certain conditions, which conditions they are also asked to specify. The survey thus gives not merely a simple forecast but a relationship which links investment of private enterprises with different economic variables (turnover, possibility of self-financing, possibility of borrowing, etc.)

The survey among businessmen is not the sole source of information concerning investment. Certain Ministries in France specialise in the study and control of the major sections of industry and are generally fairly well informed through the trade bodies on the investment projects of private business. The " Commissariat Général du Plan " is itself in contact with enterprises which submit full particulars of their investment projects to it; the same applies to the Directorate in the Ministry of Finance which is responsible for economic intervention.

As regards dwellings, a commission is responsible for consolidating all the detailed information that can be obtained on this sector. This information concerns the filing of applications for building permits, construction started in the previous year, and certain financial variables: the subsidies and loans granted directly by the Government, the limits the Government sets on the expansion of credit for house building, etc.

With regard to exports, the forecasts made centrally are compared with those prepared by the administrative departments specialising in the study of foreign trade. These departments use information which they receive from the French commercial services in foreign countries.

The same sources of information are used for imports, the Customs authorities being best placed to forecast imports some months ahead for main commodity groups.

During this stage, information is obtained not only on the principal demand factors but also on production. As regards agriculture, the forecasts of production of agricultural products are compared with those made by the trade bodies. In the other sectors the comparison is done generally through the agency of the Ministries concerned; sometimes, however, it takes place directly with the trade bodies, and, in the case of the nationalised undertakings and certain large enterprises, with their economic departments. Certain private economic research services also submit the forecasts made by the national accountants to the businesses with which they have close relations and forward the information obtained to the national accountants.

The assumptions made on the prices of each commodity group are examined with the experts of the " Direction Générale des Prix. " As regards the tariffs fixed by the Government, and particularly those at which the large national monopolies sell their products, complete operating accounts are drawn up which show whether there is consistency between the Government decisions on prices, subsidies and wages and the enterprises' projects for financing their investment.

Similarly a complete operating account for agriculture makes it possible to assess the consequences of Government decisions on agricultural prices, from the point of view of the forecasts of production of agricultural products and the forecasts of purchases of other products by the agricultural sector.

The information stage also improves the national accountants' knowledge of the expenditures and revenues of general government, though generally not to a great extent for central government, since this information is already good at the first stage; this is not the case for the local authorities, their dependent agencies, and especially the Social Security institutions.

A last series of data is obtained by comparing the financial forecasts to which we referred above with the forecasts of the various bodies and particularly the " Direction du Trésor " at the Ministry of Finance, the Bank of France, the " Caisse des Dépôts et Consignations " and the various specialist credit institutions.

4 THE THIRD STAGE OF FORECASTS

The third stage of the work is to make a synthesis of all this information and check its consistency. A first test of consistency is a purely accounting one: for each type of product, for each operation, and for each type of instrument of credit, the balance between uses and resources is checked. But a second series of tests must be carried out to ascertain whether all the behaviour equations used in the centralised preparation of the account are in fact satisfied.

The first series of tests starts with the preparation of a new input-output table. This table is in fact an extremely convenient instrument for comparing, in respect of each product, all the information obtained. The comparison is of course made more difficult by the fact that intermediate consumption of a product by a sector depends on the production of that sector and therefore on the result of the synthesis itself. Consequently efforts are made to study the balance of products in such an order that a product is only studied after the production of all the banches which consume it has been virtually finally ascertained.

The comparison of the forecasts of uses and resources is done first at the previous year's prices. The comparison often makes it possible to improve considerably the forecasts for imports or changes in stocks. To achieve balance, it is sometimes necessary for a choice to be made between information which is found to be contradictory; the methods used ensure that the national accountants responsible for making this choice are in possession of all the available information.

The preparation of the forecast input-output tables in volume and value leads to an assumption about the value added by sector and the total value added. The present tendency in the preparation of economic budgets in France is to try to break down the value added by sector into its main components: wages, taxes, income of enterprises, and compare the forecasts of incomes thus made with the forecasts made when the Plan was prepared. If considerable differences are found, special studies are undertaken in order to account for them. These differences could have three sources: they may be due to the special conditions in the year being studied; to errors in the preparation of the Plan; or to errors in the preparation of the economic budget. This comparison is one example of how the methods of forecasting used for the medium term and the short term—very different methods—complement and help to improve each other.

The next step after the study of the distribution of value added is the compilation of a forecast account for households. This account is compared with that in the global model at the outset, and also with the forecast accounts for households contained in the long term forecasts. It happens more often than not that the account differs from that obtained initially which may make it necessary to do the forecast all over again. This does not of course mean that all the information operations have to be repeated; the collection of information in the second stage is carried out with this risk in mind, and the questionnaires are framed in such a way as to give not only a forecast but also the information necessary to modify it. It sometimes happens that the work of synthesis shows why the relationships used at the beginning were not good ones and must be replaced by those which are disclosed by the final synthesis.

5 SHORTER-TERM FORECASTS

The economic budget thus constructed gives an annual forecast. Owing to its detailed nature it is possible to calculate the annual values of the items whose seasonal variation is best known: production of the industries covered by the index of industrial production, wholesale and retail prices appearing in the price indices, wages in industries covered by the quarterly survey of wages. The variation of these items during the year is then determined, taking into account what is known about the general economic situation at the end of the previous year. The probability of the trends found is assessed by the specialists in conjunctural studies. This may result in certain elements of the final synthesis being called in question. Thus very short-term, short-term and medium-term forecasts have become permanent features of French administrative practice.

CHAPTER IV

THE NETHERLANDS: SHORT-TERM ECONOMIC PLANNING AND FORECASTING

1 INTRODUCTION

As the theory of quantitative economic planning has been developed in the Netherlands and applied in practice, it owes very much to the work of Tinbergen. Although his ideas about economic policy took a more definite shape during and after the second world war, he had constructed an econometric policy model for the Netherlands as early as 1936, in order to study the effectiveness of various policy actions to cope with the depression of the thirties[1]. In 1945, immediately after the war, when the decision was taken to establish the Central Planning Bureau (CPB), he was appointed its first director. Within a few years he succeeded in extending the bureau to a size and level which has not changed considerably since.

In the present context a few remarks on the framework of Tinbergen's theory seem useful. For a more detailed account reference must be made to his own writings.[2]

The starting point of his analysis is a model of the economy for which economic policy actions have to be formulated. This model should describe in a more or less simplified way the economic mechanism of the economy concerned. If the policy actions are of an overall character—as they generally are in the Netherlands—it suffices to use a macro model in which only global concepts like total production, total employment, etc. are introduced. It goes without saying that the type of the model may vary according to the length of the period in view of which policies are to be outlined.

The model contains endogenous and exogenous variables. The first group includes the targets and other variables, irrelevant ones in Tinbergen's terminology. The exogenous variables include the external data and the instruments. The policy problem is, of course, which values should be assigned to the instrument variables in order to attain the targets set. In Tinbergen's view, the logic of economic policy is, therefore, in a sense, an inversion of the logic to which the analytical economist is accustomed. " The problem of economic policy considers the targets as given and the instrument values as unknown, or at least partly unknown "[3].

---

1. Tinbergen, J., " Is a Recovery in the Domestic Situation of this Country Possible, with or without Action on the Part of the Government, Even without an Improvement in Our Export Position? What Can Be Learned about this Problem from the Experience of Other Countries? " Paper read before the Dutch Economic Association, 1936.
2. Tinbergen, J., *Economic Policy, Principles and Design* (North Holland Publishing Company, Amsterdam, 1956).
3. Ibid., page 9.

It will not always be possible to reach a given set of targets; this is particularly true when their number exceeds the number of available instruments. In the theory of quantitative policy the way out of this difficulty can be found by means of a social welfare function. In the practice of economic policy this problem has to be solved by means of an appropriate institutional framework, which may guarantee a maximum regard to existing preferences. Therefore, a few remarks will be made below on the institutional aspects of Dutch economic planning.

The theory of quantitative economic policy, based on these concepts, has been refined in a number of ways, varying from policy formulation under uncertainty to improved methods of parameter estimation in econometric models. Notwithstanding these refinements, the actual practice of Dutch planning is still in conformity with Tinbergen's version, although the econometric model in use is regularly adapted to progress made in the field of model construction and parameter estimation.

2 CHARACTERISTICS OF SHORT-TERM PLANNING IN THE NETHERLANDS

The Dutch concept of planning

From the concept of quantitative economic policy to the definition of Dutch economic planning there is only one step. It has been explained that this theory has two principal components. The first is the model, which describes the relation between targets of economic policy and policy actions. The second is the evaluation of the targets and instruments which enables the policy maker to choose between policy alternatives. Only one step is needed to arrive at planning, because planning involves forecasting.

Forecasts are made on the basis of the expected changes in the external data. In the first instance, such predictions are usually made assuming unchanged policy. The results then have to be compared with the targets set. This confrontation may lead to a study of the implications of various policy changes. Each of them will lead to an alternative forecast, and in principle that one will be chosen that gives optimal results. It is this procedure which is characteristic of central economic planning in the Netherlands.

In the Netherlands the economic system is of the mixed economy type; it does not differ very much from the type met in several other Western economies. The policy targets are the usual global ones, referring to the rate of growth, the level of employment, balance of payments equilibrium, the level of prices and the distribution of income. Apart from these general aims there are a few more specific ones concerning regional development, residential construction, etc. They are, in the present context, less relevant.

The instruments, too, are largely familiar ones. They include budgetary and monetary policy, and also the policy of licencing construction activity. Less familiar are wage and price policies. The instruments are mainly of a macro-economic character. Differentiation of policy actions, e.g. with respect to branches of industry, is an exception rather than a rule.

Going into details one may of course find special traits. It would go too far, however, to give a detailed description of the various instruments.

Reference may be made to the existing literature in this field[1]. Here it may suffice to say that the wage policy, introduced immediately after the war, has undergone several changes leading to a strong shift in responsibility for the determination of wages from the central government to the negotiating organisations of employers and employees. At present, the general principles for their discussions are based on a report of the Social Economic Council on the general economic situation, and are worked out in the officially recognized Foundation of Labour, where the federations of trade unions and entrepreneurial organisations meet. The government has still some possibility of control. It may announce a wage pause or it may reimpose complete control over wages. However, it is agreed that this will happen in exceptional circumstances only.

The present wage policy cannot therefore be called an instrument of central economic policy in the ordinary sense of the word. But, the system which is followed in this respect, enables the authorities to form an opinion about the future rise in wages, while some safeguards have been introduced to prevent developments getting out of hand.

Although planning in the sense defined above can be applied to long and short-term planning, it is the latter which received the greatest attention during the post-war period. In practice, annual forecasts were made to find out whether the main policy targets would be attained in the short run, and which corrective policy measures would eventually have to be designed. The machinery set up to perform this task as well as the methodologies applied are discussed in the following sections.

The institutional framework [2]

The overall or macro-economic aspect of the economic policy in the Netherlands has already been stressed above. In the preparation of this policy the Central Planning Bureau (CPB) plays a characteristic rôle.

The Bureau was founded in 1945. It acquired its definite statutory basis when, in 1947, Parliament approved the so-called Central Economic Plan Act. According to this act a plan has to be prepared annually, a plan being defined as " a balanced system of forecasts and directives in relation to the Netherlands economy." In virtue of the same act, a Central Planning Committee (CPC) was set up as managing board of the CPB and advisory committee to the Minister of Economic Affairs to whom the CPB formally belongs. The members of the CPC are appointed by the Minister of Economic Affairs; they are chosen from trade union officials, representatives of employers organisations, scientific circles, etc.

The budget year in the Netherlands coincides with the calendar year. Hence it is understandable that the plans which have been designed by the CPB since 1946 also refer to calendar years.

On the third Tuesday in September the central government presents its budget proposals to Parliament. It has become customary, since 1961, to

---

1. OEEC, *The Problem of Rising Prices*, report of a group of experts, (Paris, May 1961), particularly Appendix 4, pages 359-390; OECD, *Policies for Price Stability*, report of the Working Party on Costs of Production and Prices of the Economic Policy Committee (Paris, November 1962), particularly page 45.
2. See *Scope and Methods of the Central Planning Bureau* (The Hague, 1956).

publish at the same time a preliminary version of the Central Economic Plan. This means, for example, that in September 1963 the government budget proposals for the calendar year 1964 were published, together with the first version of the 1964 plan. Essentially, such a plan is a global forecast on the basis of policies outlined by the government up to that time. The content of the forecast is entirely the responsibility of the CPB.

Before it is published, the Plan is discussed with officials representing the various ministries. The final discussion on the policy assumptions and the evaluation of the results takes place in the Council of Economic Affairs. This Council is a subcommittee of the Cabinet. Its meetings are attended by the President of the Netherlands Bank and the Director of the Central Planning Bureau. In order to facilitate the discussions alternative forecasts on the basis of alternative assumptions may be presented.

Under normal circumstances the final version of the Central Economic Plan (1964) is published in the beginning of the year (1964). The outcome of this final version may differ from the earlier one, since:

a) more statistical data are available on recent developments;
b) before closing the calculations a number of large firms is interviewed on investment plans, sales expectations, etc. This may lead to a revision of the original estimates;
c) the final estimates are not only macro-economic but also specified to branches of industry. This may also lead to revisions;
d) the policy assumptions may have to be revised.

The final version of the Plan is again discussed with the ministries, and, in the last instance, in the Council of Economic Affairs. It is also the subject of discussion in the Central Planning Commission, which is supposed to give its comments.

In connection with recent changes in wage policy, a new function has been attributed to the first version of the Plan which is being published together with the budget proposals. Before discussing this aspect the relation between the CPB and the Social Economic Council has to be described.

The Social Economic Council was established in accordance with the 1950 Act on the Industrial Organisation. It is a tri-partite body, at present consisting of 45 members. One third of its members is appointed by the federations of the trade unions, one third by the federations of employers organisations and one third by the government. These "crown members" are called upon to take care of the general interest.

The Council plays an important rôle in the public industrial organisation. In the present context, however, its advisory task is most important. According to the Act of 1950, the Government must ask the Council's advice in important social and economic problems. Unlike the CPB the Council is a political body, and the advice it has given since its establishment has had an important bearing on social and economic policy. The CPB frequently acts as technical adviser to the Council. The relations between the two are strengthened by the fact that the director of the CPB is usually appointed to be one of the crown members.

It is therefore quite natural that the Council recently decided to take the first published version of the Central Economic Plan as the starting

The Netherlands

point for its discussions on the economic situation, which according to the rules of the present wage formation system ought to end up in the indication of the desirable development of next year's wage level.

3 FORECASTING TECHNIQUES

As will be clear from what has been said before, the forecasts on which short-term planning in the Netherlands depend, are mainly based on econometric models. Such models have been developed continuously during the last fifteen years. Comparing the earlier pre- and post-war models with the most recent ones there appear to be important differences. In particular, recent models—in use since 1958—are much more dynamic than the earlier ones. Other differences result from the introduction of non-linearities and from the application of more refined methods of parameter estimation. In practice, the two and three stage least squares methods of estimation as well as the limited information maximum likelihood method were applied, in addition to the ordinary least squares procedure. On the other hand, the models show a number of common characteristics since they are all macro-economic, they are short-term, i.e. describing annual movements of the economy, and they are constructed for purposes of prediction as well as the calculation of policy alternatives.

The recent models will not be fully described here. Reference may be made to the Central Economic Plan 1961 in which the 1961 model is presented and discussed at some length[1]. Here it may suffice to say that this model contains a number of reaction equations referring to the categories of expenditure—private consumption, private investment in fixed assets, stock formation and merchandise exports—to the price levels of these expenditures (including public expenditure on goods and services), to the level of wages in industry, import demand, labour demand and supply, and to the supply of liquidities. Institutional equations for direct and indirect tax revenues as well as for unemployment benefits complete the system.

The model is not a pure demand model, in the sense that the level of production is thought to be fully determined by factors on the demand side. This is true only in case of high unemployment of the factors of production. When, however, capacity limits tend to be reached the effect on production is increasingly felt. In fact, the capacity variable plays a rôle in no less than six reaction equations. It will be understood that this also explains the non-linearities in the model.

Some variables in the model are predetermined, others are jointly dependent. The latter are predicted on the basis of the model. The values of the predetermined variables, on the other hand, are obtained outside the model.

Predetermined are the values of the lagged endogenous variables, or, more generally, the situation in the base period. As will be clear from what has been said above[2] part of the base year has to be estimated, since the prediction period is always longer than one year. This is particularly true of the first published version of the Central Economic Plan, for which the prediction period lies between one and a half and two years.

---

1. Cf. Central Economic Plan 1961. Appendix A.
2. See pages 71 and 72.

Other predetermined variables are the external data and the instrument variables. The main external data are import prices, competitive prices abroad and the volume of world trade. The latter is estimated on the basis of:
- *a)* information supplied by international organisations and the countries themselves, and
- *b)* calculations by the Central Planning Bureau itself. For this purpose use has been made, *inter alia*, of a world trade model. Thus far, however, this appears to be of too simplified a nature to give sufficiently reliable results. Further research in this field is being undertaken.

Competitive prices abroad are predicted on the basis of expected labour costs in industrial countries. Import price predictions require—in so far as raw materials are concerned—estimates of raw material prices on world markets. These have to be purely guessed, although they are not considered as completely independent of (the prospects of) world trade.

The instrument variables refer to government expenditure, tax rates, etc. Expenditures by the central government and tax rates are obtained from the central government budget. It is to be noted, however, that this budget is an authorization rather than a performance budget, which may make adjustments necessary. Expenditures by local authorities are more difficult to predict. Frequently, extrapolation must suffice. There is some connection, however, between local authorities capital expenditure and the situation on the capital market. The latter will be discussed at the end of this section where the monetary analysis is explained at some length.

At present, construction activity is subject to government licence. It appears therefore as another important exogenous variable in the model. The same is true of the wage level in industry. Though the model contains an equation for this variable, wages are under present circumstances estimated mainly on the basis of the wage reports by the Social Economic Council, taking into account also the rise in wages because of the so-called wage drift.

When the values of the external data and the instrument variables have been obtained, the forecasts follow immediately from the solution of the model. Alternative forecasts on the basis, e.g., of alternative policy assumptions are easily obtained. In fact, the number of policy actions that can be introduced in the model is rather large. The list below summarizes the possibilities in this respect.

Autonomous components can be inserted:

INTO THE EQUATION (S) FOR:	TO STUDY THE SHORT-RUN EFFECTS OF:
direct taxes	changes in tax rates on wage and non-wage income respectively.
indirect taxes	changes in tax rates on consumption, etc.
wages in industry	changes in wage policy and introduction of social security measures.
prices	price stabilization policies, rent control and changes in the rate of exchange.
supply of liquidities	changes in monetary policy.
imports and exports of commodities	trade liberalization measures.
labour supply	shorter working hours.
investments in industry	changes in licence policy.

Policy actions in the field of government expenditure on goods and services, government transfer payments and residential construction activity have to be added to the above list of instruments.

The Netherlands

The model approach of prediction suggests a purely mechanical procedure. In practice this is not so. The model outcomes are always checked on the basis of any additional information. Before closing, for example, the calculations for the final version of the Central Economic Plan a number of large firms is asked for their investment plans, sales expectations, etc. Moreover, the macro estimates are always followed by branch of industry predictions, which provide another check on the original forecasts.

It is still too early to conclude, e.g., that the model outcomes should be preferred to those obtained from the enquiry. The time series for which the results of both methods can be compared are as yet too short.

Valuable information on current events is obtained from quarterly analyses which are continuously being undertaken on the basis of seasonally adjusted data. The quarterly analysis contributes considerably to the understanding of the current state of affairs and, consequently, to the estimation of the base year figures from which the annual model starts.

The quarterly analysis plays an obvious rôle in the advisory task of the CPB. Apart from the annual plans, the CPB reports twice or three times a year on current events as well as on developments for the following three or four quarters. These reports may contain policy recommendations. They are discussed in the Council of Economic Affairs. It will be clear that policy recommendations do not necessarily originate within the CPB. Policy measures may of course be proposed by the CEA and the CPB may be charged with the task of studying their consequences.

At present, quarterly predictions are for the greater part based on interpolations of the outcomes of the annual model. In a not too distant future a more systematic approach will be possible in this respect on the basis of a quarterly model, the construction of which was started some time ago.

The foregoing makes it clear that the annual model is not used mechanically. Information from outside the model is obtained in order to analyse current events as closely as possible and to make the forecasts as realistic as possible. In this connection a few comments have to be made, finally, on the monetary analysis which constitutes an integral part of each Central Economic Plan[1]. It is true, the model contains monetary variables, viz. in the equations for private investment and private consumption. To make the monetary analysis more complete, however, the monetary flows are systematically registered in the so-called monetary survey, an abbreviated example of which is given below. In actual practice it distinguishes five sectors: households and enterprises, institutional investors, central government, local authorities and foreign countries. In the example below the number of sectors has been reduced to three.

The main function of the monetary survey is to throw light upon the creation of liquidities[2] in a given period via the three liquidity-creating sectors: the banking system, the balance of payments and the government. The

---

1. For a discussion of the various aspects of monetary analyses, see Stevers, Th. A., *Monetary Statement and Monetary Analysis*, Monograph No. 7, of the Central Planning Bureau (The Hague, 1959).

2. Liquidities in the monetary survey include primary as well as secondary liquidities. Liquidities in the 1961 model are more narrowly defined, because the 1961 model is—like all recent models—based on pre- and post-war data, and pre-war data on secondary liquidities are only partially available.

MONETARY SURVEY[1]
SUMMARY TABLE, YEAR 1963

Billions of guilders.

	PRIVATE SECTOR	GOVERN-MENT	FOREIGN COUNTRIES
1. Savings	6.46	2.44	—0.50
2. Net investments	6.23	2.17	0.00
Income surplus (1—2)	(0.23)	(0.27)	(—0.50)
3. Capital transfers received	0.33	—0.27	—0.06
Net increase in financial assets (1—2+3)	(0.56)	(0.00)	(—0.56)
reflected in:			
4. Government credits supplied	—1.38	1.43	—0.05
5. Increase in claims on account of differences between cash and accrual basis; miscellaneous[2]	—0.76	0.45	0.31
Finance surplus (1—2+3—4—5)	(2.70)	(—1.88)	(—0.82)
6. Supply on capital market	2.18	—2.28	0.10
Liquidity surplus (1—2+3—4—5—6)	(0.52)	(0.40)	(—0.92)
7. Cancellation of (primary plus secondary) liquidities through redemption	—1.30	0.40	—0.92
8. Accumulation of (primary plus secondary) liquidities (1—2+3—4—5—6—7)	1.82	0.00	0.00

1. *Source :* Central Economic Plan 1964.
2. Includes statistical discrepancies.

total amount of liquidities in circulation divided by the national income is used as a criterion for the presence or absence of monetary tensions. The survey also shows, e.g., the resort of the government to the capital market corresponding with some assumption about the creation of liquidities by the government. In this way, an important aspect of the government monetary policy finds its proper place in the analysis of current and future events.

Experience shows that monetary tensions may reflect themselves in lower government expenditure, in particular in lower capital expenditure by the local authorities. Reference was already made above to this relation between the situation on the capital market and local authorities expenditures. Strong monetary tensions will also reflect themselves in the level of private expenditure. In the case of full depletion of liquid reserves, boundary conditions will occur. The point is, that boundary conditions cannot be taken into full account by the monetary variables in the model. This is just another reason why the model cannot always be applied mechanically.

4 EVALUATION OF FORECASTS

Forecasting results

No complete account will be given here of the experience acquired with the planning system during the post-war period. Such an evaluation would of necessity be rather lengthy as it ought to pay attention to a large number of aspects such as the quality of the different models, the changes introduced and the reasons why, their effect on the results and the reliability of the forecasts, the relation between forecasts and policy measures, the rôle of structural factors interfering with the short-term policy consideration in the final choice of measures, etc. Research has been done in this respect and information on these aspects can be found in a recent CPB monograph about developments since 1950[1]. In the present section, a few words will be said only on the forecasting results in the last ten years, on the basis of comparisons between forecasts and realizations.

The quality of the predictions by the Netherlands Central Planning Bureau has been analyzed in a recent study[2]. In this study, which covers the period 1953–1962, a comparison is made between the forecasts published in the Central Economic Plans and the most recent national accounts figures published by the Netherlands Central Bureau of Statistics. In general, the forecasts were taken as they stand. Adjustments were made, however, for unforeseen policy changes. The revaluation of the guilder in March 1961, for example, was not foreseen in the Central Economic Plan 1961. In a case like this the forecasts were corrected for the consequences of the change in policy. Such consequences had of course to be estimated. This was done on the basis of the 1961 model.

Denoting by $R_{i,t}$ the realization, i.e. the observed percentage change of the i-th variable in period t, and by $F_{i,t}$ the corresponding forecast change, the predictive error is

$$U_{i,t} = F_{i,t} - R_{i,t}$$

Using as a measure of predictive accuracy:

$$U'_{i,t} = \frac{U_{i,t}}{\bar{S}_{R_i}},$$

where $\bar{S}_{R_i}$ denotes the root-mean-square of the observed changes in i, taken from zero. This statistic is meant to represent the normal intensity of change of the variable i in the period of observation.

For a number of m variables (i = 1, 2, ... m) the inequality coefficient is defined as follows

$$U'_t = \sqrt{\frac{1}{m} \Sigma U'_{i,t}{}^2}.$$

An accuracy measure of the forecasts of one variable over a number of periods can be obtained similarly.[3] It will be clear that $U'_t = 0$ in case of perfect forecasts. The coefficient has no finite upper boundary. When its

---

1. Van den Beld, C.A., *Conjunctuurpolitiek in en om de jaren vijftig*, Monograph No. 8 of the Central Planning Bureau. An English translation entitled *Dutch Short-term Economic Policy in the Fifties*, will appear shortly.
2. De Wolff, P. and van den Beld, C. A., "Ten Years of Forecasts and Realisations, Inquiry into the Quality of the Predictions by the Netherlands Central Planning Bureau, 1953-1962", paper presented at the Ottawa meeting of the International Statistical Institute, August 1963.
3. Ferber, R. and Verdoorn, P. J., *Research Methods in Economics and Business* (Macmillan, New York, 1962), pp. 476 ff. This inequality coefficient has been published earlier by P. J. Verdoorn and C. J. van Eijk, in *Experimental Short-term Forecasting Models* (Central Planning Bureau, 1958).

value approaches unity, however, the prediction results have to be considered as very unsatisfactory, in the case of prediction by variable over time as unsatisfactory as no-change extrapolation.

A number of inequality coefficients by variable are given in Table 1, for the ten year period 1953-1962 as well as for the five years 1958-1962. A distinction is made between exogenous variables, controlled and non-controlled, and endogenous ones. The predicted controlled variables have been corrected for unforeseen policy changes in a limited number of cases only, for a complete correction would at least in a number of cases render the comparison of forecast and realization senseless. Predicted government expenditures were not corrected at all, since supplementary budgets played a minor or even negligible rôle in the period of observation.

The predictions of the controlled variables have been considerably improved in recent years. This is not true of the remaining exogenous variables, the external data. This reflects the extreme difficulties involved in predicting developments abroad.

The endogenous forecasts, in turn, were definitely better in recent years. Apart from improved statistical information and cumulative experience, this result has to be ascribed to the construction of the new, more dynamic models in use since 1958. The quarterly analysis, which was started in 1957 to follow short-run economic developments more closely, also contributed to the higher accuracy of these predictions.

TABLE 1. INEQUALITY COEFFICIENTS

	1953-1962	1958-1962
Exogenous variables		
Controlled:		
Wage level in industries	0.29	0.20
Government wage bill	0.29	0.12
Other public consumption expenditure	0.69	0.47
Public investment expenditure	0.92	0.22
Volume of residential construction	0.70	0.54
Non-controlled:		
Price level of commodity imports	0.56	0.56
Volume of world trade	0.63	0.54
Competitive price level on foreign markets	0.74	0.68
Endogenous variables		
Employment in industries	0.30	0.18
Price level of consumption	0.42	0.46
Volume of private consumption	0.42	0.16
Volume of commodity imports	0.42	0.20
Volume of production in industries	0.48	0.38
Price level of exports	0.54	0.59
Unemployment	0.56	0.48
Volume of commodity exports	0.58	0.57
Balance on current account of the balance of payments	0.75	0.44
Volume of gross investment in industries[1]	0.77	0.50
Price level of gross investment	0.80	0.53
Non-wage income	0.82	0.64
Formation of stocks	1.04	0.44

1. Residential construction not included.

The Netherlands

In Table 2 the inequality coefficients are summarized by Central Economic Plans. For some plans (1954, 1956, 1958, 1961), the quality of the predictions is illustrated by means of the traditional graphs, in which the actual changes are plotted against the predicted ones.

TABLE 2. INEQUALITY COEFFICIENTS BY CENTRAL ECONOMIC PLANS

	1953	1954	1955	1956	1957	1958	1959	1960	1961	1962
Exogenous variables:										
controlled	0.71	0.74	0.91	0.54	1.06	0.46	0.18	0.38	0.23	0.42
uncontrolled (external)	0.43	1.06	0.69	0.76	0.38	0.68	0.78	0.57	0.50	0.34
sub-total	0.63	0.85	0.83	0.63	0.87	0.55	0.50	0.46	0.36	0.39
Endogenous variables: *of which:*	0.86	0.93	0.84	0.66	0.50	0.53	0.58	0.48	0.36	0.22
targets[1]	0.67	0.90	0.89	0.66	0.39	0.50	0.77	0.28	0.37	0.18
All variables:	0.79	0.90	0.84	0.65	0.67	0.54	0.55	0.47	0.36	0.28

1. Balance of payments current account, unemployment, volume of investment and price level of consumption.

The figures of Table 2 show again the considerable improvement in the prediction of the controlled variables (after 1957). The external forecasts appear to be highly inaccurate in years of rapid expansion of world trade (1954, 1959). In general, the inequality coefficients of the external variables tend to become lower. The trend, however, is small.

It is much more marked for the endogenous forecasts. In this case, too, the deviations from the trend are of interest. The coefficients tend to rise in periods of rapid expansion (1954/5, 1959/60). The reverse holds for years of relative stagnation (1956/7, 1961; cf. also the graphs). This illustrates the general point that bold projections are difficult to make. Turning points are relatively well predicted, as is evident from the few number of points appearing in the second and fourth quadrant of the graphs.

The inequality coefficients of the targets of economic policy, given separately in Table 2, are of the same order of magnitude as the overall coefficients. Since policy actions tend to be mainly based on the predictions of the target values, the conclusion follows that the predictions have become a considerably more reliable guide line for such actions in recent years than they were in the more distant past.

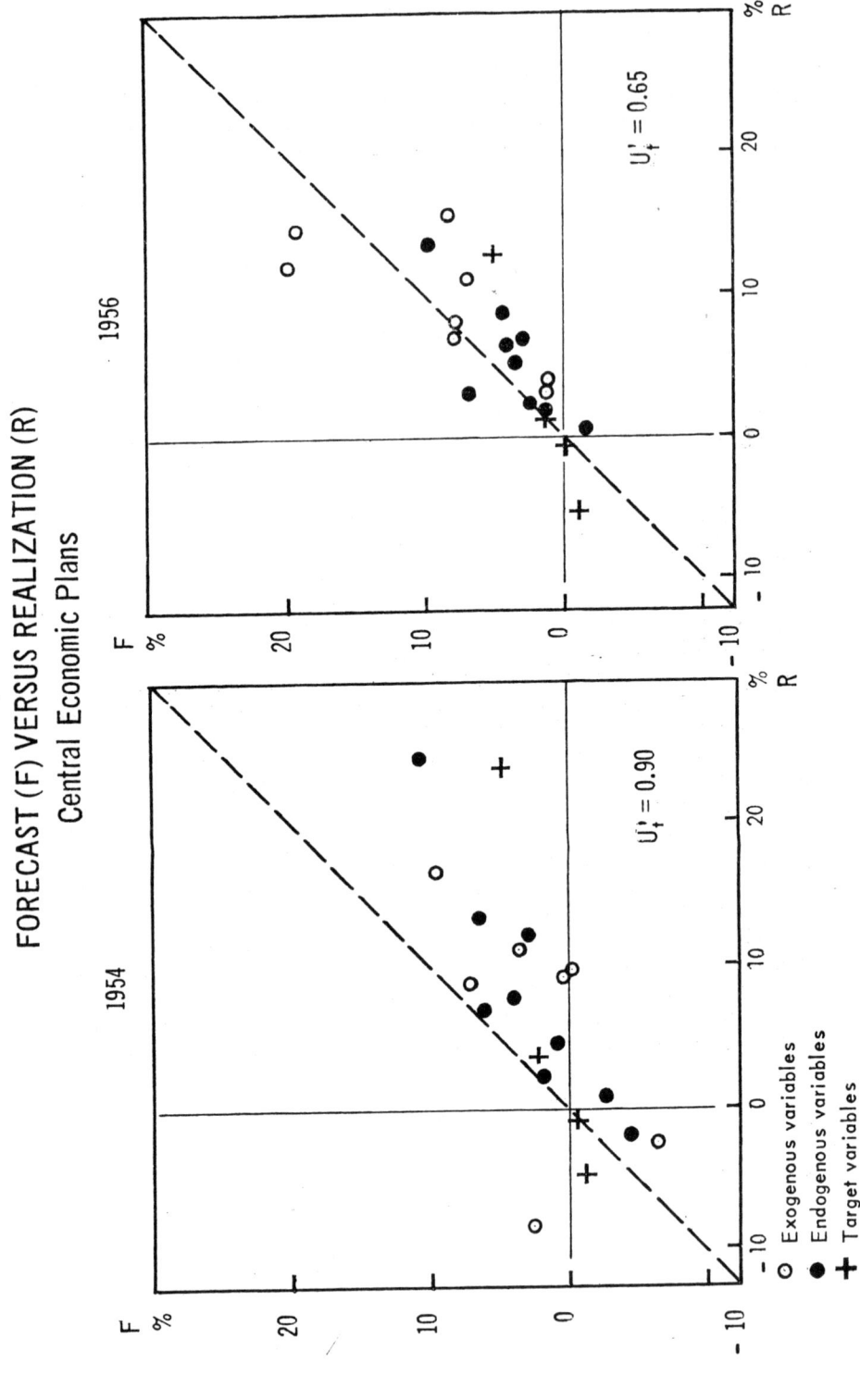

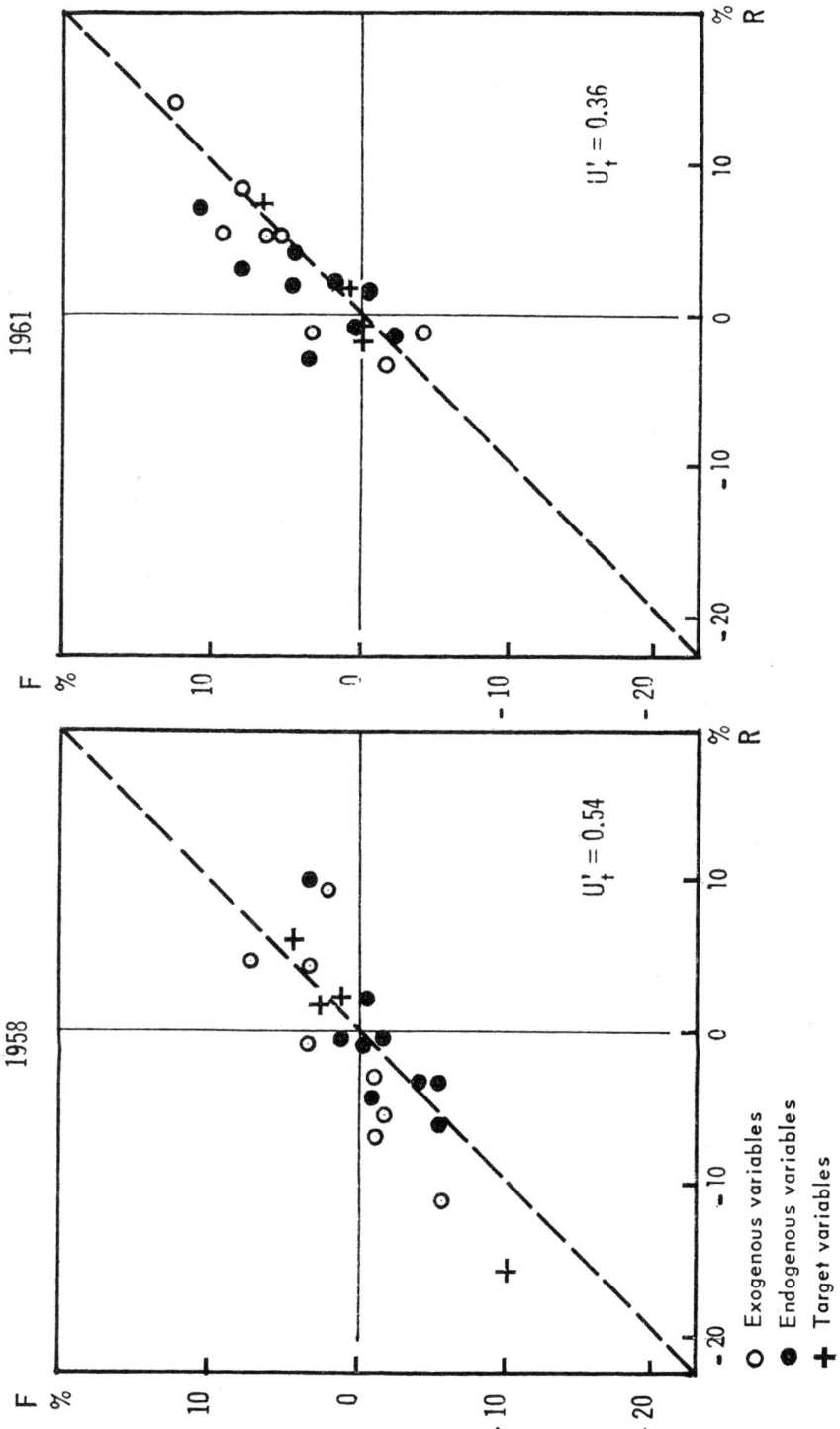

CHAPTER V

SWEDEN: SHORT-TERM FORECASTING

1 GENERAL PRINCIPLES FOR ECONOMIC FORECASTS

During the depression of the 1930's economic policy changed from passive registration to active intervention. The need and demand for economic statistics and analysis therefore increased greatly. In order to meet these increased requirements the National Institute of Economic Research was established in 1937. The Institute was given the task to follow up and analyse economic developments.

The problems connected with insistent pressure of demand against resources during the second World War led the National Institute of Economic Research to undertake inflationary gap calculations, i.e. calculations of the *ex ante* discrepancies between supply and demand in the commodity markets. Thereby a method was developed for appraising the probability of overstraining the resources of the economy. This method was for several years essential for the work on forecasts. The calculations were transferred to the work of the Ministry of Finance by the creation of the National Budget Delegation in 1947[1].

From 1948 onwards, a National Budget has been presented in connection with the Finance Bill at the opening of the Parliament in January. The National Budget provides background material to the economic policy proposed in the Finance Bill. Since 1956, a revised National Budget has been presented at the end of the spring session of the Parliament. This Revised Budget forms the basis of the Supplementary Finance Bill, summing up the various Bills presented after the Finance Bill and containing also a revision of the estimated income for the next fiscal year. In addition, a Research Council for consultation and supervision was founded in 1954. The members bear, however, no responsibility for the form and judgments of the National Budgets. The Research Council consists of the heads of the Industrial Institute for Economic and Social Research, the Agricultural Research Institute, the National Institute of Economic Research, the Research Departments of the Federation of Trade Unions, of the Swedish Employers Association and of the Organization of Salaried Employees. The chief of the Economic Division of the Ministry of Finance is chairman.

In October at the opening of the autumn session of the Parliament the National Institute of Economic Research presents a forecast. This forecast as well as the Preliminary and Revised National Budget are now published in the series *The Swedish Economy*.

---

1. The office of the Delegation of the National Budget was transformed into the Economic Division of the Ministry of Finance in 1957.

As earlier mentioned the gap technique was used for forecasting work during a long succession of years. During some of the latest years this technique has, however, been departed from. Particularly during years with divergent development for different sectors an inflationary/deflationary gap calculation has been considered insufficient or misleading; therefore direct prognosis has been made instead. More work has also been devoted to sector analysis. In the following the gap technique will first be described and then the methods of sector forecasts also will be briefly outlined.

The gap calculation is based on mutually independent *ex ante* estimates both from the demand side and the supply side[1]. If demand is larger than supply, an inflationary gap is apparent; if the opposite is the case, a deflationary gap. In practice the calculations are based on the levels of the previous year and the result is presented as changes from these levels. The calculated gap is thus an order of difference—one has to take the initial gap situation into consideration. This is dependent both on the gap of the preceding year and on the manner in which this gap might have been closed. The whole calculation is made under the assumption of no change in economic policy.

The supply side of the balance of resources consists of gross national product and imports. The growth in the GNP is estimated by means of data on the development of the labour force and of calculations of the development of productivity on the assumption of unchanged economic policy. If there is idle capacity of production at the outset, the above estimation does not provide the answer of how great the maximum increase in production during the next year will be. The necessary prerequisite for making this estimate is knowledge of the initial degree of capacity utilization. This is one of the complications that make this method most easily applicable to a situation with marked full capacity utilization.

Next item on the supply side, i.e. imports, is calculated under the assumption of constant marginal relations between imports and certain sectors of demand and production. If the over-all calculation results in an inflationary gap, it might, however, not be consistent with the above-mentioned assumption. In such cases, one should thus consider the possibility that part of the inflationary gap corresponds to an underestimation of imports.

The supply as well as the demand side of the balance of resources is basically made at constant prices. On the demand side private consumption cannot, however, be directly estimated in terms of volume changes since it is based on calculations of disposable nominal income. The increase in the disposable nominal income has been calculated on the assumption of equilibrium in the labour market. In order to obtain the increase in disposable real income the increase in the disposable nominal income is deflated by the price increase that can be estimated from the cost side. The calculation is thus not adjusted for the impact of factors that might influence prices from the demand side. The other demand components are mainly obtained from plan statistics and survey information.

A calculated gap can motivate an economic policy that strives to close the gap and thereby actually realizes the equilibrium, from which the calcula-

---

1. In Table 1, an example is given of the numerical estimate in which the National Budget work results, viz, the Balance of Resources.

tions on the supply side started. If in a (correctly estimated) gap situation the government takes no action, equilibrium will not be attained. But the calculation is not constructed in such a way as to give information about the ensuing process and the *ex post* situation it will lead up to. The calculation of the gap thus aims directly to give a guideline to economic policy rather than to be a pure forecast. This can be illustrated by a diagram using a technique that is well-known from economics textbooks.

In the initial situation income is Y_1. Increases in productivity and in the labour force are expected to raise the *possible* income level to Y_3 in the forecast period. But planned investment will increase only from I to I_2 thus leaving a deflationary gap of ΔI. The gap analysis aims at predicting this gap by-passing the forecast of the income Y_2 which would take place if the gap is *not* closed by some sort of economic policy. In the earlier years of national budgeting when intense inflationary tendencies prevailed the procedure can be said to have been the other way round. Then the desired amount of investment was taken as a starting-point and the possible scope for private consumption was obtained as residual.

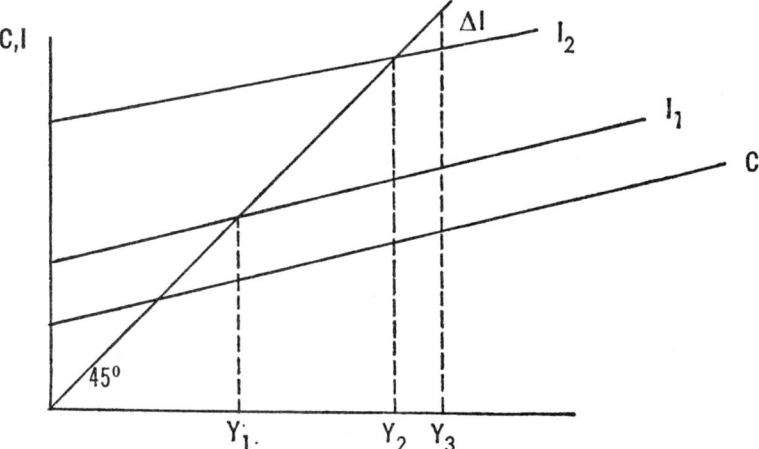

C = Consumption
I = Investment
Y = Total Income

It must, however, be recalled that the gap is of the order of a difference. Interpretation of a gap is therefore considerably more difficult when we start from a non-equilibrium position than an equilibrium position. (Point Y_1 in the diagram then does *not* represent an initial full employment situation.) Then we cannot assume that *ex ante* equilibrium is by itself an optimum situation. This reasoning will be illustrated below by a closer study of the National Budget for 1959.

The initial situation for the National Budget work was the slack economic activity which persisted during 1958. On the supply side the production increase for 1959 was estimated in the manner described earlier. In this way the calculation resulted in an *ex ante* equilibrium as is indicated

Economic Forecasting

TABLE 1. REVISED BALANCE OF RESOURCES FOR 1959

Million kronor in 1958 prices.

	1958	CHANGES 1958-59	
		MILLION KRONOR	PER CENT
Supply:			
Production	59,600	+1,400	+ 2.5
Imports	12,250	+ 250	+ 2
Inventory decrease	100	+ 400	..
Total	71,950	+2,050	+ 3
Demand:			
Gross private investment	10,750	+ 350	+ 3
Gross Central Government investment	4,400	+ 500	+12
Gross local authorities' investment	3,350	+ 200	+ 6
Exports	12,000	0	0
Private consumption	33,850	+ 700	+ 2
Central Government consumption	3,000	+ 100	+ 3
Local authorities' consumption	4,600	+ 200	+ 4
Total	71,950	+2,050	+ 3

by Table 1. The increase in production could not, however, be considered as the maximum conceivable increase, since in the initial situation the factors of production were not fully utilized. The change on the demand side thus only corresponded to the change on the supply side. On the other hand, there were no signs that demand could make use of the resources which were idle in the initial situation.

In order to assess the gap it was therefore necessary to evaluate the initial situation, in addition to the changes presented in the Balance of Resources. The maximum conceivable production was obtained by starting from the latest preceding year of full employment, which was 1957, and cumulating the successive changes in utilization—in this case only the intermediate year 1958. This calculation was undertaken in the Revised National Budget for 1959. Table 2 presents the result of the calculation. The degree of uncertainty is naturally considerable, and the calculation serves only as a numerical illustration—thus the figures have been rounded to a half per cent.

TABLE 2. CALCULATION OF A CUMULATED GAP

	1958	1959 FORECAST
1. Increase in active population	+1	+1
2. Legal shortening of work hours	−1.5	−1.5
3. Labour reserve left over from previous year	0	+0.5[1]
4. Labour supply disposable for production increase	−0.5	0
5. Productivity reserve left over from previous year	0	+1.5[1]
6. Hypothetical productivity increase	+3	+3
7. Possible production increase (4+5+6)	+2.5	+4.5
8. Actual production increase	+0.5	+2.5
9. Deflationary gap (7—8)	2	2

1. The sum of items 3 and 5 equals the preceding year's deflationary gap.

Sweden

The shortening of the hours of work in 1958 was so large that, despite the increase in the active population, it resulted in a decrease in labour supply. Productivity is, owing to capital formation and rationalization etc., assumed to increase 3 per cent per annum. Since the labour supply decreased by 0.5 per cent, the possible increase of production was 2.5 per cent. The actual increase of production, however, amounted only to 0.5 per cent. The deflationary gap, measured as the difference between possible and actual increases of production, was thus 2 per cent of the total production of 1957.

The active population was assumed to increase during 1959 as much as during 1958, in other words, by 1 per cent of the total labour supply. The continued legal shortening of hours of work reduced the labour supply by 1.5 per cent. As the unemployment during 1958 gave rise to a labour reserve of 0.5 per cent, the labour supply disposable for increase of production was zero. The deflationary gap of 1958 seems to have corresponded partly to the above-mentioned unemployment and partly to " underemployment " and losses of production caused thereby. The productivity reserve left over from the previous year, on these assumptions, was 1.5 per cent. When the hypothetical productivity increase was added, the total possible productivity increase became 4.5 per cent. Since the actual " spontaneous " increase in production as estimated in Table 1 was 2.5 per cent, the calculated deflationary gap was maintained during 1959.

The gap calculation can be criticized on the grounds that the simplification has gone too far when one sums up in an inflationary or deflationary gap the current economic tendencies. In many cases the economic situation varies both as between different commodity and factor markets, and between different regions. There may thus exist serious shortages in certain markets at the same time as there exists large excess capacity in other markets. These discrepancies may be averaged and disappear in an over-all calculation. Under these circumstances a calculated *ex ante* equilibrium does not have any great informative value. It is therefore necessary to pay attention to the separate markets.

Besides the above views the inflationary/deflationary analysis can be criticized on the grounds that it is only a forecast of an *ex ante* gap and not of the different variables one is interested in. As the gap-forecast furthermore in practice is a magnitude of change, the appraisal is still more complicated.

The alternative which is available besides the inflationary/deflationary gap analysis, and which also has been exploited during recent years, is the direct forecast. This method is of a trial-and-error nature, as initial assumptions have to be revised and re-revised when compared with successive forecasts of production and employment. The logical way of simplifying this procedure is, naturally, to use a complete econometric model. Work is also under way in this field. An argument in favour of the more " verbal " method is, however, that the national budget to a very considerable extent relies on information of plans and intention surveys which are difficult to incorporate into a model. It is furthermore difficult to give a " model forecast " a form which is intelligible for politicians and businessmen, who now, after 15 years of education, seem to be well acquainted with the present form of the National Budget. A " model " forecast therefore, for some time to come, for several reasons can be expected to play only a subsidiary role in the national budgeting.

The future development of the scope and the methods of economic forecasting in Sweden will be along the following lines:

a) The national budget work is, at present, to a large extent, based on plan statistics and survey material. Only to a minor extent are econometric relationships used. As a supplement to the present method it is intended to extend the econometric relationships so as to comprise systematically the whole economy.

b) Financial aspects of economic development have hitherto often been given a very rudimentary treatment. The problem of the consistency between the forecast in terms of the balance of resources and the envisaged financial developments will, however, in the future be given increased attention. In the econometric relationships the role of liquidity and financing may also have to be ascertained in certain cases.

c) In order to provide a better background for economic policy, work is underway at the Institue with a view to making possible quarterly forecasts of GNP and its components as well as to stretch the forecast horizon to embrace at least the fiscal year ahead. Occasionally this requires a forecast of one year and a half.

d) More attention will be paid to studies of economic developments in different economic sectors. The " balance-of-resources " approach has, as a matter of fact, been applied also for several manufacturing industries[1] for the building sector and for the forestry sector. Lack of statistical information so far prevents the extension of this analysis to other sectors. In an economy with such large geographical dissimilarities as those of Sweden there is also a need for a regionally differentiated economic policy.

A comparison between the national budgets, preliminary and revised, and the actual outcomes, is given in *The Swedish Economy, 1961, No. 2* published by the National Institute of Economic Research. A similar comparison for the years 1961–63 is given below in Table 3.

In the following sections a more thorough description of the forecasting methods, used in 1963, is given for the various items included in the balance of resources.

2 PRODUCTION

As indicated above one part of the forecast is " built up " from the expenditure side. The estimates of the separate expenditure components are described in the following sections. On the other side total production is estimated in the form of the contributions from different producing sectors. These estimates are based on calculations of changes in productivity and labour force. The way in which these forecasts have been used is indicated by the discussion of a " deflationary gap " in the preceding section of this report. In this case the calculation is made with the purpose of getting

---

1. See pages 89 and 90.

Sweden

TABLE 3. BALANCE OF RESOURCES 1961-1963, FORECAST AND OUTCOME
CONSTANT PRICES

	PER CENT CHANGES 1960-61			PER CENT CHANGES 1961-62			PER CENT CHANGES 1962-63		
	PRELIMINARY NATIONAL BUDGET	REVISED NATIONAL BUDGET	OUTCOME	PRELIMINARY NATIONAL BUDGET	REVISED NATIONAL BUDGET	OUTCOME	PRELIMINARY NATIONAL BUDGET	REVISED NATIONAL BUDGET	OUTCOME (PREL.)
Supply:									
Production	+4	+4	+5.9	+3.5	+4.0	+3.5	+3.5	+4.5	+3.5
Imports	+4	+4	+0.4	+5.0	+6.0	+5.8	+3.0	+4.0	+7.0
Demand:									
Gross private investments	+3	+5	+6.3	0	+2.0	+0.5	+0.5	+1.5	+0.5
Gross Central Government investments	0	0	+1.3	+5.0	+8.0	+2.0	+6.0	+5.5	+2.0
Gross local authorities' investments	+4	+4	+8.9	+10.0	+13.0	+14.0	+12.0	+11.5	+14.0
Exports	+6	+6	+3.7	+6.0	+7.0	+7.7	+3.0	+6.5	+7.0
Private consumption	+5	+5	+5.4	+3.5	+4.0	+3.0	+4.0	+4.0	+4.0
Central Government consumption	+5	+5	+6.1	+5.0	+5.0	+6.5	+6.0	+7.0	+7.5
Local authorities' consumption	+4.5	+5	+3.0	+6.0	+6.0	+4.6	+6.6	+5.0	+5.0

an idea of total possible production. Besides, this estimate serves as a rough consistency check on the *ex ante* calculation made from the expenditure side. This check is expected to be considerably improved when the present work on input-output tables becomes available and can be currently utilized.

The labour force estimates are made by the Labour Market Board in the usual way by considering the natural growth of the population, net immigration, changes in participation rates. Lately efforts have been directed especially towards the way in which regional imbalances between the supply of and demand for labour may affect total production.

Forecasts concerning the yearly contributions to total production are made for each main sector of the economy. These forecasts are based on information of various kinds, acquired from hearings, local employment boards and other authorities, enquiries concerning production plans, the inflow of orders and the like, the budgets of the state and local government authorities, etc. When making the calculations, consideration is also given to possible bottlenecks other than manpower, such as production capacity, raw materials, fuel and electricity.

The GNP forecast is arrived at as the sum of production in the following sectors.

Manufacturing

For 1963 the production forecasts are based on balance of resources for some of the most important branches of industry, being most detailed for engineering products and finished iron and steel. For engineering products, the 1957 input-output survey provided basic information for estimating the proportion of engineering products in Central Government and local authorities' consumption and the input of engineering products into current industrial production. The development from 1957 to 1962 (in 1954 prices) has been extrapolated according to the changes of the Central Government and local authorities' consumption (excl. wages) and, in the case of the input of products in mining and manufacturing, on the basis of the volume development in the different sectors of industry. Input of engineering products in buildings and construction has been extrapolated on the basis of the volume development of gross investments, including maintenance, in building and construction (excl. roads). The remaining items in the balance, i.e. imports, private consumption, exports, investments and stock changes have been taken, after certain adjustments, directly from the Institute's calculations for the different items in question. The sector production has then been estimated as the residual of the balance (consumption + investment + stock increase + exports + input into other branches — imports = production) and *ex post* been compared with available indications of production, before using as forecast. Table 4 shows the results of the calculations which were made in December 1963.

TABLE 4. BALANCE OF RESOURCES FOR ENGINEERING PRODUCTS
(EXCL. SHIPS)

Million kronor; 1954 producer prices.

	1961	1962	1963 (PRELIMINARY)	1964 (FORECAST)
Production (Residual)	9,833	10,395	10.655	10,983
Imports	3,883	4,060	4,344	4,583
Total supply	13,716	14,455	14,999	15,566
Private consumption	2,795	2,840	3,093	3,309
purchases of new cars	963	1,047	1,225	1,354
other	1,832	1,793	1,868	1,955
Public consumption	14	15	16	18
Investment in machinery etc.	4,764	5,008	5,100	5,165
private	3,231	3,234	3,278	3,267
public	1,533	1,774	1,822	1,898
Change in inventories	+365	+321	+233	+230
Exports	3,350	3,758	3,908	4,049
Input into other manufacturing and building	2,428	2,513	2,649	2,795
other manufacturing	1,181	1,205	1,275	1,367
building and construction	1,246	1,308	1,374	1,428
Total use	13,716	14,455	14,999	15,566

Source: National Institute of Economic Research, Stockholm.

The balance of resources for finished iron and steel is constructed in a similar way. The production forecast is here a residual calculated as exports + stock increase + input — imports. The Institute has also compiled balance of resources for iron ore, sawn and planed softwood, pulp and paper. These balances may be seen mainly as an effort to check the consistency of total forecasts of production and GNP components.

Sweden

Power works

Information of production plans is obtained from the National Power Board. As technical capacity is well known estimates must be made of the demand for electric power (which is dependent on activities in other sectors of industry, mainly in manufacturing).

Building and construction

The methods of calculation are the same as those described in the section on investment.

Agriculture

Estimates of agricultural output (based on the assumption of normal weather conditions) are made by the Agricultural Marketing Board. The contribution to the GNP is calculated as the difference between the output value and the value of inputs (such as fodder, artificial manuring, power, etc.).

Forestry

Production plans of regional forestry boards and big firms are collected by the National Forest Service.

Housing

The contribution of housing to the GNP is estimated with regard to the construction of new dwellings.

Trade and communication

It has not been possible to make direct forecasts for trade and communications. It is, however, assumed that these activities will increase their contribution to the national product at the same rate (or a slightly higher one) as that of the goods-producing industries exclusive of stock-piling.

Public services

The contribution of the central government and of the local authorities to the GNP is equal to wages and salaries in the public sector (defence, education, administration etc.). The volume of employment has been used for the estimate of the contribution of this sector (the sum of wages and salaries at unchanged levels of earnings according to the budget proposal).

Other private services

The production calculation is based on previous trends of developments.
It will be noted that the production estimates of the various sectors are primarily worked out independently. At a later stage of the analysis corrections are made by gradual adjustments of the various items to one another as the total supply of manpower and estimated changes of productivity are taken into consideration.

The estimates described above have been made on a yearly basis only. For some sectors quarterly data are, however, available in the form of qualitative judgments, which can be used as a support of the quarterly forecasts made from the expenditure side.

Business Tendency Surveys—applying methods established by the Ifo-Institute in Munich—have been used for the engineering industry and the textile and clothing industries since 1955 and since 1959 for all branches of mining and manufacturing. Since the first quarter of 1962, Business Tendency Surveys are also conducted for the construction sector.

Data are gathered on a quarterly basis concerning recent developments and short-term expectations with regard to the following variables: volume of production, spare capacity, incoming orders (domestic and export markets), delivery periods, sales prices, value of purchases, stocks of raw materials and of finished goods, employment, investments in and maintenance of buildings and machinery. Information is also asked for in the form of " as-of-now " judgments concerning order stocks, shortage of labour, stocks of raw materials and of finished goods.

The data are collected separately for the following sectors: mining, iron and steel works, engineering industry, quarrying and manufacture of stone, clay and glass products etc., wood industry, manufacture of pulp, paper and paper products, printing and allied industries, food manufacturing industries, beverage and tobacco industries, manufacture of leather, furs and rubber products, manufacture of chemicals and chemical products, textile and clothing industry, and construction.

The firms included in these surveys have been chosen according to strict statistical principles—stratified random sampling being used. The results are published within two weeks after the collection of questionnaires has been finished. They are presented in tables showing the weighted replies to the different questions together with a brief analysis of these answers. Diagrams based on the surveys are also presented in *The Swedish Economy,* the review published by the National Institute of Economic Research. This type of information has become increasingly important as a complement to the short-term forecasts using quantitative data.

3 EXPORTS

In March and in December every year the Board of Trade makes estimates of imports and exports for the current as well as the following year. These estimates form part of the basis for the foreign trade forecasts in the National Budget. It should be noted, however, that the estimates made by the Board of Trade are not called forecasts, as they are valid only on the assumption that business tendencies remain the same as known at the time of forecasting.

The estimates are made at current prices for groups of commodities. Volume changes are then estimated for aggregates of groups of commodities by means of very schematic assumptions about the price development.

The most substantial and valuable information is received by way of long standing contacts maintained between the Board of Trade and export organizations and exporting firms, especially in industries producing stock commodities like pulp, timber, paper and ores. As to imports, good coverage is received for raw materials like fuel, textile fibres, metals and agricultural products. Information on other groups of commodities is more sporadic and incomplete. This is the case for exports and imports of machinery, apparatus, metal manufactures and transport equipment. Within this group of commodities, the foreign trade in transport equipment (automobiles, aircraft and ships) is, however, fairly well covered. For the remainder, the information is derived from discussions with representatives from some of the larger enterprises in engineering and from certain qualitative estimates of the investment development in Sweden and in foreign countries (especially Western Europe). In recent years, the Board of Trade has also used the results of the export surveys for iron and steel and engineering products made by the Institute (described below).

Rough commodity balances of resources are made for the estimation of foreign trade in iron and steel, automobiles, and food and agricultural products, under certain assumptions with regard to the development of consumption and production in Sweden of each of these groups of commodities. One of the main difficulties here is to estimate correctly the changes in stocks. Such changes affect the outcome of both the export and import calculations.

The National Agricultural Marketing Board undertakes calculations on exports and imports of *regulated agricultural products and food*, which in recent years have been made also on a half yearly basis. Foreign trade in agricultural products is to a large extent regulated with the express purpose of adjusting agricultural production to the level of consumption. As variations in harvests are difficult to foresee, forecasts of agricultural exports and imports become very tricky too. Surplus exports of regulated products are usually sold at a given price. All exports of food do not, however, consist of regulated agricultural products. A number of commodities included in the food group should rather be considered as a separate export group, including, e.g., fish, fish preserves and certain types of manufactured food. These products comprise only one quarter of total exports of food. The group is, however, steadily expanding.

In regular meetings of the Institute with representatives of Swedish timber exporters the demand situation and current conditions of competition are discussed. The forecasts derived in this way are compared with forecasts of imports and of building activity in the most important buyer countries. The Institute also collects current statistics on sales and deliveries of timber exports in Finland and Sweden. Seasonally adjusted series on sales and deliveries give a fairly good idea of tendencies in the short run.

The Institute also keeps close contacts with the organization of *pulp* producers. When forecasting production and exports of pulp, the Institute has access to the pulp producers' confidential statistics on production, deliveries, orders and stocks. These statistics, together with other relevant information, make it possible to estimate pulp exports to different countries.

Exports of *paper and board* are, compared to exports of timber and pulp, considerably more differentiated as to numbers of products and qualities and thus to demand development. It is therefore relatively difficult to get a correct view of export prospects by means of contacts with the branch organization. The consumption calculations for Western Europe, based on

GNP developments and made by FAO, are of some help. But the Institute has as yet no satisfactory material for checking the forecasts of the branch organization on paper exports.

Swedish exports of *ore* are dominated by a single seller from whom the Institute regularly obtains information on production, stocks and exports. According to contracts, the iron ore to be delivered during one year is sold in the late autumn of the preceding year. Therefore, the yearly forecasts are firmly based. One remaining problem is to estimate the rate of delivery in view of conditions in the steel market in the purchasing countries. The Institute therefore keeps under special surveillance the demand situation abroad and the development *during* the calendar year.

Until recently predictive information on exports of *base metals and engineering products* has been rather scarce. Calculations of the relation between Swedish exports of engineering products to Western Europe and investment developments in that region have given certain indications, but they are not quite efficient for forecasting purposes. Furthermore a relation between Swedish exports of base metals on the one hand and engineering production in Western Europe on the other has been calculated, but this relation has not proved suitable for forecasting purposes. A different method to create a reliable method for forecasting these groups of exports was used by the Institute for the first time in 1962. In two surveys, plan statistics were collected from a stratified selection of firms in engineering and from all firms producing iron and steel. Similar surveys were also carried out in February and August 1963. The forecasts of the value development for these groups of commodities have been based on the results of these surveys.

The surveys for engineering exports have included firms listed in the register of the Business Tendency Surveys of the Institute. All larger firms and a sample of the smaller firms have been surveyed. The sample has continuously been enlarged in order to decrease the uncertainty of inference in total exports. One hundred and eighty three engineering firms were included in the latest August survey.

Out of a total of some 800 engineering firms listed in industrial statistics, 60 cover about 80 per cent of exports of engineering products. This concentration of exports in a few larger firms has permitted a limitation of the number of firms surveyed, and still made it possible to give an acceptable estimation of total exports of engineering products. The surveys for iron and steel works have included all 33 enterprises in Sweden. The frequency of answers has on all occasions been very satisfactory—it has never fallen below 90 per cent.

Information gathered through these surveys refers to actual delivery values for the immediately preceding two or three half-years, and estimated delivery values for the two coming half-years. The questionnaire has gradually been made more detailed by way of requesting break-downs of delivery values into various countries and groups of countries. In order to permit a rough conversion of the estimated values to fixed prices the firms have also been asked to make an approximate assessment of average price changes in their exports from the immediately preceding half-year to the respective half-year forecast. The firms have also been asked for information on the delivery value of their total export order book and on how deliveries will be distributed over the forthcoming periods.

Sweden

The selection of engineering firms which at present constitutes the basis for the Business Tendency Surveys of the Institute was made in 1959. The changes that since then have occurred among the engineering firms and the fact that exports of engineering products also are carried on by firms not registered as engineering firms cause the exports of engineering products reported in the surveys to fall short of the corresponding group of exports according to foreign trade statistics. The coverage of the surveys has hitherto varied between *ca.* 85 and 90 per cent of total exports of engineering products. The iron and steel surveys give about the same coverage.

For those groups of firms which have been sampled, total levels of deliveries and orders have been acquired by mean per sampling unit estimation. Alternative methods of estimation have not yet been tested but should be realized in the near future.

The total difference between the firms' estimation *ex ante* and *ex post* of their exports has been 2-3 per cent. The surveys have indicated that the ability of the firms to appraise the developments of their exports is clearly correlated with the export value of the firms.

There have been some difficulties in estimating the total exports of engineering products and iron and steel from the surveys. This is partly due to a systematic variation in coverage of the surveys between the half-years, partly to a displacement of the exports towards the second half-year in comparison to foreign trade statistics. The experience of the surveys is still too limited to allow an evaluation of this problem.

Exports of *ships* are on the whole determined by contracts concluded years in advance, and a forecast for a current or a following year poses no fundamental problem. Figures on the shipyards' expected deliveries are collected by a survey covering all shipyards. Such surveys are made each spring and autumn and also serve to get figures on investments in ships for the national accounts. These surveys, used in combination with current information on new contracts, launched and delivered ships, give a fairly good idea about ship exports. The remaining problem is to estimate exactly when a ship will be delivered. A random variation in the delivery of one single ship by a couple of weeks at the turn of the year or half of a year can cause an error in the forecast for the exports of ships by several per cent and even add a noticeable error to the forecast for total exports.

There is a residual group that can be said to consist of all commodities on which information for a forecast is lacking. However, this group, which has a heterogeneous composition of commodities and a wide distribution between purchasing countries, on the whole changes in the same direction as the total production (GNP) in the different purchasing countries, although at a much higher rate. This relation is used to get some idea about the developments of this group.

For several years, research has been under way in the Institute in order to clarify the main characteristics of international demand for Swedish exports. Established relationships in the export sector can then be used to check and modify the exporters' judgments on their own exports. Attempts have been made to estimate demand relationships in the form of area forecasts. These attempts show that it is possible to find quite stable relationships for some parts of exports to Western Europe and North America. It is, however, difficult to use these relationships for forecasting, as the independent and sometimes "leading" variables (viz. various economic series for Western Europe) cannot be obtained but for the most general economic indicators like GNP and total industrial production. Co-operation and work in this field could be most useful and improve national forecasts by providing additional information.

A description is given below of the regression equations and methods used during 1961-1963 in forecasts by commodity groups. This analysis is still in the experimental stage. The calculations are made at current prices.

Western Europe

$$V_t = -1{,}743.53 - 161.52\,Q_1 - 106.48\,Q_2 - 37.29\,Q_3 + 19.81\,P_{xt} - 7.99\,P_{it} + 16.85\,X_t - 0.076\,(\log.\,Z_t - 2) \quad R^2 = 0.9825$$

V_t = Value of exports to Western Europe excluding ships and food, million kronor

P_{xt} = Swedish average value index for total exports excluding ships and food   1953 = 100

P_{it} = Total import price index for Western Europe   1953 = 100

X_t = Total index of industrial production for Western Europe   1953 = 100

Z_t = Total unemployment index for Western Europe   1953 = 100

$Q_1;\ Q_2;\ Q_3$ = seasonal (quarterly) constants, adjusted to the fourth quarter

($Q_1 = 1;\ Q_2,\ Q_3 = 0$ during the first quarter,
$Q_2 = 1;\ Q_1,\ Q_3 = 0$ during the second quarter etc.)

The equation is estimated for the period 1954 to 2nd quarter 1963. P_{it} X_t and Z_t are weighted means, each country given a weight corresponding to its share in Swedish export value during the previous year. This equation seems to give a fairly exact forecast of exports, provided that the forecasts for the independent variables are correct. The main deficiency of this model is that changes in stocks of these commodities, which are prominent in Swedish exports, are not taken into consideration.

It may be pointed out that the parameters for prices are insignificant. The seasonal adjusting constants seem to cause a slight bias in the estimates.

U.S.A.

$$V_t = -79.71 + 0.45\,Y_t + 2.06\,S_t - 0.51\,S_{t-1} - 0.51\,P_{xt} - 0.75\,P_{it} + 8.17\,P_{Dt} - 1.66\,Z_t \quad R^2 = 0.904$$

All series are seasonally adjusted. The equation is estimated on data for the period 1954-1962.

V_t = Swedish export value to U.S.A., million sw. kronor

Y_t = U.S. Final sales = GNP — inventory changes, in billions of dollars

$S_t,\ S_{t-1}$ = Inventory changes in quarters t and t—1, in billions of dollars

P_{xt} = Swedish average value index of exports   1954 = 100

P_{it} = U.S. import price index   1954 = 100

P_{Dt} = U.S. wholesale price index (excl. farm products)   1954 = 100

Z_t = Rate of unemployment in U.S.A.

Canada

$$V_t = -48.38 - 2.16\, Q_1 + 2.17\, Q_2 + 0.61\, Q_3 + 0.195\, P_{xt}$$
$$-0.62\, P_{it} + 0.53\, P_{Dt} + 0.49\, X_t + 0.08\, Z_t \qquad R^2 = 0.839$$

V_t = Swedish export value to Canada in quarter t, million sw. kronor
P_{xt} = Swedish average value index of total exports $\quad$ 1953 = 100
P_{it} = Canadian import price index $\quad$ 1953 = 100
P_{Dt} = Canadian wholesale price index $\quad$ 1953 = 100
X_t = Canadian industrial production index $\quad$ 1953 = 100
Z_t = Rate of unemployment in Canada
$Q_1; Q_2; Q_3$ = seasonal constants.

The equation is estimated on data for the period 1954-1962.

These two equations for North America have been used only recently and their efficiency in forecasting cannot be judged yet. Compared with the relation for Western Europe they show a lower degree of correlation. The model seems to be rather poor in judging short-run changes in exports as compared with the model for Western Europe.

Other areas

Special efforts have been made by the Institute in order to estimate Swedish exports to the *primary producing countries*. The imports of primary producing countries seem to vary—with a certain time-lag—with their exports to the industrialized countries, owing to their generally weak foreign exchange position. Attempts have been made to use this relation in forecasting Swedish exports to this group of countries. The exports of primary producing countries to industrialized countries are, however, on the whole very difficult to obtain for recent periods. Statistics of the O.E.C.D. countries' imports from this area can, on the other hand, provide the required figures with a lag of 1-2 quarters. An indication of the prospects for Swedish exports can then be obtained by using these series for exports by primary producing countries. The primary producing countries have in this context been divided in three groups: Latin American countries, sterling area countries, and other countries. These relationships appear, however, to be extremely unstable and can give only vague guidance as to the development of the exports concerned.

Sweden has bilateral trade agreements with *Eastern Europe* and *China*, which by and large regulate our trade with these countries. Therefore, one can get a fairly good forecast of exports to these countries. Exports to *Japan* are forecast in a rather summary fashion.

Finally, it should again be noted that the regional forecasts are viewed as complementary to the commodity group forecasts but that neverthelesss the two forecasts are made independently of each other.

Table 5 shows the differences between half-year forecasts and outcome for the latest eight forecast occasions. The table gives the absolute differences in millions of Swedish kronor and gives also these differences expressed as a percentage of the outcome, i.e. of the registered half-year exports. The forecasts for Western Europe are comparatively satisfactory.

In order to improve the relationships used one needs much statistical information which is not available now. However, small improvements may

TABLE 5. EXPORT FORECASTS AND OUTCOME ACCORDING TO THE AREA AND COMMODITY GROUP METHODS, 1961 (II)—1963 (I)

	EXPORT VALUE 1962 EXCL. SHIPS MILL. SW. KR.	2ND HALF-YEAR 1961		1ST HALF-YEAR 1962	2ND HALF-YEAR 1962			1ST HALF-YEAR 1963	
		JULY[1]	OCT.	MARCH	MARCH	SEPT.	NOV.	NOV.	MARCH
		Difference between forecast and outcome, area method in millions of Sw.kr.							
Western Europe	10,522	+46	−38	−85	−23	−120	−25	−95	−52
North America	958	+18	+41	−22	+13	+40	+9	+16	+42
Latin America	644	+22	−42	−27	+72	+59	+10	−17	−16
Other primary producing countries	1,102	+5	+67	+32	+78	+70	−38	−52	+58
East Europe, China and Japan	850	+5	−30	+2	+48	+9	−62	−73	−32
Total	14,076	+91	−2	−100	+188	+40	−106	−221	0
	Shares of Swedish exports 1962	*Percentage difference*							
Western Europe	75	+0.9	−0.7	−1.7	−0.4	−2.2	−0.5	−1.8	−1.0
North America	7	+4.2	+9.5	−4.5	+2.7	+8.5	+1.9	+3.3	+8.8
Latin America	4	+2.4	−11.7	−7.8	+24.0	+19.7	+3.3	−5.7	−5.4
Other primary producing countries	8	+12.2	+6.0	+13.7	+12.3	+6.7	−9.6	+10.7	
East Europe, China and Japan	6	+1.2	−7.3	+0.5	+10.6	−2.0	−13.7	−18.8	−8.2
Total	100	+1.3	−0.0	−1.5	+2.6	+0.6	−1.5	−3.1	0
		Difference between forecast and outcome, commodity group method							
Total exports excl. ships: mill. of kronor		−130	−300	−300	−170	−170	−86	−17	+93
Total exports excl. ships: percent		−1.9	−4.3	−2.1	−1.2	−2.4	−1.2	−0.2	+1.3

1. Month during which the forecast is made.

still be possible. The same may be said about North America. Forecasts for the primary producing countries have the largest relative errors, but are nevertheless difficult to improve.

As can be seen from the table the area forecasts are at least as good as the commodity group forecasts. We have, however, too little experience to say that one method is better than the other. The area forecast is a promising method for further development to the limits of the method, which may be rather close to the results already obtained.

4 IMPORTS

Section 3 on export forecasts gives an account of the estimates of both exports and imports made by the Board of Trade and used in the National Budget as well as in the Institute's reports. The description in this section will therefore be limited to the regression analyses of imports made by the Institute and used as a complement to the estimates of imports made by the Board of Trade.

The Institute's report of May 1961 described the results of some regression calculations concerning the relations between Swedish imports and certain economic variables, which—at least to some extent—are supposed to " explain " the import development. In that report the forecast of import development during 1961 was based mainly on the regression estimates. These along with the calculation by the Board of Trade, have also been used in the Institute's import forecasts on later occasions. The October 1962 issue of the *Swedish Economy* gives the latest published description of these regression analyses.

In the course of time, the regression analyses have been modified in several ways, as is apparent from the reports. Below a description is given of the models for the October 1963 issue. The main deviation from the earlier analyses concerns the change of the time span. The new regression relations cover the years 1953 through 1962 as compared to the earlier 1950-61. The change of period is mainly because import restrictions during the Korean boom distorted the estimate of the average propensity to import of the previous calculation. Several economic variables, used in " explaining " imports, have also been modified, partly on account of minor inconsistencies in the approach and partly because of low correlation.

The regression calculations are based on yearly statistics for the period 1953-62. If not otherwise stated the variables are estimated in millions of kronor at 1954 prices (with one exception discussed below). The reason for this is that most of the explaining variables are taken from the national accounts. The only constant price calculation so far available for these items is at 1954 prices.

As before, four different approaches have been used with regard to the relationship expressed by the regression equations. In three of these alternatives total imports are taken as the dependent variable. In the fourth alternative total imports are obtained as the sum of estimates of separate import items. The following relationships were obtained.

I. $Y_1 = -9{,}592 + 0.416\,X_1$
$r^2 = 0.974$
Y_1 is total imports, X_1 is GNP

For this alternative, a logarithmic regression equation was also calculated:

$\log Y_1 = -4.681 + 1.857 \log X_1$
$r^2 = 0.963$

II. $Y_1 = -4,843 + 0.477 X_2$
$r^2 = 0.989$

Y_1 is total imports and X_2 is total expenditures (exports, consumption and investment), the following items being deducted: investment in building and construction, military investment in machinery, services in private consumption, consumption of central and local government, exports of ores, forestry products and foodstuffs, stock increases in mining, quarrying and forestry, the correction for variations in the stock of cattle and in timbercutting.

In this case, also, a logarithmic regression was fitted to the data.

$\log Y_1 = -2.456 + 1.436 \log X_2$
$r^2 = 0.984$

III. $Y_1 = -4,539 + 0.465 X_3 + 0.718 X_4$
$R^2 = 0.990$

Y_1 is total imports and X_4 is net increase in total stocks exclusive of stock changes in mining, quarrying and forestry, and of variations in stocks of cattle and in timber cutting. X_3 stands for the X_2 of equation II net of X_4.

IV*a*. $Y_2 = -2,034 + 0.323 X_5$
$r^2 = 0.943$

Y_2 is imports of foodstuffs including raw materials to the foodstuffs industry and the beverage and tobacco industries and X_5 is private consumption of foodstuffs, alcoholic beverages and tobacco.

IV*b*. $Y_3 = -771 + 0.435 X_6$
$r^2 = 0.972$

Y_3 is imports of non-durable consumer goods (exclusive of foodstuffs) and raw materials to textile and clothing industries and X_6 is private consumption of non-durable consumer goods exclusive of foodstuffs, beverages and tobacco.

IV*c*. $Y_4 = -333 + 0.337 X_7$
$r^2 = 0.955$

Y_4 is imports of durable consumer goods including the share of automobiles supposed to go to private consumption, and X_7 is consumption of durable consumer goods plus increase in stocks of automobiles.

IV*d*. The import equation described below has been found to give a higher degree of correlation if the variables are in *current prices*. The reason is probably that the price indices for investment goods are rather unreliable. In order to get a forecast of the volume development (of total imports) the value change of this group of imports according to the regression equation has been deflated by an estimated price development.

$Y_5 = -834 + 0.404 X_8$
$r^2 = 0.972$

Y_5 is imports of capital goods (including passenger cars for the business sector and excluding ships, aircraft and ordnance), and X_8 is gross investment (including maintenance) in machinery, apparatus and appliances within the sectors agriculture, forestry, fishing, mining and manufacturing, communications exclusive of shipping, and medical and social services.

IV*e*. $Y_6 = -1{,}443 + 39.131\, X_9 + 0.297\, X_{10}$
$R^2 = 0.944$

Y_6 is imports of raw materials for industrial production and X_9 is a weighted production index (1953 = 100) calculated in the following way: from the Swedish input-output survey for 1957 the imports of raw materials for industrial production by different branches of industry can be obtained. The following branches accounted for the major part of total imports of the raw materials concerned: iron and metal works, shipyards, other engineering industries, chemical industry, pulp industry and iron ore mines. The production index of each branch has been given a weight in accordance with the respective share of imports in 1957. X_{10} is the change in stocks of raw materials in the above-mentioned branches of industry.

IV*f*. $Y_7 = -436 + 0.039\, X_1$
$r^2 = 0.799$

Y_7 is imports of fuel and lubricants and X_1 is GNP.

IV*g*. $\log Y_8 = -4.773 + 1.850 \log X_{11}$
$r^2 = 0.909$

Y_8 is imports of raw materials for building and X_{11} is investment in building and construction.

The regression calculations of alternative IV do not include all imports. The remainder is, however, relatively small and consists of raw materials for agricultural production, ships, aircraft and ordnance.

The goodness of fit between the values of total imports calculated according to the four different methods described can be measured by the mean difference in percentage points—irrespective of sign—between actual and calculated imports, 1953-62. This difference was 2.4 for alternative I, and 1.5, 1.6 and 2.4, respectively for alternatives II-IV. (The comparison for alternative IV refers only to the part of total imports for which regression calculations have been made.)

Although the differences were smaller for alternatives II and III than for alternative IV, the latter has mainly been used for the forecasts. The reason for this is that information about the economic situation, available at the time of the forecast has often suggested deviations from the trend. This information can most easily be considered in a forecast based on calculations of disaggregated imports.

Forecasts of the remainder, for which no regression calculations have been made in alternative IV, have been taken directly from the import estimates by the Board of Trade. These estimates have also been used for the Institute's forecasts of imports of fuel, the explanatory value of the regression being too weak.

In an effort to improve the forecasts, the relation between import prices and prices of domestic production was included as a separate independent variable in the equations. The inclusion of this relation did not, however, increase the correlation significantly. Still another reason for not using these variables in forecasting imports is the difficulty of estimating the price development.

Regression calculations for groups of imports on a half-yearly basis have been worked out but are not yet evaluated. They may possibly be used for forecasting imports later on.

Forecasts for special import groups

In the section on production, a description of the balance of resources for engineering products and iron and steel was given. These groups of commodities do not correspond to any of the above-mentioned import groups. It has therefore been necessary to calculate separate import regression equations for these two groups, both based on yearly data 1953-62.

a) *Imports of engineering products*
$Y_9 = -113.0 + 0.848\ X_{12} + 1.408\ X_{13}$
$R^2 = 0.923$

Y_9 is imports of engineering products expressed as a volume index (1953 = 100). X_{12} is a weighted production index (1953 = 100), the production indices of mining and quarrying, iron and metal works industry, shipyards, other engineering industry and chemical industry being weighted by their respective share of imports of engineering products in 1957. These shares of imports have been obtained from the Swedish input-output survey for 1957. X_{13} is an index consisting of private consumption of durable consumer goods, investment in machinery and equipment and investment in building and construction, each weighted by its share of imports of engineering products in 1959. This regression calculation does not give a satisfactory goodness of fit. A new regression equation, based on half-yearly figures and with the various explanatory variables separated, will presently be calculated.

b) *Imports of iron and steel*
$Y_{10} = -29.87 + 1.351\ X_{14} + 0.035\ X_{15} - 9.685\ X_{16}$
$R^2 = 0.857$

Y_{10} is a volume index of imports of iron and steel (1953 = 100). X_{14} is a volume index (1953 = 100) of production and of investment in building and construction. The production index is a weighted index of production in mining and quarrying, iron and metal works industry, shipyards, other engineering industry, and chemical industry, the weights being the shares of imports of iron and steel in 1957 according to the input-output survey. This production index (1953 = 100) is weighted together with a volume index for investment in building and construction (1953 = 100), the weights being the imports of iron and steel for industrial purposes and for building and construction. In this case the weighting is done for each year of the period covered. X_{15} is the change in stocks of raw materials in the five industries mentioned above. X_{16} is a trend variable, designed to express the substitution effect of new Swedish industrial capacity within this group of commodities. Its values are 0 for the years 1953 through 1960, 1 ½ for 1961 and 2 for 1962.

In order to improve the import forecasts for this group, the regression equations will soon be recalculated on the basis of half-yearly figures. The different components included in X_{14} will then be separated.

In Table 6 belows, the import forecasts and outcome of the latest years are listed. The first column refers to the forecast in the Preliminary Budget made in November of the preceding year. The " Revised National Budget " is made in April of the current year. It should be noted that the methods described above have been used only since 1961.

TABLE 6. FORECASTS OF THE VOLUME DEVELOPMENT OF IMPORTS AND ACTUAL OUTCOME
PERCENTAGE CHANGE FROM PRECEDING YEAR

	PRELIMINARY NATIONAL BUDGET	REVISED NATIONAL BUDGET	OUTCOME
1957	−1	+3	+ 7
1958	±0	±0	+ 2
1959	+2	+2	+ 5
1960	+7	+8	+18
1961	+4	+4	+ 1
1962	+5	+6	+ 6
1963	+3	+4	(+ 7)[1]

1. Preliminary.

5 INVESTMENT

The methods for forecasting investment activity in Sweden are to a very large degree based on statements and surveys of planned expenditures in various sectors. This method is natural as far as the public sector is concerned and quite consistent with a general view of public investment as an exogenous variable. Plan statistics are, however, also used in forecasting private investment. During most postwar years up to and including 1957 investment in building and construction of the private sector was subject to rigorous control and thus more or less of an exogenous nature. The plan figures had then to be supplemented with a lot of data from investment control agencies. As these conditions have changed during recent years the methods used in the forecast now call for an interpretation of plan figures of investment in the light of other relevant variables. This interpretation is partly circumstantial which makes it necessary to go rather much into details when describing the methods used and the results actually achieved.

Housing

The volume of residential construction is estimated on the basis of calculations of monthly figures of the number of dwelling units started and completed. The purpose is to obtain figures on the production value in fixed prices for each quarter. On the basis of statistical material showing the number of starts each month subdivided according to the duration of the production period, each dwelling unit is, according to certain criteria, distributed by fractions over the appropriate production period. The fractions from every dwelling unit which fall into a given quarter are then added and multiplied with an average cost[1] per dwelling unit, which gives an estimate of the amount invested during the quarter in question.

The *ex ante* calculations are carried out in the same way as the *ex post* calculation. The forecast thus concerns estimates of the duration of future construction periods as well as the number of future starts. Furthermore, the possibility of changes in the size of apartments must be considered.

Forecasts or assumptions on construction periods (in number of months) must be made for dwelling units that are started but not yet finished as well as for dwelling units that will be started in the future. There is not much material that can be used to throw light on the development of construction periods for the latter units. For the former, however, monthly figures on the expected date of completion have been available from the contractors since the middle of 1961. These figures have to some extent been compared with the *ex post* data. As the changes, but not the level, of the planned building periods turned out to fit the data well, the former have been applied in the forecasts presently used. The number of building starts is chiefly determined by the housing programme and the amount of government building loans made available. In the Finance Bill presented at the beginning of each year, proposals are made concerning the housing programme and expenditure limits for government building loans to become effective during the current year and the immediately following calendar year. Building starts of apartment houses are furthermore determined both as to scope and timing by the labour market boards of the various provinces—the decisions of which, however, are made only after consultation with the local building authorities. Each quarter the county unemployment agencies present forecasts on building starts during the two following quarters. All these sources, together with direct information from the authorities concerned, provide the basis for the estimate of building starts.

As to the construction of one- and two-family houses, general permission has been granted during the last few years to exceed the volume of government loans. In addition, construction of one- and two-family houses is not subject to the law requiring building permits. Therefore, the forecasts on building starts of one- and two-family houses have to be based on estimates of the income development of households and on the situation in the credit market. Any changes in the stipulations of state loans will also, of course, have to be considered. The conditions now regulating this building sector are, however, so changed that no quantitative relations between the above-mentioned variables and the building of one- and two-family houses have as yet been established. As further information is lacking we have in the last forecasts used the figures calculated in the housing programme uncorrected.

---

1. When calculating the average cost, changes in the size of apartments are taken into consideration. Other quality aspects are, however, neglected because of lack of information.

Sweden

In Table 7, investment forecasts are compared with the actual [outcome]
according to the latest available estimates. The figures in the t[able include]
maintenance costs, which are mainly calculated separately by me[ans of trend]
extrapolations.

TABLE 7. INVESTMENT IN DWELLINGS INCLUDING MAIN[TENANCE]
PERCENTAGE CHANGE IN VOLUME COMPARED TO PREVIOUS YE[AR]

	FORECAST IN DECEMBER PREVIOUS YEAR
1957	+2
1958	+6
1959	+1
1960	−2
1961	+1
1962	+1

Mining and manufacturing

The Investment Surveys by the Board of Trade (p[resently the Central]
Bureau of Statistics) constitute the most important sour[ce of the forecast of]
investment in mining and manufacturing. Since 1955, th[ese surveys were car]-
ried out twice a year, and are now—since 1962—carr[ied out on a quarterly]
basis. In the October survey, the investment plans in m[ining and manufac]-
turing for the following year are presented, together with a preliminary calculation of the outcome of the current, not yet concluded, year. The March
survey gives information on the plans then valid and—still to some extent
preliminary—figures on the outcome of investment during the past
year.

Statistics on investment plans in mining and manufacturing are available for a long sequence of years. The years up to and including 1957 were,
however, characterized by policy measures tending to limit investment:
building restrictions, investment fees etc. Since the investment forecasts have
to be based on a hypothesis of the relation between planned investment and
actual outcome in an approximately unchanged environment (e.g. with
regard to policies) the plans for the years preceding 1958 are of little interest
at present. Thus, useful statistics on planned investment in mining and
manufacturing are available for a period of four to five years only. If an
investment forecast is to be regarded as statistically well covered, in spite of
the fact that it is based on knowledge of the outcome of plans for the very
short period of five years, the following requirements will have to be met:
a) firstly, the five years should be fairly homogenous as to both general
economic conditions and economic policy, *b)* secondly, the relation between
planned change and realized change should not vary too much, *c)* thirdly,
conditions during the year that the forecast refers to should be similar to
those mentioned under *a)*. If neither of the two first requirements is fulfilled the deviations from the " normal pattern " in the *b)* requirement must
be possible to explain by changes in requirement *a)*. Furthermore, an

estimate must be made as to which of the five years will most resemble the year to be forecast. The chosen year will then be given greater weight than the others in the interpretation of past experience.

Actually, none of the above-mentioned requirements is fulfilled. The beginning of the period 1958-1962 was characterized by a slight decline in business activity followed by a pronounced boom, while towards its end there were some tendencies of stagnation. Economic policy was first expansive and later became contractive and then expansive again. In addition, the removal of the investment fees in 1958 and the introduction, in 1960, of the general sales tax caused shifts in the timing of registered investment. These shifts were to some extent real but to some extent due only to adjustments in accounts.

The experience with statistics on investment planning in mining and manufacturing indicates that the October surveys—especially with regard to investment in machinery—underestimate and the March surveys usually overestimate the change. This pattern is presumably connected with the fact that in October the plans for the coming year are still incomplete. This should especially apply to purchases of machinery, the plans for which probably are more short-term than those for building and construction. At the time of the March survey, the plans are probably fully worked out but the firms seem to overestimate the possibilities of delivery, building capacity, credit facilities etc. The figures in the March surveys of the last years seem, however, to give a satisfactory indication of investment demand. A comparison between plans in October and in March therefore gives a measure of the degree of underestimation in the former plans, which can be used to estimate the investment demand during the following year on the basis of an October survey only.

The relations between the plans in October and in March, respectively, and the actual outcome have, however, since 1957 been characterized by considerable variation. This is evident from Table 8. The figures in the table are corrected for changes in prices but not for systematic over- or underestimation in planned investment. The directions of the variations usually seem explicable though, in view of the special conditions prevailing on each occasion. Thus the plans for 1959—the year that the boom started—were adjusted by an unusually large amount from the October to the March survey. Furthermore, the March plans overestimated the actual outcome of investment less during 1958—a year of low business activity—than during 1959 and 1960. In 1961, the March plans fully materialized—the tendency towards overestimation was probably then counter-acted by a certain increase in investment at the end of 1961, caused by the efforts to avoid the increased rates of the general sales tax, effective after the turn of the year. The March plans were, however, again realized in 1962. This fact may be ascribed to the effects of the expansive credit policy from the middle of the year and of the release in May of the Investments Reserves for investment in building and construction.

Investment forecasts in the Preliminary National Budget can be made only by means of the October figures adjusted to the level of the March survey. The forecast in the Revised National Budget can be based on the March survey. In years characterized by some idle capacity and favourable conditions of delivery the investment demand might be obtained directly

Sweden

TABLE 8. INVESTMENT IN MINING AND MANUFACTURING
UNADJUSTED PLANS
PERCENTAGE CHANGE IN VOLUME COMPARED TO PREVIOUS YEAR

	BUILDING AND CONSTRUCTION EXCLUDING MAINTENANCE			MACHINERY AND EQUIPMENT EXCL. CARS AND MAINTENANCE		
	PLANNED		OUT-COME	PLANNED		OUT-COME
	IN OCT. PREV. YEAR	IN MARCH SAME YEAR		IN OCT. PREV. YEAR	IN MARCH SAME YEAR	
1958	+16	+20	+17	+ 7	+25	+23
1959	− 1	+19	+ 9	− 4	+ 9	+ 5
1960	+16	+22	+18	+14	+17	+13
1961	+13	+21	+21	+10	+20	+19
1962	− 9	− 5	− 3	+ 1	+ 4	+ 4

from the survey after minor corrections only. Naturally, one must consider the extent to which firms have been able to pay attention to recent changes in credit policy, financial policy, liquidity etc. A forecast of the actual outcome of investment necessitates, in addition, an evaluation of the probable future development of certain strategic variables such as those related to changes in the economic policy.

In Table 9, the forecasts of investment in mining and manufacturing for the period 1957-62 in the national budgets, based on the (adjusted) plans and including maintenance are compared with outcome. The table shows clearly that the investment plans—together with other information used—have provided a rather unreliable basis for the forecasts, especially so in October. Some comments on the table may, however, be of value. Thus, the revised forecast for 1958 was made with some regard paid to earlier experience of overestimation in the March surveys. It was very difficult to estimate the net effects of, on the one hand, the recession and, on the other, the liberalized investment policy—manifested for instance in the removal of the 10 per cent excise duty at the beginning of 1958.

The inaccuracy of the forecast made in March 1961 coincided with the fact that the March plans were realized—for the first time in the history of the investment surveys. To some extent this absence of overestimation probably can, as mentioned above, be explained by the investment rush at the end of 1961 which could not be foreseen in March. Furthermore, the revised investment forecast for 1961 was made at the same time as the enterprises were recommended to postpone their investments planned earlier for the spring half-year. The firms themselves estimated that this recommendation would be followed to the extent of a reduction of the original forecast for 1961 by 60 million kronor in building and construction (about 4 per cent) and by 40 million kronor in machinery (about 2 per cent). This was of course taken into consideration in the calculations of the forecast.

Besides the plan statistics described above, the forecasts of construction investment usually exploit calculations based on administrative statistics on buildings starts and buildings under construction in industry. These calculations were of great value especially during the years when plan statistics were difficult to use because of the restrictive building regulations. Other auxiliary

TABLE 9. INVESTMENT IN MINING AND MANUFACTURING
PERCENTAGE CHANGE IN VOLUME COMPARED TO PREVIOUS YEAR

	BUILDING AND CONSTRUCTION INCLUDING MAINTENANCE			MACHINERY AND EQUIPMENT INCLUDING MAINTENANCE		
	FORECAST			FORECAST		
	IN DEC. PREV. YEAR	IN MARCH SAME YEAR	OUT-COME	IN DEC. PREV. YEAR	IN MARCH SAME YEAR	OUT-COME
1957	+ 4	+ 3	0	− 2	− 1	0
1958	+ 5	+ 5	+12	+ 6	+ 6	+11
1959	− 3	+ 9	+ 8	− 3	+ 2	+ 5
1960	+12	+24	+15	+13	+10	+17
1961	+13	+13	+19	+10	+10	+17
1962	− 2	− 2	− 3	+ 1	+ 4	+ 2

information used for the forecasts are the Business Tendency Surveys of the Institute, statistics on the stocks and inflow of orders in engineering industry, etc.

Local authorities

The basis for the forecast of investment by local authorities is provided by survey material published by the Central Bureau of Statistics in November and March. The November surveys have been carried out for a long period of years, the March surveys since 1960 only. The existence of restrictive building regulations before 1958 makes earlier experience from plan statistics of local authorities—whose investment is dominated by building and construction— inapplicable for later use.

The survey material refers to investment and investment plans of primary communes and county councils. Experience from recent years has shown that the investment plans in November by and large give accurate forecasts of the actual outcome of investment in current prices. This means that a price increase will reduce the real scope for investment increases, and a forecast must accordingly be made for the price development of investment goods.

The fact that local authorities—contrary to firms in mining and manufacturing—can give reliable figures on plans already in November does not seem unreasonable in view of certain institutional factors. It seems peculiar, however, that all the March surveys that have been conducted have shown—as proved later—an unjustified upward revision.

In the November survey, figures on the expected income development and on the planned borrowing of the local authorities are also gathered. As the tax revenue of local authorities is largely determined by the income assessments of previous years, they can quite accurately forecast their income development. It is however of importance as a consistency check to compare their planned borrowing with the situation in the credit market and the actual intentions of monetary policy.

Investment plans for construction by local authorities can, as in the case of mining and manufacturing, also be compared with statistics and calculations of projects initiated.

Sweden

A great deal of the investment by primary communes is undertaken by public enterprises. These invest mainly in residential building. The plan statistics of these investments have, however, often proved to be quite unreliable. For this reason the forecast of investment in residential building by local authorities has to be made in connection with the calculations of total residential building.

In Table 10, forecasts of investment in building and construction by local authorities are compared with actual outcome. The notable discrepancy between the forecast and the outcome in 1960 results probably to some extent from the government's recommendations to public authorities and public enterprises in the spring of 1960 to be restrictive in their investment activity. Furthermore the figures concerning 1959 and 1960 are rather shaky as a result of partly real, partly purely accounting shifts in the investment amounts, caused by the introduction of the general sales tax at the turn of the year 1959/60.

TABLE 10. BUILDING AND CONSTRUCTION INCLUDING MAINTENANCE BY LOCAL AUTHORITIES
PERCENTAGE CHANGE IN VOLUME COMPARED TO PREVIOUS YEAR

	FORECAST		OUTCOME
	IN DECEMBER PREVIOUS YEAR	IN MARCH SAME YEAR	
1957	+ 9	+11	+10
1958	+ 1	+ 3	+ 4
1959	+ 5	+ 7	+ 8
1960	+ 5	+ 6	− 2
1961	+ 4	+ 4	+ 5
1962	+11	+13	+14

Central government

Investment by public enterprises is determined mainly by the expenditure limits laid down in the government budget. Investment may not exceed these limits or be reserved for expenditure during the following fiscal year. The frames should therefore give a fair forecast of investment during the fiscal year. (The fiscal year in Sweden runs from July 1st to June 30th.) The forecasts of the National Budgets apply, however, to the calendar year, and it is difficult to arrive at a half-yearly distribution of investment that reflects real investment activity and not cash expenditures. Furthermore, the frames are fixed in nominal amounts, and the scope for real investment is therefore diminished by price increases. The same difficulties also apply to military investment, but here forecasting is further complicated by the fact that the approved expenditure may be carried over to the next fiscal year. The forecasts of expenditures actually obtained are also very difficult to interpret, as they concern only cash payments. Table 11 indicates the forecasts of the National Budget for investment by public enterprises and for military investment.

TABLE 11. CENTRAL GOVERNMENT INVESTMENT INCLUDING MAINTENANCE
PERCENTAGE CHANGE IN VOLUME COMPARED TO PREVIOUS YEAR

	PUBLIC ENTERPRISE AND GOVERNMENT INVESTMENT FOR CIVIL PURPOSES			MILITARY INVESTMENT		
	FORECAST			FORECAST		
	IN DEC. PREVIOUS YEAR	IN MARCH SAME YEAR	OUTCOME	IN DEC. PREVIOUS YEAR	IN MARCH SAME YEAR	OUTCOME
1957	+ 3	+ 2	+ 6	0	− 2	− 1
1958	+ 4	+ 5	+ 6	0	+ 8	+ 3
1959	+ 9	+14	+16	+ 6	+ 8	+ 5
1960	+ 2	+ 1	− 4	+ 7	+ 8	0
1961	− 3	− 3	+ 1	+ 6	+ 8	− 4
1962	+ 4	+ 5	+ 1	+ 7	+13	+22

Other sectors

Statistics on investment plans for private power stations, for communications in the private sector and for the merchant marine are also available and can be used as a basis for forecasts. In addition, statistics on investment plans are available for forestry, private as well as state-owned. As to building investment in commerce, the forecasts are based solely on the above mentioned type of calculations derived from statistics on starts and projects under construction. There are no statistics on investment in agriculture or on the majority of car purchases. There are also no statistics on planned maintenance expenditures in the private sector. Forecasts of investment in these sectors can be made only by means of extrapolation of the trends.

Total investment

Total investment forecasts and outcome of total investment activity—distributed according to investment in building and construction and investment in machinery—are indicated in Table 12. The table shows that the forecasts—even the revised ones—have often been rather misleading. The discrepancy between forecasts and outcome is especially notable for 1960. As to this discrepancy, it should be mentioned that the calculations of outcome for 1959 and 1960 are rather shaky as a result of party real, partly purely accounting shifts in the investment amounts, caused by the introduction of the general sales tax at the turn of the year 1959/60.

Possibilities of improving the investment forecasts

It seems to be generally agreed that the calendar year is too long a period for the purpose of business cycle analysis. For this reason interest has recently been focused on short-term statistical data. The most important way of improving the investment forecast is therefore to obtain short-term statistics on investment plans. However too little is yet known about when plans are made, about planning periods, frequency of plan revisions, etc. The half-year has been selected as the *ex ante* statistical period. In the *ex*

Table 12. INVESTMENT FORECASTS AND OUTCOME
PERCENTAGE CHANGE IN VOLUME COMPARED TO PREVIOUS YEAR

	FORECAST		OUTCOME	DEVIATION	
	IN DEC. PREVIOUS YEAR	IN MARCH SAME YEAR		PERCENTAGE POINTS	
				DECEMBER	MARCH
Building and construction including maintenance					
1957	+4	+4½	+3	+1	+1½
1958	+4½	+6	+6	—1½	0
1959	+4	+8½	+9½	—5½	—1
1960	+2	+4	+1	+1	+3
1961	+2½	+4	+7½	—5	—3½
1962	+4	+5½	+4½	— ½	+1
Machinery and equipment including maintenance					
1957	+3	+3½	+2	+1	+1½
1958	+2½	+6	+5	+2½	+1
1959	+ ½	+2	+6	—5½	—4
1960	+9½	+9½	+8	+1½	+1½
1961	+2½	+3½	+5	—2½	—1½
1962	+2	+4	+6	—4	—2

post statistics, the quarter was chosen. This decision was partly based on a survey of short-term accounting by enterprises. Half-year plan statistics on investment in mining and manufacturing were collected for the first time in October 1961. The figures concerned 1962. In Table 13 these figures are given, together with figures on revised plans and on outcomes collected in surveys during 1962 and 1963.

Table 13 shows that the October plans—as suggested above—are a rather incomplete forecast for what is going to happen during the second half of the following year. What makes the interpretation of half-year plan statistics more complicated than those on a yearly basis is the existence of a seasonal pattern in the *ex post* data, which probably has no correspondence in the *ex ante* data. This makes the seasonal components of the *ex post* statistics inapplicable to the *ex ante* data.

This will probably result in continuous problems of interpreting the short-term investment plans during a period of transition. Until a series of

Table 13. INVESTMENT IN MINING AND MANUFACTURING, 1962

Current prices, million kronor.

	BUILDING AND CONSTRUCTION EXCLUDING MAINTENANCE		MACHINERY AND EQUIPMENT EXCLUDING MAINTENANCE AND CARS	
	1ST HALF-YEAR	2ND HALF-YEAR	1ST HALF-YEAR	2ND HALF-YEAR
Planned in October 1961	735	561	1146	1146
Planned in March 1962	749	739	1340	1250
Preliminary outcome (estimated in August 1962)	609	782	1182	1516
Definite outcome (estimated in June 1963)	652	855	1162	1459

half-year plans, sufficiently long to allow accurate seasonal adjustments, is achieved, a seasonally adjusted short-term forecast seems impossible to calculate so as to be consistent with seasonally adjusted *ex post* data.

One of the reasons why forecasts of central government investment have been so inaccurate—at least in comparison with the possibilities of accuracy—is probably that the above-mentioned type of analysis has not been applied. The transformation of fiscal year figures into figures for the calendar years is, however, by its nature a problem which for its solution necessitates consideration of the relation between the *ex post* and the *ex ante* seasonal accounting patterns. The forecasting methods for the central government sector are impaired by a certain inconsistency in this respect. For these reasons, inquiries are presently made with the purpose of establishing an accounting of the *ex post* figures by public enterprises and the central authorities that better reflects the actual investment development than the present accounting. Simultaneously, the newly received figures on half-year plans have to be examined as to their proper significance, i.e., if they refer to planned cash expenditures or if they concern actual deliveries.

Because of the transitional problems that are to be expected before the half-year plan statistics can effectively be used for short-term investment forecasts, an extension of the afore-mentioned calculations for building, based on permits and starts, is planned. Because of the relatively shaky statistical material presently available, these calculations seem rather unreliable when concerning whole years and all the more so for half-years. Their great advantage lies, however, both in that the forecasts are consistent with the outcome for whole years and half-years, and in that they can be collected currently.

Another problem is that interpretation of information on investment plans is made difficult by the fact that conditions for the investment plans are not at all specified in the surveys. The firms are asked to report only the total sum of calculated investment for a given period to come. For certain investment projects, plans may virtually be unconditional, whereas plans for other projects may in a high degree be dependent on development tendencies in many respects, e.g. financing possibilities and general economic development both inside Sweden and abroad.

As has been shown above there have been evidenced not only discrepancies of certain magnitudes between plans and outcomes in the survey but also a high degree of variation in the magnitudes of discrepancies. This can, of course, be to a large extent explained by changes occurring during the plan period which in all probability have not been taken account of in the plans. Changes in economic policy are a case in point. To a certain extent, however, the variations might have been caused because the plans were formulated on the basis of (unspecified) assumptions which appear to have been unrealistic and inconsistent with the general economic forecast. It seems, therefore, necessary to supplement the surveys so as to obtain additional information that will facilitate the interpretation and evaluation of investment plans. Such information would possibly also provide an indication of the strength underlying investment activity in the longer run than in the period covered by the plans.

Sweden

Stockbuilding

Forecasts of total inventory investment in industry are based on the changes in stocks of raw materials, goods in process and finished goods calculated for the various branches. In estimating these branches' changes in stocks, forecasts of those variables that are assumed to be of primary importance for these stocks are taken into account. Those variables have been mainly production and prices of various commodity groups. In a way forecasts of production and of inventories were adapted to each other successively. In the same way inventory trends in trade have been calculated.

When the last inventory forecasts were calculated an attempt was made to formalize the relations for inventories in industry mentioned above. So the following inventory functions for the engineering industry and the rest of industry were estimated.

Engineering industry:

$$r^It = -4{,}096.0 + 9.42\Delta_v O_{t-1/12} + 15.33\Delta_r P_{t-1/4} + 16.59_r P_{t-1} +$$
$$+ 1.80 \frac{vV_t}{BNP_t} + 0.0655\Delta_v OR_{t-1/3} \qquad R = 0.9156$$

$$w^It = -339.7 + 27.13\Delta_v O_{t-1/4} - 10.99\Delta_i P_{t-1} + 3.02 P_{t-1}$$
$$R = 0.9063$$

$$f^It = 106.5 + 17.48\Delta_v O_{t-3/4} - 2.42\Delta_i P_{t-1} - 0.17_i P_{t-1} -$$
$$- 0.272 \cdot a \cdot \frac{d^2 v OR_{t-1/3}}{dt^2} \qquad R = 0.9098$$

All other industries:

$$r^It = 603.9 + 0.0162\Delta_r O_{t-1/6} + 12.58\Delta_r P_{t-1/4} + 0.0385\Delta_{tm} O_{t-1 1/6} \quad R = 0.9070$$
$$w^It = 27.9 - 0.522\Delta_w O_{t-1/3} + 0.023\Delta_i P_t$$
$$R = 0.7176$$

$$f^It = 113.2 - 0.0164\Delta_f O_t + 1.70\Delta_i P_t - 0.0296 \frac{\Delta^2_t O_t}{\Delta t^2}$$
$$R = 0.9202$$

r^It = change in stocks of raw materials during year t
v^It = change in goods in process during year t
f^It = change in finished goods during year t
$\Delta_v O$ = change in production in engineering industry
$\Delta_r O$ = change in industrial production, excluding engineering, weighted with changes in raw material stocks
$\Delta_w O$ = change in industrial production, excluding engineering, weighted with changes in goods in process stocks
$\Delta_f O$ = change in industrial production, excluding engineering, weighted with changes in stocks of finished goods
$\Delta_{tm} O_t$ = change in industrial production in wood and pulp industries
r^P = price index of commodity-input of industry
i^P = price index of industrial products
$\frac{vV}{BNP}$ = gross profit in engineering industry in relation to gross national product
vOR = orders received in engineering industry
a = dummy variable

Economic Forecasting

6 HOUSEHOLD INCOMES AND EXPENDITURES

The first quarterly calculations (covering 1954 onwards) of household incomes and expenditures were completed at the beginning of 1961. The quarterly estimates follow the definitions which are used in the yearly national accounts but the available short-period statistics are not completely consistent with the yearly. Efforts have, however, been made to improve existing short-period statistics in different fields and to obtain new statistics in the fields which have not been covered earlier. The calculations are therefore not definitive, while the methods of compiling *ex post* statistics and of forecasting have to some extent been established. Short-term forecasts are made by the Institute three times a year, namely in March, September and November.

Forecasts for the household sector are made from the income side. Separate forecasts are made for each series of income category and transfer payments which are included in *ex post* statistics (see Table 14). A seasonally adjusted aggregate of these series, i.e., disposable income of households, is used to estimate consumption. Price movements must also be forecast for deflating both income and consumption. No forecasts are yet being made of consumption of individual goods and services but possibilities for such forecasts are being investigated.

TABLE 14. FACTOR INCOME, INCOME REDISTRIBUTION, DISPOSABLE INCOME AND CONSUMPTION

Current prices, million kronor.

		1962
1.	Wages, salaries and pension allowances (assessed)[1]	45,181
2.	Income of independent entrepreneurs (assessed)	5,749
3.	Miscellaneous	4,221
4.	Income redistribution	—7,595
	of which : a) interest and dividends (net)	604
	b) direct transfers from Central Government	4,253
	c) direct transfers from local authorities	1,033
	d) insurance claims	2,242
	e) direct taxes	—13,550
	f) fees to Central Government and local authorities	—813
	g) insurance premiums[1]	—1,364
5.	Disposable income (items 1 to 4)	47,556
6.	Consumption	42,973

1. Excluding employers' contribution to social security.

Wages and salaries

The yearly calculations of wages and salaries for the national accounts are made from the official statistics of assessed income. Total net income registered in the tax statistics does not, however, cover the whole flow of incomes to households. Estimates of non-taxable income and of costs deductable from gross income have to be added. The quarterly total wage and salary bill is in principle calculated as the product of a wage rate and the number of employees working during the quarter concerned. To this quarterly total the value of pension allowances accrued is added. The quarter to quarter development of the total of wages and salaries (including pensions) calculated in this way is then adjusted to the level of the yearly calculations in the national accounts.

The forecast of pension benefits is made on the basis of the estimated change in the number of pensioners and information about the way in which general wage developments influence the level of pension benefits.

The quarterly calculations of wages and salaries cover the following sectors: 1) agriculture, 2) forestry, 3) mining and manufacturing, 4) building and construction, 5) trade, 6) transport and communication, 7) Central Government and local authorities, 8) other. For each sector sums of wages and salaries can be calculated from *ex post* material with different time lags. With these sums as starting points forecasts are made for their development between corresponding quarters of two consecutive years. The forecasts are based on estimates of negotiated earnings, wage drift and changes in employment for the different sectors. As far as can be judged from available statistics wage drift is negligible except in mining and manufacturing and in building and construction. Forecasts of wage drift and of employment in different sectors are derived partly from forecasts of production and productivity in these sectors and partly from the assessments of the over-all economic situation made at the same time by the Institute.

The methods for judging the development of negotiated earnings vary according to when the forecast is made. As a rule the negotiations end in March and the agreements have hitherto been in force one or two years, generally from the middle of the first quarter of a year. March forecasts in most cases concern the remaining three quarters of the current calendar year and preliminary data are in general available for that purpose.

September forecasts concern the fourth quarter of the current year and the first two quarters of the following year. For the fourth quarter definite figures are obtainable from the negotiations. For the following two quarters preliminary data are available if these quarters belong to the second year of an agreement period of two years. If this is not the case there is, of course, no firm basis for a forecast and the Institute must therefore make estimates on the basis of current tendencies of wages and salaries and of general economic prospects.

In November, finally, the forecasts generally concern all of the four quarters of the following year. Here the problems are similar to those mentioned in respect of the September forecast of the following year's first two quarters.

Incomes of independent entrepreneurs

Incomes of independent entrepreneurs are estimated separately for the following three income categories, namely agriculture, forestry and other unincorporated businesses both in *ex post* calculations and in the forecast. The quarterly breakdown is made very roughly for each group by adopting a percentage distribution which is retained unchanged for all of the years concerned. The forecasts generally refer to changes between the full years except the September forecasts which concern changes between the first half of the current year and the first half of the following year.

Forecasts of income from agriculture are made in March and November by the National Agricultural Marketing Board on the basis of data collected for the price regulation system of agricultural products. The forecasts of income from farming are built up from very detailed estimates of output and expenditure. When these forecasts are not available rough extrapolations must be made.

Incomes from forestry owned by farmers are determined by timber prices and cutting. The prices are estimated by the National Board of Crown Forests and Lands taking into account previous sales as well as other relevant market conditions. The cutting is estimated by the Institute in connection with the construction of a balance of resources for timber.

The yearly calculations of income of other independent entrepreneurs and from real estate (other than agricultural real estate and related businesses) are based on tax assessment statistics. Forecasts are made in collaboration with the General Accounting Office and are guided by an assessment of general economic development.

Interest and dividends (net)

Calendar year estimates of incomes of capital are based on the tax assessment statistics, and forecasts of these incomes are made by the General Accounting Office. Changes in the stock of housing loans, estimated by the Central Bank of Sweden, are used to arrive at total outstanding housing loans. A fixed proportion of this total is treated as loans to owner-occupied houses. Interest costs for owner-occupied houses, estimated from this sum and an interest rate calculated by the National Rent Council, are deducted from the gross incomes of capital.

When assessing the future development of housing loans the Bank of Sweden takes into account the Institute's forecast of production of dwellings. The National Rent Council conducts periodical investigations of the interest rates for loans on certain types of dwellings. The Institute's forecast of interest rates is mainly based on the prediction of the National Rent Council.

Miscellaneous

In the Swedish national accounts gross national product is primarily calculated from the expenditure side. This calculation does not entirely agree with estimates made from the income side. The residual is treated as consisting of two parts, namely, the regular part which is allocated to income of households and the irregular part which is included in corporate saving. The results of the Institute's investigation of household savings in 1957 have been utilized for estimating household saving and the regular part of the residual. For years other than 1957 the regular residual is calculated as the same percentage of factor incomes of households as in 1957.

Sweden

Insurance premiums and claims

Insurance premiums and claims are calculated on the basis of official annual statistics and of slightly less detailed short-period statistics. The insurance sector is subdivided into three parts: national insurance, private insurance and other insurance.

Forecasts are in many cases based on extrapolations of trends indicated by current statistics. (Short-period statistics on private insurance companies appear with a time-lag of about two months.) The extrapolations may be modified if information about future developments calls for a change.

For national insurance, the scope and the size of premiums and claims are stipulated by law, amendments to which are generally preceded by investigations which often indicate the estimated effects. New regulations usually come into force at the turn of the year.

Transfers between households and the public authorities

Direct taxes and fees from households to the authorities consist of the following items:

A-tax (Preliminary taxes paid by wage-earners)
B-tax (Preliminary taxes paid by taxpayers other than wage-earners)
Supplementary tax payments
Tax arrears
Miscellaneous tax payments
Deductions: excess tax advances
real estate tax
Fees to Central Government
Fees to local authorities

Income taxes are in principle collected on a pay-as-you-earn basis in the form of A-tax or B-tax. A-tax is paid by persons whose main income originates from employment, while others pay B-tax. A-tax is preliminarily deducted from wages and salaries before they are paid out. Supplementary A- and B-tax payments may then be made until April of the year following the income year. If the preliminary tax paid exceeds the final tax assessment, the surplus will be reimbursed to households, while households pay tax arrears in the opposite case. Reimbursements are made during the final quarter of the year following the income year, while tax arrears are paid during the period of January-April two years after the income year. The preliminary A-taxes currently account for more than three quarters of total direct taxes and fees.

The forecast of preliminary A-tax payments is based on the following equation:

$$A_t = -884.8572 + 2.7734 \, _1Y_t + 0.1046 \, _1T_t$$

$$R = 0.9949$$

A = A-tax
$_1Y$ = total wages and salaries
$_1T$ = changes in tax rates

The equation is estimated on seasonally adjusted quarterly data.

Towards the end of every year the amount of tax arrears to be paid during the following year is known. For the September forecast, however, this information is not available and extrapolations of the trend have to be made.

Also for *other* tax items as well as for *fees to Central Government*, forecasts are made by way of linear extrapolations. This method is to some extent justified by the relative stability observed for the largest item here—preliminary B-tax.

Fees to local authorities are obtained yearly from the surveys of local authorities' finances which are conducted in the autumn and contain data on both the current and coming calendar year. The yearly figures are evenly distributed over the quarters.

Income transfers from the public authorities direct to households include old-age pensions, children's allowances and other.

Old-age pensions as well as children's allowances can be rather reliably forecast over a year. For children's allowances account is taken of the expected change in the number of children in the relevant age group as well as of the amount of allowance per child. Any change in this amount, actually decided on, will of course be taken into account. When forecasting old-age pensions account is likewise taken of the expected change in the number of pensioners and of the amount of pension per pensioner. The amount of pension per pensioner furthermore is subject to a kind of escalator-clause, which means that a price rise exceeding a fixed amount gives rise to a compensatory payment called index allowance. In the forecast of old-age pensions account is thus taken of the price forecast. The forecast of pensions is facilitated to the extent that an index allowance is put into effect with a time-lag of three months in relation to the minimum fixed price rise.

Consumption forecast

An analysis of the quarter to quarter development of the seasonally adjusted value of disposable income and private consumption during 1954-62 shows that consumption varies less than disposable income. Saving acts as a buffer when the income changes are exceptionally large or small. Therefore the relative income change has been included, besides the income in absolute terms, as an independent variable in the consumption function. Consumer prices are also supposed to influence consumption and, therefore, the consumer price index has been included as an independent variable.

The consumption function has changed a little from time to time. The latest consumption function, which was used in the Preliminary National Budget 1964, is presented below.

$$C_t = -3{,}502.716 + 0.6443\ _d Y_{t-1/6} - 55.0 \frac{\Delta_d Y_{t-1/6}}{_d Y_{t-1\,1/6}} + 76.92\ _k P_t$$

$$R = 0.9993$$

C_t = consumption during half-year t, million kronor, current prices.

$_d Y_{t-1/6}$ = disposable income during half-year $t-1/6$, million kronor, current prices

$\dfrac{\Delta_d Y_{t-1/6}}{_d Y_{t-1\,1/6}}$ = percentage change of income between half-year $t-1/6$ and half-year $t-1\,1/6$

$_k P_t$ = consumer price index during half-year t.

Sweden

Consumer prices

In deflating the forecast of current consumption a forecast of the total consumer price index is used. The forecast of price movements is made on the basis of statistically covered development of costs, trade margins, agricultural producers' prices, import prices, expenditures on housing, etc.

About 40 per cent of the total weight in the consumer price index consists of services (exclusive of housing), processing costs in commodity production without international competition and trade margins. Costs and prices in this sector mainly depend on wages. Besides the rise in wage costs, which can be derived from the wage forecast, it is also necesary to estimate productivity increases in order to arrive at changes in unit costs.

About 12 per cent of the total weight of the consumer price index is affected by changes in agricultural producers' prices. The price regulation of agricultural products provides some guidance for anticipating developments. The pricing system now in force covers a 6 year period between September 1, 1959 and September 1, 1965. Its main purpose is to achieve income parity for farmers as compared with wage-earners in manufacturing.

7 PUBLIC CONSUMPTION

Public consumption is broken down into Government consumption and local authorities' consumption. Each of these measures outlays on wages and salaries (including pensions) and those expenditures on goods and services which are not considered as investment expenditure. It should be noticed that public enterprises are not included here as they are treated in the same way as private enterprises.

Government consumption

Government consumption appears, in the same way as Government investment, in different appropriation items in the fiscal Bugdet. For the current and the coming year, budget figures are available only on a full fiscal year basis, while figures on actual outcome are available on a half-year basis. It is therefore necessary to make a rough breakdown of the budget figures with the guidance of the half-year distribution of actual outcome for previous fiscal years. Besides, an observed regular bias to overestimating wages and salaries (including pensions) entails a downward revision of this item.

In the December calculations for the Preliminary National Budget, forecasts for the following calendar year are made on the basis of a regrouping by economic categories partly of the budget figures for the current fiscal year and partly of the figures of the forthcoming Finance Bill. For the calculations for the Revised National Budget in March there is no further information available for new forecasts except such proposals, if any, for increased appropriations submitted since the turn of the year. As is evident from Table 15 such increases have not been of such magnitude for the period covered as to give rise to revisions of the forecasts made in the Preliminary National Budgets.

TABLE 15. GOVERNMENT CONSUMPTION
PERCENTAGE CHANGE IN VOLUME COMPARED TO PREVIOUS YEAR

	FORECASTS		OUTCOME
	IN DECEMBER PREVIOUS YEAR	IN MARCH SAME YEAR	
1957	+4	+4	+2
1958	+2	+2	+1
1959	+4	+4	+8
1960	+5	+5	+3
1961	+5	+5	+5
1962	+5	+5	+6

Local authorities' consumption

The basis for forecasts of local authorities' consumption is a survey of local authorities' finances conducted by the Central Bureau of Statistics. The survey is made three times a year, namely in March, in September and in November and consists partly of a complete survey covering cities, municipalities and county councils and partly of a sample survey covering rural communes. The March and September surveys do not, however, cover information on all of the items constituting local authorities' consumption. Thus, expenditure on goods and services must be estimated on the basis of information on the planned outlays on wages and salaries (including pensions).

Local authorities' expenditure plans for the coming calendar year are worked out in the autumn and they can largely be regarded as fairly firmly established when the information on them is returned in November. It is therefore natural that no major revisions for such a continuously growing item as local authorities' consumption occur in the March survey.

In Table 16 forecasts on local authorities' consumption are compared with actual outcome.

TABLE 16. LOCAL AUTHORITIES' CONSUMPTION
PERCENTAGE CHANGE IN VOLUME COMPARED TO PREVIOUS YEAR

	FORECASTS		OUTCOME
	IN DECEMBER PREVIOUS YEAR	IN MARCH SAME YEAR	
1957	+7	+7	+4
1958	+4	+4	+5
1959	+4	+4	+4
1960	+5	+5	+1[1]
1961	+5	+5	+5
1962	+6	+6	+6

1. This low figure results partly from a reorganization of statistics on local authorities' finances in 1960.

Sweden

8 THE CREDIT MARKET

Up to and including 1960, during which period the Institute published reports only once or twice a year, the treatment of the credit market was relatively extensive. Since the introduction of quarterly reports, the credit market chapter has been given rather limited space. One of the reasons for this is that this chapter had included more historical material and fewer elements of forecasting than the other sections of the report. A general limitation of the historical material has been made in connection with the transition to quarterly reports, and this has especially affected the credit market analysis. At the same time, however, endeavours are being made to create a method of analysis which is directly aiming at forecasts. The first results of this work were published in the Preliminary National Budget for 1961[1] and in the report of the 1959 committee on economic development 1960-65[2]. The latter uses the most disaggregated model. The purpose is, however, basically the same: to provide firstly a consistency test of the national budget from financial points of view, and secondly some guidelines for financial policies.

The GNP forecast partly states explicitly, partly implies, certain developments of incomes and expenditures and therefore also of the difference between these magnitudes, i.e. of the financial savings of certain sectors. Some sectors will show negative, others positive financial savings, i.e. net borrowing and net lending respectively. In the household sector the estimated relationship between disposable income and consumption is used in forecasting the latter. Financial savings are therefore automatically consistent with the GNP forecast. The forecast of private investment, on the other hand, is to a great extent based on surveys of investment plans and is not systematically related to income (profits) in the business sector. An important consistency test therefore is a comparison between the financial savings of enterprises on the one hand and the investment calculations used in the GNP forecast on the other. The assumptions about prices, sales, wages and productivity used in the forecast of the GNP and its components imply a forecast of profits. This forecast can be compared with the forecast of private investment and the comparison results in an estimate of the need for net borrowing by enterprises. (The borrowing can take the form of an increase of liabilities and/or decrease of assets.) The question is if this borrowing, the implication of which until that stage cannot be considered in the forecast, is consistent with the predicted investment activity. One has of course also to consider the stocks of financial assets and liabilities held in the period used as a basis for the forecast. Investment incentives (and, for that matter, also consumption incentives) will to some extent depend upon the initial financial situation. If e.g. the enterprises have passed through a prolonged period of extensive self-financing in spite of shrinking financial savings and thus in the process have decumulated their financial assets, they will be compelled to turn to borrowing to a larger extent than otherwise would have been the case. The assessment of this initial situa-

---

1. Addendum 2 to appendix 1 to the finance bill 1961 also published as SOU 1961: 10, Chapter IX.
2. " Sveriges Ekonomi ", SOU 1962: 10, appendix B.

tion in itself gives rise to various problems as the statistical coverage of certain sectors is far from satisfactory. Surveys of financial assets and liabilities of enterprises have, however, lately been used for this purpose. To some extent these surveys can be checked with regular credit market statistics.

The consistency test just described might result in an adjustment of the GNP forecast or to a recommendation with regard to measures aiming, e.g., at a strengthening of investment incentives by a general easing of credit market conditions. The second stage in the credit market forecast is of a different although closely related kind and usually involves other, more special, types of credit market policies. In the preceding stage of the analysis the credit system is treated as one single sector, the other sectors being households, private enterprises, public enterprises, central and local governments and the external sector. In the second stage the credit system is split up into subsectors: the Central Bank, commercial banks, savings banks, private insurance companies, the General Pension Fund, mortgage institutions etc. The estimates of financial savings are now translated into an analysis of the demand and supply of the credit market. The demand will generally arise from the central and local authorities, the housing sector and from " deficit " enterprises. The supply will come from households and " surplus " enterprises—the government's pension fund may also be considered as a " real " sector with financial savings supplied directly to the credit market. This supply and also the funds channelled by other collectors of institutional savings such as savings banks and private insurance companies (and also by the " open market ") is possible to predict rather accurately. The difference between total demand in the organized credit market and the supply from " institutional " lenders indicates the lending by the commercial banks that is needed in order to obtain the overall balance in the credit market that corresponds to the distribution of financial savings and thereby to the GNP forecast.

This consistency test can be carried one step further in considering the balance between supply and demand in the different subsectors of the credit market. Granted, e.g., the need and willingness of enterprises to borrow a given amount in the organized credit market in order to finance predicted investments one has to assess the corresponding availability of funds to be channelled through the proper credit institutions where also other borrowers are competing for funds. Likewise the demands for funds from other sectors such as government and housing have also been assessed by the calculation of financial savings in the first stage of the analysis and have to be allocated to the proper subsectors of the credit market. The supply of funds, on the other hand, can be forecast, e.g., by the way in which households and other " surplus " sectors distribute financial savings to different credit market institutions and to the " open market " outside these institutions. (One increasingly important and rather accurately predictable item in this calculation is the accumulation of the General Pension Fund.) As there furthermore exist comparatively stable patterns of the distribution of lending to different " real " sectors with typical differences, e.g., between commercial banks, savings banks and insurance companies, it is finally possible to " match " the distribution of borrowing demands from these sectors with the corresponding distribution of supply both of which are to some extent implied in the GNP forecast. Discrepancies between the two distributions reveal " bottle necks " in the credit market.

Such bottle necks have at times existed, e.g., with regard to the financing of housing. Mortgage institutions being " loaned up ", funds might have to be transferred mainly from the commercial banks which calls for action by the Central Bank. Either the commercial banks can be forced by reserve ratio regulations to lend directly to the housing sector or the Central Bank can buy mortgage bonds and restrict the total lending capacity of commercial banks correspondingly. Otherwise there might occur building stops or at least delays. Real resources might be unused or used in ways other than have been originally forecast or planned. In the opposite case a desired expansion of industrial investment might be curbed or delayed by lack of lending capacity of the commercial banks. In either case the credit market forecast will indicate not only inconsistencies in the National Budget but also the policy or alternative policies, which the monetary authorities will have to undertake in order to make the GNP forecast consistent from the point of view of the implied development in the financial sphere. Technically the analysis takes the form of a related series of " credit market matrices, " where the actions of the monetary authority will appear as one or several " degrees of freedom " which have to be utilized in order to close the system.

In order to give a somewhat more concrete description of the methods of analysis, three tables, Tables 17–19, used in the forecasts, are presented below. The first two tables are taken from the report of the Committee on Economic Development and the third one from the quarterly reviews of the National Institute of Economic Research.

Table 17 is used for assessing the financial requirements of the different sectors in the organized credit market. The sectorization has varied according to the purpose of the analysis. In this case housing has been taken as a separate sector, the financing requirements of which have thus been given special attention. Usually sectors A and C are divided into subsectors. The estimates of financial savings taken over from the GNP calculations represent the starting point for Table 17. From there one moves to "monetary savings " via the estimated net lending between sectors, i.e. outside the organized credit market. The residual which appears in the column F of " foreign countries " is the same that is encountered in balance of payments tables and is usually labelled " statistical errors and omissions. " The residuals of the other sectors are of the same kind and appear *ex post* in all sector accounts. Their total equals zero as also does the total of net advances between sectors. " Lending to the credit market " (item 5) is, just as item 2, an indication of the elasticity of the financial system. As far as, e.g., business enterprises are concerned a negative figure for item 5 may indicate not only self-financing from accumulated funds but also intra-sector lending i.e. from surplus to deficit enterprises. Such lending, *ceteris paribus,* reduces the requirements of the sector as a whole for borrowing in the organized credit market, a borrowing which is indicated by item D6 and for the other borrowing sectors by A6, B6, and F6.

The borrowing sectors of Table 17 appear as column headings in Table 18 with the exception that an extra column has been added for the transactions between credit market institutions (column E). The sum of this column is, with minor adjustments, equal to the financial savings (with a minus sign) of the institutions and also equal to the difference between their borrowing and lending. The other sums of the columns (A8-D8 in Table 18) correspond to the borrowing requirements of the different sectors already calculated as items A6, B6, D6 and F6 in Table 17. The right hand column of Table 18 (column F) predicts the distribution of the supply of funds via credit institutions inclusive of insurance companies (F 1-5) and via the " open market " (F6-F7). The grand total (F8) corresponds to total lending (G5) according to Table 17. The lending by the commercial banks is, as indicated before, in a sense obtained as a residual, i.e. as the difference between total demand and the " institutional " supply. The lending in the bond market may on the other hand to some extent be considered as a parameter of economic policy and can be affected, e.g. by changes in the rate of interest.

The " interior " of the matrix represents an attempt to itemize the supply and demand according to lending and borrowing subsectors partly based on established lending patterns of the credit market institutions. The actual forecast also contained alternatives for monetary policy to ensure a balance between supply and demand implying changes in the items recorded with regard to the Central Bank and corresponding reactions in relevant parts of the matrix.

TABLE 17. FINANCIAL SAVINGS IN 1965

Million kronor.

	CENTRAL AND LOCAL GOVERNMENT INCL. PUBLIC ENTERPRISES	RESIDENTIAL BUILDING	INSURANCE COMPANIES	OTHER BUSINESS ENTERPRISES	HOUSEHOLDS	FOREIGN COUNTRIES	TOTAL
	A	B	C	D	E	F	G
1. Financial savings	—1000	—3800	3600	—3500	4600	—300	— 400
2. Net lending between sectors	— 700	700					
3. Residual				200		— 200	
4. Monetary savings (=1+2+3=5+6)	—1700	—3100	3600	—3300	4600	— 500	— 400
5. Lending to the organized credit market			3600	200	4600		8400
6. Borrowing from the organized credit market (—)	—1700	—3100		—3500		— 500	—8800

NOTES. 1. *Financial savings.* Financial savings of the credit institutions (exclusive of insurance companies) have been removed from the business sector and are included in the total (column G).
2. *Net lending between sectors.* The lending of insurance companies has been excluded and is moved to the credit market (line 5). Net advances between business enterprises and households have been impossible to calculate.
3. *Residual.* This is the difference between the financial savings on the one hand as calculated in the national accounts and on the other hand as indicated by credit market statistics. The residual for " Foreign Countries " refers to the residual of the balance of payments. *Ex post* this residual appears in all sector accounts.
5. *Lending to the organized credit market.* The figures given for Central Government etc., and Foreign Countries refer to changes in deposits with credit institutions. " Other Business Enterprises " and " Households " include both deposits and purchases of shares and bonds.
6. *Borrowing from the organized credit market.* The figures refer to borrowing from the credit institutions **and** borrowing by means of shares and bonds, bought by the public and the credit institutions.

Sweden

TABLE 18. LENDING AND BORROWING IN THE CREDIT MARKET IN 1965

Million kronor.

	BORROWING SECTOR					
	GOVERN-MENT AND PUBLIC ENTER-PRISES	RESIDEN-TIAL BUILDING	BUSINESS ENTER-PRISES	FOREIGN COUN-TRIES	INTERNAL TRANS-ACTIONS	TOTAL LENDING
	A	B	C	D	E	F
1. Central Bank of Sweden				500	—200	*300*
2. Commercial Banks	— 300	300	1100		—100	*1000*
3. Other banks	700	1300	100		—100	*2000*
4. Private insurance companies	400	300	200			*900*
5. Public insurance companies	600	1100	1000			*2700*
6. Bond market	300	100	600			*1000*
7. Stock market			500			*500*
8. *Total borrowing*	*1700*	*3100*	*3500*	*500*	*—400*	*8400*

NOTE : The figures of column F and line 8 correspond to lending and borrowing (lines 5 and 6) of table 17. Items E1-E5 include financial savings of the credit market institutions (as a negative item) and the net lending between them. E6-7 refer to purchases by business enterprises and households of debentures and shares issued by credit institutions.

TABLE 19. MONEY MARKET
CHANGES IN STOCKS

A. 1. Foreign exchange reserves
    2. Central Government surplus of total expenditures over current income
    3. Net sales of Government bonds etc. to the sectors outside the commercial banks (—)[1]
    4. Enterprises' investment reserves deposited in the Bank of Sweden (—)[1]
    5. Notes held outside the commercial banks (—)[1]
    6. Swedish bonds held by commercial banks except Swedish Government bonds
        Total A
B. Commercial banks
    1. Cash
    2. Treasury bills
    3. Swedish bonds
    4. Foreign currencies
        Total B (=A)

1. The sign (—) indicates that the figures have been given an inverse sign, i.e. minus sign as an increase and plus sign as a decrease in the stock-figures.
    NOTE. Item A6 is also included in B3 and thus appears on both sides of the balance; It is generally, however, of minor importance. (This arrangement is undertaken in order to include under B all liquid assets of the commercial banks.) Other variables under A can be considered as data (A5) or as parameters of economic policy.

Finally the changes recorded in Table 18 with regard to the commercial banks can be taken as a starting point for a detailed analysis of the liquidity position. The standard form used for this purpose—*ex post* as well as *ex ante*—is shown in Table 19. In this table the different components of the liquid assets of the commercial banks are recorded under heading B, and the factors " determining " the changes in liquidity are recorded under the heading A. Given the initial liquidity ratio of the commercial banks—the ratio between liquid assets and certain liabilities—and the initial reserve requirements, the surplus or deficit lending capacity at the starting point of the forecast period can be calculated. This capacity will be affected both by the lending of the commercial banks as envisaged in Table 18 and by the operations of the Central Bank, forecast in Table 19. The confrontation of Table 18 and Table 19 therefore gives guidelines with regard to the actions to be taken by the Central Bank in order to achieve a consistent development in the money market.

CHAPTER VI

THE UNITED KINGDOM: SHORT-TERM ECONOMIC FORECASTING[1]

Short-term forecasts are made in the United Kingdom of the movement of total demand, domestic activity and the balance of external payments. They are considered an essential basis for short-term management of the economy, that is, for decisions influencing the level of domestic activity and the balance of external payments. All the government departments concerned either with the individual components of the forecast or with the implications of the outcome in aggregate terms collaborate in their preparation under the leadership of the Treasury.

Forecasts are usually made three times each year looking some twelve to eighteen months ahead, on the assumption that current fiscal and credit policies are unchanged. In addition interim reassessments may be made from time to time to take into account new developments or fresh pieces of information. The timing of the three main forecasts is geared to the annual Budget which is normally in the first half of April. In the autumn a preliminary appraisal of the outlook to the end of the following calendar year is prepared. In the new year forecasts are made spanning the whole of the coming financial year (April-March) as part of the material required in the preparation of the Budget. In the early summer a third set of forecasts is made, taking into account any changes made in the Budget and other developments and again extending the forecast period further ahead.

1 FORECASTING DOMESTIC ACTIVITY

The forecasts of gross domestic product (GDP) are built up primarily by forecasting changes in the individual components of expenditure. They are expressed in terms of seasonally adjusted series at constant prices, although forecasts of incomes and price movements are a necessary step in the process. The relative magnitudes of the components of expenditure are illustrated by Table 1 relating to 1962[2].

The predominant aim is to forecast the level of activity at the end of the period under consideration and, so far as possible, its course between the base date and the end of the period. The result is typically expressed as a change between the present or recent past and a quarter near to the end of the forecast period. Forecasts are not set out in terms of changes between the

---

1. This chapter has been previously published in substantially the same form in the August, 1964, issue of *Economic Trends* (Central Statistical Office, London).
2. The figures in this table and elsewhere in the paper are taken from " Preliminary Estimates of National Income and Balance of Payments, 1963 " (Cmnd. 2328).

TABLE 1. GROSS DOMESTIC PRODUCT AND ITS COMPONENTS, 1962

At 1958 prices.

	£ MILLION	PER CENT OF TOTAL
Personal consumption	17,101	55
Public authorities' consumption	4,126	13
Fixed investment	4,438	14
Investment in stocks	113	1
Export of goods and services	5,274	17
Total final expenditure	31,052	100
less Imports of goods and services	−5,553	
less Net indirect taxes	−3,102	
Gross domestic product at factor cost	22,397	

totals for whole years since a given change in these terms is consistent with many different patterns of change between the beginning and end of the period under review. A conclusion, for instance, that output would rise two per cent between one year and the next would be consistent with either a rise or fall in output between the beginning and end of the second year so that the policy implications of changes between whole years would be quite uncertain. There is no suggestion that it is possible to forecast precisely individual quarterly movements of demand and output over a period of, say, fifteen months. But such a layout, building up to a forecast of the level of activity around the end of the period, is intrinsically much more informative about expected trends. The forecasts are therefore always cast in a quarterly framework, each component of expenditure and the related quantities (employment, wage rates, etc.) being set out quarter by quarter for the base period and for the whole future period under consideration.

Statistical background

It is useful, before discussing the forecasting in detail, to give a brief account of the nature of the statistics available. The GDP is estimated in three ways:

a) The sum of expenditures: personal consumption, public authorities' consumption, investment (fixed and in stocks) and exports, from the total of which are deducted imports and net indirect taxes. The GDP derived from expenditure data is measured at current prices and also at the prices of a base year.

b) The sum of factor incomes: income from employment, income from self-employment, profits, rent and the surpluses of public undertakings. This is a measure of GDP equal in principle to the GDP estimated at current prices in *(a)* above.

c) Finally, the GDP is estimated from output data. Roughly half the GDP is accounted for by industrial production for which a monthly index is available. The other components of output are estimated at present on an annual basis. The GDP measured from output data is in principle equal to the GDP measured from expenditure data at constant prices.

The United Kingdom

Each estimate of the GDP is comprehensive in the sense that every component is individually estimated; none contains a residual category.

The GDP measured from income (at current prices) and from expenditure (at current and constant prices) is available quarterly; usually the majority of the figures are available about three months after the quarter to which they refer. The GDP measured from output is at present available only annually, but some approximate indication of its movement is provided by the index of industrial production.

Apart from the national income and expenditure and production figures there are a large number of indicators available on a monthly basis which help in the task of diagnosing trends in the most recent period (i.e. the last four or five months). Perhaps the most important are the figures relating to demand for labour, especially those for overtime, registered job vacancies and unemployment; the figures for retail sales (which account for about half personal consumption), for registrations of new cars and for hire purchase transactions; for exports and imports; and for new housing starts and completions. There is also a considerable amount of information about new orders and orders on hand and about investment intentions which is mainly forward looking.

Organisation of material

The first step is to organise the statistical material for the recent past in a suitable way to provide a starting point for the forecast. There are two main problems. Each of the seasonally adjusted series is liable to a degree of random or erratic fluctuation and some attempt has to be made to establish its underlying trend. A good deal can be done, for example, by processes of averaging, to smooth out erratic fluctuations but there remain difficulties in handling the most recent observations. Secondly there are problems of consistency between series. For instance, although variations in the timing of payments in relation to work done should be reflected in counterpart changes in recorded stockbuilding, in practice this does not always happen; and some series, for example those for changes in stocks and imports, are not always consistent for each quarter. Not infrequently, there are discrepancies in the measurement of GDP from income data and from expenditure data although both are estimates of the same thing. Bearing in mind that each component of the GDP measured both from expenditure and income data is separately estimated, usually on the basis of sample enquiries, and that separate corrections are made for seasonal variations, it is not surprising that in practice these measures sometimes move differently. The GDP estimated from output data is not so far available on a quarterly basis, but it sometimes happens that the index of industrial production by itself suggests a movement in total output different from one or both of the other measures.

The preparation of an account of past developments which is consistent as far as possible with all the information available, including statistics which are not national income statistics (such as those of unemployment) and other indicators such as retail sales or wage rates for the very recent past, is therefore an important preliminary stage of the work. There are various methods of dealing with these problems and the choice between them depends on the nature and extent of the inconsistencies. It should be emphasised that these difficulties and discrepancies cast some doubt on the validity of precise statements about the recent past.

The forecasting process

The forecasting process relies rather extensively on programme or survey material (e.g. for public authorities' consumption and fixed investment) and also on the detailed knowledge of the relevant government departments about particular items (e.g. for imports and exports, detailed studies of particular commodities and markets; for wage rates, an examination of current settlements and claims). The components of demand are then built up, largely by a process of successive approximation, into a total which is internally consistent on the basis of past experience. The methods employed are always under review. They have been evolved gradually as the practice of forecasting has developed and are still being modified fairly continuously to take advantage of new techniques or new pieces of information. For example, the growing quantity of quarterly national income data and the availability of computers are making possible more refined mathematical investigations which in turn make possible the use of predetermined relationships at various stages of the forecasting process. The following paragraphs thus describe the present state of a developing system.

The first step is to make preliminary forecasts of all components of expenditure other than personal consumption; these are treated as more or less independent variables. Given the basic assumption of unchanged fiscal and credit policies the final outcome of any forecast is critically dependent on the changes in exports and fixed investment.

Exports

A forecast of exports of goods and services is required both for assessing demands on the home economy and for estimating the prospects for the balance of payments. The way in which this is prepared is described below in the section on forecasting the balance of payments. For that purpose forecasts in current values are needed, and these are translated into volume terms (i.e. at constant prices) for purposes of forecasting demands on the home economy, export prices being forecast primarily by reference to past trends, and the outlook for home costs.

Fixed investment

As regards fixed investment, a good deal of information is available about intentions and plans in both the public and private sectors and this is supplemented by other indicators, for example, statistics of engineering and building orders, of industrial development certificates required before an industrial building can be constructed and the figures for architects' commissions, etc., collected and published by the Royal Institute of British Architects. At present forecasts are made separately for eight headings which provide an approximate division between the private and public sectors.

The United Kingdom

The five headings for the private sector are manufacturing, distribution and other services, shipping, private housing and a residual category. The Board of Trade conducts sample enquiries into the investment intentions of the first three categories. Until 1963 three such enquiries were made for each year, the first being in the middle of the previous year, the second at the end of the previous year, and the third in the middle of the year in question (coinciding with the first enquiry for the following year). Late in 1963 the timing of the enquiries was modified. A first estimate for 1965 was collected then (at the same time as the second enquiry for 1964) instead of in the middle of 1964. In addition, a qualitative enquiry was instituted in the spring of 1964, asking firms if plans for 1964 and 1965 had been revised up or down or left unchanged since the previous main enquiry at the end of 1963. The mid-year full enquiry (giving final forecasts for 1964 and a second main forecast for 1965) was postponed until the early autumn of 1964. Except in the new spring enquiry, firms are asked to forecast their expenditure in terms of the money they expect to spend in the calendar year taken as a whole.

There are various problems in using these surveys as the basis of a forecast of the change in investment at constant prices during the forecast period. First, there is the question of obtaining from the individual forecasts supplied by contributors an estimate of the aggregate level of expenditure in the year concerned. While the relationship between forecast and out-turn has varied very much from company to company it has been found that, in the aggregate, firms' forecasts are in excess of actual expenditures in a fairly systematic way. The proportionate excess varies with the first, second and third forecasts (the constancy of the pattern from year to year depending on there being no great change in business outlook). The practice therefore is to take as the forecast of the change in expenditure between one year and another, the change between the aggregated forecasts for the first year and the comparable forecasts for the second year (i.e. first forecast to first forecast, second to second, and third to third). Secondly, the price basis on which firms make their forecasts is not precisely known since they are asked to return the intended value of expenditure. In the normal way it is assumed that some allowance should be made to reduce the expected rate of change to a constant price basis.

Having derived a percentage change between whole years in this way the important questions to consider are how closely to rely on it as the basis of the forecast and what quarterly path to interpolate. This depends somewhat on which of the intentions enquiries is available. Experience has shown that first forecasts, made in the middle of the year preceding the one to which they relate, can be unreliable at times when there is about to be a change of trend. Third forecasts, on the other hand, made in the year to which they relate, have generally given more reliable results. The approach used in evaluating the available survey results is to try to set them in a cyclical context. With the accumulation of experience in handling the results of the intentions enquiries, attempts can be made to anticipate the effects of changes in the level of activity that have occurred since the last enquiry or which may be in prospect as a result, for example, of a recent Budget.

The other forward looking indicators already mentioned are used as corroborative evidence, particularly in assessing the timing of possible cyclical turning points. For example, the balances of " ups " over " downs " in the answers to the questions, " Do you expect to authorise more or less expenditure on (a) buildings, (b) plant and machinery in the next twelve months than you authorised in the last twelve months ? " included in the four-monthly industrial trends enquiry, conducted by the Federation of British Industries show a clear cyclical fluctuation related with a time lag to actual investment expenditures by manufacturing industry.

For private housing the main indicators are the recent figures for starts and completions which are available monthly and the direct, half yearly, enquiries by the Ministry of Public Building and Works into the number of starts intended by builders. The enquiry to builders and property developers, who account for over 85 per cent of private enterprise housing, is also made three times for each year, the first being in the middle of the previous year, the second at the end of the previous year, and the third in the middle of the year in question (coinciding with the first enquiry for the following year). The forecast also takes into account the likely financial position of building societies and the level of interest rates.

For the residual category (which includes agriculture) the normal practice is to extrapolate past trends.

The three headings considered for public investment are nationalised industries, public services and public authority housing. In all cases the forecast is derived from the plans of the various authorities and departments concerned which are agreed by the Treasury and published every autumn. The total of expenditure (and, in the case of housing, the number of tenders) authorised relates to financial years and there may be difficulties in assessing the quarterly evolution particularly when authorisations are changing substantially from one financial year to the next. The problem is aggravated by the tendency of some of the quarterly expenditure data for the past to fluctuate rather erratically (perhaps because some figures are of cash payments) which makes it hard to measure recent performance at all closely. In the past big changes in plans have generally taken longer to achieve than has been anticipated. If on occasion the change authorised between two financial years is large and implies a very rapid change of pace, either upward or downward, in investment, the quarterly figures written into the forecast may provide for some carry forward into a succeeding year or even beyond the forecast period.

The enquiries on which the forecasts of investment are based make possible a breakdown of the total among the main types of asset, i.e. plant and machinery, vehicles, and building. Sometimes the asset picture makes necessary some modifications to the forecast of total investment if, for example, the implied demand for building exceeds what is believed will be the capacity of the industry (though such unfulfilled demand is taken into account in the general assessment of the forecast pressure of demand).

The initial investment forecast, built up in this way, may be modified at a later stage in the exercise in the light of the forecast for total demand which finally emerges. But in the ordinary way such changes would be slight because the feedback from future trends in activity to fixed investment is likely to be fairly small within the twelve to eighteen months reviewed by a forecast.

The United Kingdom

Public authorities' consumption

The forecasts of current expenditure by the central government on goods and services are derived from the Budget Estimates and, for the period after the Budget year, from forward estimates which departments are required to submit as part of a survey of total public expenditure. This information covers a great many other payments than current expenditure on goods and services (e.g. subsidies, grants to persons and capital expenditure). The first step therefore is to extract the total of items of current consumption. This has then to be corrected for price changes between one year's Estimates and those of the previous year. Since the price basis used by departments in preparing their estimates is not uniform, departments are asked to make the necessary revaluation. Finally there are the familiar difficulties of assessing the quarterly evolution of expenditure from the past into the future. These difficulties are at least as important for public authorities' consumption as for investment because of the difficulty of eliminating fluctuations from the payments figures which do not represent any change in the underlying trend.

Information about future current expenditure on goods and services by local authorities is derived mainly from the estimates of expenditure on education, health and certain other services used for determination of the general grant by the central government, and from estimates of relevant expenditure for specific grants such as for roads and police. The expenditure covered by this information comprises about three-quarters of current expenditure on goods and services by local authorities, though the total of grants from the central government amounts to a smaller proportion.

Investment in stocks

The function of stocks in the economy makes it particularly difficult to forecast changes in them precisely. The general approach to the question is based largely on an analysis of how stocks have moved in relation to changes in output in the past. Over the whole period for which quarterly stocks and output figures are available (i.e. from the beginning of 1955) stocks in total have tended to rise about as fast as output but with fairly marked short-term differences. The ratio of total stocks to total output has fluctuated cyclically, but about an apparently rather stable level. In periods when, for example, demand other than stockbuilding has risen sharply there has tended to be some initial counterpart movement in stockbuilding in the opposite direction and the stock/output ratio has fallen abruptly. This has tended to be followed by subsequent increases in stockbuilding and a recovery in the ratio.

In forecasting, the idea of a tendency to restore or maintain a long-run average value for such ratios is a useful way of establishing some presumptions about possible rates of stockbuilding which would over a period be consonant with the rest of the forecast. In dealing with the initial part of the forecast period, however, more weight is given to cyclical considerations, starting from the recent history of the rate of stockbuilding and making allowance for the character of the coming phase of the cycle as indicated by the forecasts of other elements of demand.

The stock/output ratio is examined by detailed sectors (i.e. manufacturers' stocks held as finished goods, work in progress and materials, and stocks held by retailers and wholesalers) as well as in total. In manufacturing industry there has been some shift from stocks classified as materials to stocks classified as finished goods within a roughly constant long-term ratio for the total.

Personal consumption, first estimate

The forecast of personal consumption is built up by forecasting individually all the main components of personal income, direct taxes, consumer prices and personal saving. To a large extent changes in income, and hence in consumption, are dependent on the change in output, a large part of which is represented by personal consumption itself. An iterative method is used to obtain forecasts of personal consumption and total output which are mutually consistent. The first step is to postulate (largely by reference to past experience) changes in personal consumption and in total output that appear to be likely to result from the forecasts so far made for other changes in demand. Given the assumed change in output a forecast for income from employment can be built up and with this a complete personal income and expenditure account. If this results in a forecast of consumption different from that postulated, the output forecast is modified accordingly and the personal account revised to bring the relationships into order.

Personal disposable income

The relative magnitudes of the components of personal income before tax are indicated in Table 2 relating to 1962:

TABLE 2. COMPONENTS OF PERSONAL INCOME, 1962

	PER CENT OF TOTAL
Wages and salaries	65
Forces' pay	2
Employers' contributions[1]	5
Current grants from public authorities	8
Rent, dividends and interest	11
Income from self-employment	9
Total personal income before tax	100

1. To national insurance, pension funds, etc.

The practice at present is to make a single forecast of the combined wage and salary bill, partly because some of the statistics cannot be adequately separated between wage incomes and salary incomes. The framework of thought that has been used is illustrated (on an annual basis) in Table 3. For the first column, the wage and salary bill. published information is used. Column 2 is derived in a fairly simple way from published civil employment data and column 3 is obtained by dividing column 1 by column 2. The hourly wage rate index (column 4) is published and the relation of its

The United Kingdom

TABLE 3. WAGES AND SALARIES
PERCENTAGE INCREASE ON CORRESPONDING FIGURE IN PREVIOUS YEAR

	TOTAL WAGES AND SALARIES	NUMBERS OF WAGE AND SALARY EARNERS	WAGES AND SALARIES PER HEAD	HOURLY WAGE RATES INDEX	EARNINGS DIFFERENTIAL	
					IRREVERSIBLE	REVERSIBLE (residual)
1959	4.8	0.5	4.3	2.8	0.6	0.9
1960	7.8	2.0	5.7	4.2	0.6	0.9
1961	8.1	1.4	6.5	6.4	0.6	—0.5
1962	4.7	0.7	4.0	4.5	0.6	—1.1

movement to the movement of the wage and salary bill per head (column 3 divided by column 4) yields the " earnings differential. " This is a composite residual embracing for example, the effect of changes in the amount of overtime and in bonus payments and in the relative number of wage earners and salary earners. For forecasting purposes the earnings differential is divided into two parts. First, a trend factor (shown in column 5 as the irreversible earnings differential) which is estimated to be an increase of 0.6 per cent a year. Secondly, a residual factor (shown in column 6 as the reversible earnings differential) which has fluctuated roughly in proportion to fluctuations in the pressure of demand for goods and services in the economy as a whole (defined below). The relationship is conceptually very imperfect because the hourly wage rates index covers only manual operatives and excludes all salary earners so that the " reversible earnings differential " in reality reflects not only changes (such as the amount of overtime pay) which can be directly ascribed to fluctuations in the pressure of demand but also any unusual changes in the composition of the wage and salary bill.

The field of knowledge about the determination of earnings is one in which rapid development is taking place, centred particularly on the analysis of the wage and salary bill and the nature and causation of " wage drift. " The improvement in understanding should lead to the adoption of alternative and more refined methods of forecasting.

In forecasting, each component of the analysis is estimated in turn. For wage rates, the main considerations are what has happened in past periods of similar pressure of demand for labour and current information about the state of wage negotiations. The rate of change of wage rates has shown some cyclical fluctuation in the past but the bargaining processes have been much influenced by habit and convention and in practice past experience has generally proved a useful guide, though in assessing its relevance to any particular circumstances attention has to be paid also to developments in prices (which may influence collective bargaining) and, nowadays, to the development of incomes policy. In addition to these rather general considerations there is always a good deal of information available about the current size of wage settlements, the intervals between them, the main claims outstanding and the actual monthly increases in the wage rates indices all of which help to determine the forecast, particularly for the earlier part of the forecast period.

The " irreversible earnings differential " is extrapolated at the same rate of increase as in the past. The forecast for the " reversible earnings differential " and the forecast for employment are inter-related. The form of the relationships between output, employment and output per head (and also between output, employment and unemployment which is discussed below) is not fully identified or understood. Various rules of thumb have been deduced from analyses of past changes in output, employment and the labour force, and work is proceeding both on the nature of the relationships and their magnitudes. The convention used at present is that a change in the level of activity (i.e. a change in the pressure of demand for goods and services) will be reflected roughly equally in a change in the reversible earnings differential and in an abnormal change in employment (abnormal in the sense of being additional to the absorption of the underlying change in the labour force). The pattern of changes may allow for some time lag, especially in the response of employment to a change in the pressure of demand. The employment forecast may also be modified if, for instance, there is an unusual supply of particular types of labour, e.g. immigrants or juveniles, or if there has been a large change negotiated in the length of the standard working week.

Dividend income paid to persons is assumed to be related after a time lag to changes in profits. Other property income (rent and interest) is normally assumed to continue recent trends. Income from self-employment has in the past tended to move sluggishly but with some cyclical variation in its rate of change. A continuation of the recent trend is normally assumed with some allowance for the cyclical character of the whole forecast.

Almost all the other components of personal disposable income can be forecast from the government's own information. Forecasts of Forces' pay, current grants to persons, and national insurance contributions are based on information about the numbers involved and current or prospective rates of pay, benefit and contribution. Direct tax payments are built up by applying the appropriate marginal rates of tax to the various kinds of personal income.

Consumer prices

Most of the analysis and forecasting of prices is in terms of the monthly retail price index, a linked Laspeyres index, excluding from its coverage expenditure by the relatively higher income groups. One advantage of using this index, apart from the fact that it is available monthly, is that a very detailed breakdown of its components is available.

The retail price index is forecast in three broad categories:
a) Those kinds of foods of which the price fluctuates largely as a result of short-run changes in domestic supplies
b) Rent and rates[1]
c) Other goods and services

The average price of the foods considered separately has large short-term fluctuations about its trend. The procedure is usually to assume that these prices will be normal at the end of the forecast period. This part of the forecast is particularly subject to error but it is useful to take separate account of it especially when prices are abnormal in the base period.

---

1. Local authority taxes on property.

The forecast of the rent and rates index is usually an extrapolation. Sometimes (as when there was legislation to remove certain kinds of rent control) a more elaborate study is carried out. Allowance is also made when unusual changes in local authority rates are expected.

The average price of the remaining group of goods and services (about 80 per cent of the total) is assumed to move, after a time lag, in the same way as costs, which are made up of import prices, specific indirect taxes and normal labour costs.

Import prices are derived from the work on the balance of payments. Specific indirect tax rates are assumed to remain constant in line with the general assumption of unchanged fiscal policy. For labour costs the relevant concept is taken to be the change in the cost of labour, defined below, less a trend increase in output per man, whether or not this is the actual increase in output per man expected in the forecast period. The theory underlying this assumption—which past experience in the United Kingdom broadly supports—is that business men generally fix their prices on the basis of a standard or normal degree of capacity working; in other words that, given the cost of labour, short term variations in the level of total output and output per head make little difference to the price level.

The cost of labour is defined as average hourly earnings (corrected to remove the effect of changes in overtime) plus average employers' insurance and pension contributions, all of which are derived from earlier stages of the operation. Hourly earnings are corrected for the effect of changes in overtime because it is believed that changes in average earnings due to more or less overtime being worked are not a factor affecting prices. An exception is the rise in overtime that may result when the standard working week is cut. This manifestly puts up normal costs and attempts are made to allow for any substantial changes of this kind.

The resulting forecast of prices may be modified if special factors are known or expected to be present. One fairly recent example was the larger than usual rise for a time in prices charged by the nationalised industries which followed a review of their financial and economic obligations.

Finally it is necessary to convert the forecast changes in the retail price index into a forecast of the consumer price index which is the average value index covering the whole of consumers' expenditure. On an annual basis the consumer price index has usually risen by about nine-tenths of the increase in the retail price index though this may be upset by, for example, a sharp change in the pattern of consumer spending following a sharp change in price relativities. The relationship is much weaker on a quarterly basis. In the ordinary way the nine-tenths relationship is used to provide forecasts of annual changes, but it is not applied automatically to each quarter partly because the consumer price index required is a seasonally adjusted one and because there are frequently difficulties in reconciling the data on such a short term basis.

Real personal disposable income (RPDI)

The individual forecasts of personal incomes, direct tax payments and national insurance contributions, and of consumer prices yield a forecast of real personal disposable income (RPDI). As already indicated, the rate of change in RPDI is associated with the rate of change in total output. In practice, consistency of the relationship can be disturbed by a large number of factors including changes in the distribution between sectors of the national income or within the field of personal income, changes in taxes, import prices or seasonal food prices. It is never easy to handle the complex combinations of special factors that can occur and have occurred in the past but, nevertheless, it is worth comparing the forecast of RPDI built up in successive steps with the forecast growth of non-consumption demand and of output to test the plausibility of the relationships between them.

Personal saving

Since the beginning of the 1950's there has been a very large rise in the proportion of RPDI saved, with considerable fluctuations from year to year. The fluctuations in the saving ratio appear to have been associated to some extent with fluctuations in net lending on hire purchase and by banks. In Table 4 net saving is equal to the difference between disposable income and consumption (the conventional national income definition of personal saving). Gross saving is equal to net saving plus an adjustment for the assumed effect on consumption of changes in hire purchase debt and bank advances.

TABLE 4. SAVING AS A PERCENTAGE OF PERSONAL DISPOSABLE INCOME

	GROSS SAVING	NET SAVING
1956	5.8	6.3
1957	6.4	6.2
1958	5.9	5.1
1959	7.9	6.1
1960	8.8	8.4
1961	9.8	10.0
1962	8.8	8.7

There is no hard and fast way of making this adjustment. It seems unlikely that an increment in net lending would result in an equal addition to consumption over and above what it otherwise would have been, and reasonable to suppose that the addition to spending on consumption is considerably smaller in the case of bank lending (some of which is in respect of, for example, house buying) than hire purchase lending. For forecasting purposes rule of thumb conventions have been adopted about the extent to which such borrowing generates additional consumption.

Real net saving is forecast in two stages, first the " borrowing effect " and, secondly "real gross saving." So far as hire purchase debt is concerned, the change in debt in any period is equal by definition to credit extensions less repayments of debt. Although the method of forecasting hire purchase business explained in an article " Hire purchase and instalment credit statistics " in *Economic Trends,* September, 1961, seemed to work fairly

The United Kingdom

well in the later 1950's, it has not been so successful in recent years. Presumptions about the future course of hire purchase business are now established from the size and structure of existing debt, from the credit policy of the government and from any special features in the prospects for the main categories of goods bought on hire purchase.

The change in bank advances classified as personal and professional is also separately estimated. There is little to go on here apart from rather general inference from the government's credit policy. But useful presumptions about the likely future change in net lending can sometimes be established simply from recent developments and from experience of comparable periods in the past.

The year to year changes in RPDI, gross saving and the difference between them (spending out of income) is shown in Table 5.

TABLE 5. CHANGES IN INCOME, SAVING AND SPENDING

£ million at 1958 prices.

	REAL PERSONAL DISPOSABLE INCOME	REAL GROSS SAVING	REAL SPENDING OUT OF INCOME	CHANGE IN REAL GROSS SAVING AS PERCENTAGE OF CHANGE IN RPDI
1951-52	244	261	—17	107
1952-53	660	159	501	24
1953-54	486	—1	487	—
1954-55	708	93	615	13
1955-56	413	201	212	49
1956-57	294	112	182	38
1957-58	213	—73	286	—34
1958-59	885	399	486	45
1959-60	1,072	237	835	22
1960-61	689	259	430	38
1961-62	37	—183	220	—495

NOTE. Estimates prior to 1956 are considerably less reliable than the later ones.

The table shows that there have been substantial fluctuations in the marginal propensity to save (even after allowing for the supposed effects of borrowing on saving). Their causes are not fully understood. One possible factor in the short term is a time lag before spending habits adjust to a change in the rate of growth of RPDI, so that when there is a sharp upturn in RPDI the marginal saving ratio is for a time unusually high, and vice versa. For forecasting purposes the usual assumption is that the marginal (gross) saving ratio will be roughly what it has been on average over a run of years, but this is modified if the forecast rate of growth of RPDI represents a sudden change from the past.

Personal consumption, second estimate

The forecast for personal consumption emerges by subtracting the forecast for net saving from the forecast for RPDI.

Imports

The next step is to consider how the change in total final expenditure given by the sum of the preceding demand forecasts will be met by changes in imports of goods and services and changes in home output. The way in which the forecast of imports is made is described in the section on forecasting the balance of payments.

The subtraction of the forecast of imports of goods and services and of the forecast value at constant tax rates of net indirect taxes from the aggregate forecast for total final expenditure yields the forecast of the gross domestic product at constant factor cost.

Pressure of demand and unemployment

The relationships between output, employment and unemployment are at present the subject of a good deal of investigation both here and in other countries. The system of thought now used to assess the implications of the GDP forecast for the pressure of demand for goods and services and for unemployment, is based on the idea that the change in unemployment can be explained as a consequence of differences between the actual growth of output and what may be called its potential rate of growth. The latter is defined as that growth of output which would ensure a constant pressure of demand as measured by unemployment and other labour market indicators, with allowance for time lag. There is no way of measuring this rate of growth directly but it is possible, for example by means of multiple regression analysis, to allow for the effect on output of changes in the pressure of demand and by this means to estimate values for past rates of change of output associated with a constant pressure of demand. The analyses that have been made suggest that in the period 1952–62 the potential rate of growth was $2\frac{1}{2}$–3 per cent per annum, with a rather higher rate, perhaps a little in excess of 3 per cent, in the latter part of the period. An index of the potential rate of growth interpolated as a quarterly series from estimates obtained in this way, compared with an index of actual quarter by quarter output provides an indicator of the degree of utilisation of the productive potential of the economy.

Unemployment has tended with a considerable degree of consistency to move after an interval towards the level appropriate to the degree of utilisation. Because the process takes time unemployment tends to be low in relation to the concurrent level of utilisation on the downswing of a cycle and high in relation to it on the upswing. This approach suggests that a variation of one per cent in the degree of utilisation of the productive potential has been associated with a change of the order of 50,000 in the number unemployed by the end of a period of adjustment.

The forecast for the potential rate of growth is based on an extrapolation of the current estimates of recent experience with some allowance for any known special factors such as fluctuations in the rate of change in the population of working age, large changes in the standard working week and the recent rate of fixed capital formation. A comparison of this rate with the output forecast yields an implication for the pressure of demand and hence for the change in unemployment.

The United Kingdom

2 FORECASTING THE BALANCE OF PAYMENTS

As already noted, forecasts of the balance of payments are made concurrently with those of domestic economic activity and the two are closely inter-related at many points. The material on imports and exports of goods and services, which is required for both purposes, is combined with estimates of property income, transfer payments and long-term capital flows to reach an assessment of how the "basic" balance of payments of the United Kingdom (on current and long-term capital account) is likely to move.

As in the case of the domestic economy, the organisation of the statistical material for the past is an important preliminary step, since much depends on a correct understanding of past relationships and a proper assessment of the trend of developments at the time the forecast is made.

World economic prospects

The first stage in assessing prospects for the external accounts is an appraisal of prospects for the world economy. Forecasts are made of the movement of gross national product (GNP), and its main components, in the main industrial countries, drawing on the information available from these countries and from parallel studies made both in the United Kingdom and by international organisations. From this material a forecast is made of the short-term trends in world industrial production and in the exchange of manufactures between industrial countries. For primary producing countries attention is focused on potential export earnings and aid receipts, since their external financial resources are often the dominant factor determining the level of their imports. The forecast of their export earnings depends on the implications of the review of industrial countries' activity for demand for the major industrial materials and for changes in commodity prices; and also on a review of prospects for international trade in the main foodstuffs. It is supplemented for the countries of the sterling area by more detailed country by country appraisals of their balance of payments prospects. This leads to a forecast of industrial countries' exports of manufactures to primary producing countries which, combined with the forecast of trade between industrial countries, gives a view about the trend of world trade in manufactures.

Exports

In the short run it is primarily conditions in overseas markets which determine the value of exports of goods. The forecast is thus essentially a demand forecast, founded upon the prior study of world economic prospects. The views of official British representatives in a number of the most important markets are sought on the likely development of United Kingdom exports to these markets. Separate forecasts are made of the value of exports to each of the main areas to which the United Kingdom exports—Western Europe, the sterling area (each accounting for over one-third of total exports), North America, the rest of the world and, in a few cases, for sub-areas or important individual markets.

The particular method by which the forecast is made varies from area to area depending on the amount of background information available and on indicators which the analysis of past experience suggests are the most relevant to demand for United Kingdom exports. For example, from past experience it appears that the trend of United Kingdom exports to the United States follows fairly closely the trend in GNP of the United States, with changes in stockbuilding playing an important part in the short run. Forecasts of the GNP of the United States and its main components thus provide a basis for this element in the export forecast. It is necessary, however, to make an independent assessment of prospects for exports of transport equipment, especially cars. The forecast of exports to Western Europe is based as far as possible on reviews of the economic outlook in the principal countries concerned, though statistical information about short-term changes is not sufficiently comprehensive to allow more than a broad assessment of their prospects to be made. The changes that have occurred over the past decade in factors affecting United Kingdom exports to Western Europe (e.g. the removal of import restrictions, the growth of tariff discrimination and the growth of interest of United Kingdom exporters in these markets) all add to the difficulties of establishing from past data relationships useful for forecasting. Figures for past periods, however, show that the development of private investment in Western Europe has an important effect on United Kingdom exports of capital equipment; changes in rates of stockbuilding also may have an important effect. For the sterling area and the rest of the world—comprising mainly primary producing countries—the forecast is based on the study of prospects for their export earnings and their likely aid receipts, since these largely determine their ability to import. Any knowledge or expectation of changes in import restrictions is also taken into account and the domestic prospects of the more developed sterling area countries are examined in more detail.

Such commodity information as is available, for example from statistics of orders, is examined for its consistency with the market forecasts. The forecast is reviewed in the light of expected relative movements in United Kingdom costs and prices and is compared with the forecast for world trade as a whole, derived from the study of world economic prospects. The implications for the United Kingdom " share " of world exports of manufactures provides an alternative viewpoint from which the forecast can be judged, though by no means an unambiguous one. It is not easy to discern the relative importance of the factors influencing the United Kingdom share of world exports of manufactures, and there have been large short-term and cyclical movements in the share in the past (even after seasonal adjustment) which make it difficult to establish the trend and to form a view about the future. This approach, however, helps to bring explicitly into the forecasting process considerations such as the competitive position of the United Kingdom in world trade.

Imports

Over a run of years the volume of imports of goods has risen somewhat faster than home output (a phenomenon common to most, if not all, industrial countries) with fluctuations about the trend in part associated with fluctuations in the rate of stockbuilding, which has an import content considerably higher than that of final expenditure as a whole. The relationship, however, is not a simple one because of the incidence of special or short-term factors whose effects are not easily measured. Examples are the progressive liberalisation of imports from quantitative restriction, the varying size of harvests, and the variability of fuel imports due to abnormal weather or changes in the pattern of international oil sales. An important feature of the import forecast is the attempt to accommodate such factors. The forecasts of import prices, especially for food and industrial materials, make use of the commodity price forecasts in the review of world economic prospects (allowing for differences in the commodity composition of world trade and of United Kingdom imports).

The approach to the total import forecast is two-fold. There is the detailed commodity by commodity approach designed to bring any special features or information about particular commodities within the framework of the general forecast for final demand and stockbuilding. There is also the aggregative approach which deduces imports (by volume) as a function of the forecast changes in total final sales and in stockbuilding (the latter being assumed to have an import content of about one half) allowing for some upward trend in the use of imports. This provides a general check on the results of the detailed approach.

The main features of the commodity approach are as follows:

a) Food imports (about a third of the total) appear to have a very slow upward trend but in the short term they are influenced a good deal by home and overseas supply prospects.

b) Imports of industrial materials (two fifths of the total) are forecast by considering possible consumption and stock changes for major industrial materials in the light of trends in the using industries based on the forecast growth of industrial production. At this stage any special factors expected to affect imports of particular industrial materials, e.g. sales from United Kingdom government stockpiles, can be taken into account as well as recent trends in these imports. The forecast built up in this way is compared with one based on an estimated relationship between industrial production, stockbuilding and imports of industrial materials derived from past experience.

c) The forecast of imports of oil (a tenth of the total) is based upon an assessment of future internal and export demand. The effect of expected stock changes is allowed for and advice is sought about possible changes in refinery throughput which would affect the distribution of imports between crude oil and oil products.

d) Imports of finished manufactures (about a seventh of the total) are forecast within two broad heads: consumer and capital goods. The former are related to the forecast of consumers' expenditure and stockbuilding (bearing in mind the likely trends for particular commodities such as cars or clothing) and the latter to the investment forecasts, having regard to possible changes in the share of imports. Attempts are made to allow for the effects of any recent or expected tariff changes or measures of liberalisation.

Invisibles

Forecasts are made separately of each of the main debit and credit items in the invisibles account, against the background of the expected developments in economic conditions in the United Kingdom and overseas. There are indications that, if certain items are excluded, e.g. government transactions and interest on sterling liabilities, the remaining invisible debits and credits are in some degree connected with the growth of output in the United Kingdom and in other industrialised countries. It is possible to get a broad check on the results of more detailed estimation by using such relationships, even though they have not as yet been very fully developed.

Government current expenditure and receipts are mainly built up from Budget Estimate figures revised in the light of the latest information. Forecasts of shipping credits and debits are derived from the forecasts of the volume of United Kingdom imports and exports and of freight rates; account is taken of the likely trend of the share of British shipping in world trade (cross trades and own trade). Forecasts of travel debits and credits are made in terms of transactions vis-à-vis the main areas concerned: Western Europe, North America and the sterling area. Extrapolation of recent developments is supported by some forward guidance from information about bookings. The forecast of other imports and exports of services is little more than an estimate of a trend value.

Interest, profits and dividends (IPD) is the most important item in the invisibles account, for debits and credits are large and the balance between them fluctuates considerably. The forecasts of income from direct investment are derived from views taken of the prospects for company earnings overseas and in the United Kingdom, bearing in mind the industrial and, for credits, the area distribution of investments. For oil companies' earnings use is made of forward estimates by the major companies.

Long-term capital

Official transactions are forecast from the current programme for loan drawings and loan repayments. Repayments are usually known, but loan drawings cannot be forecast with any precision for the timing of drawings is often uncertain (even where the amounts are specific and settled) and contingent expenditure can rarely be foreseen.

Private investment flows have been found most difficult to forecast with confidence. This is partly because, as with some of the components of IPD, much of the information underlying the figures has been available only from 1958; as a result, there is little experience of the way in which changes in investment flows are associated with other related variables.

Direct investment flows, like the debits and credits arising from these investments, are influenced by economic prospects here and abroad. It has also been found that the proportion of profits which are re-invested by companies operating abroad tends to be fairly stable. For oil investment reliance is placed on forward estimates made by the major companies. Portfolio investment is sensitive to unforeseeable movements of relative interest rates and of confidence. The forecasts of a number of the remaining items within the private investment account are little more than extrapolations of past experience adjusted for any perturbations which can be foreseen. It is recognised that the forecast of total private investment is subject to a wide range of error, which has been increased by the emergence of a widely fluctuating flow of inward portfolio investment in recent years.

Balancing item and monetary movements

The methods described above lead to a forecast of the identified balance of current and long-term capital transactions. In order to arrive at an implied forecast of the balance of monetary movements (broadly, the balance of changes in short-term assets and short-term liabilities) it would be necessary to forecast the balancing item (which represents the net total of errors and omissions throughout the account). The balancing item has fluctuated widely in recent years and, although it is possible to advance some speculative hypotheses about these movements, they provide no basis for a quantitative forecast. Nevertheless, the apparent existence of a persistent positive element in the balancing item, reflecting errors and omissions in the current and long-term capital accounts, is borne in mind in judging the significance of the forecast of the identified balance. No attempt is made to make a quantitative estimate of likely changes in the items that make up monetary movements—the reserves, net sterling liabilities and other short-term capital movements. But some light may be thrown on these by the separate estimate of the balance of payments of the overseas sterling area mentioned above.

CHAPTER VII

THE UNITED STATES: SHORT-TERM FORECASTING BY THE PRESIDENT'S COUNCIL OF ECONOMIC ADVISERS

1 ORGANIZATION OF ECONOMIC FORECASTING

Quarterly projections of national income and product are prepared by staff economists in a number of agencies of the Federal government, including the Departments of Agriculture, Commerce, Labor, and Treasury, the Bureau of the Budget, the Council of Economic Advisers, and the Board of Governors of the Federal Reserve System. There is a continuous flow of information and frequent exchanges of views among the staff economists charged with responsibility for forecasting, but they may agree to disagree. In such instances, staff economists will pass up the line their own forecasts and a comparison of these with the opinions of other government economists. Also, the government forecasters weigh—and, when relevant, report—the projections of economists outside government. The financial press and periodicals publish a considerable number of projections of business conditions; government people have access to the forecasts of economic consulting services and, on an informal basis, receive forecasts used for internal purposes by private business firms. Furthermore, the Treasury and the Council of Economic Advisers meet regularly with consultant groups of academic and business economists to obtain their quantitative and qualitative appraisals of the economic outlook.

Wherever there are a number of trained economists appraising business conditions, views with different shadings are bound to emerge. A synchronized and uniform government forecast could be practically obtained only if all efforts at business forecasting were consolidated in one locus, with projection activity banned, in effect, for other agencies. In view of the nature of the relationships among government economists and among agencies, such a ban is out of the question. And fortunately so. It would harm the formation of sound economic policies. The range of predicted paths of the economy is important information to the policy-makers in the Administration. Decentralized, but coordinated, efforts at forecasting help to point up uncertainties, whereas a single government view might appear more precise and definite than would ever be justified.

Quantitative forecasts of national product have many uses in guiding policy. Certain government agencies use them—much the same way private business firms use forecasts—as a guide to their management decisions and plans in operating programs that are affected by economic activity. For example, the Post Office Department finds that the demand for its services is closely related to personal income. Agricultural programs are influenced by business conditions through effects on farm prices and incomes and on migration of the rural population. Lending and loan-guarantee activities of housing agencies vary with the strength of the housing market. The services provided by the Commerce and Labor Departments must be geared to the state of the economy.

In addition to its uses in the management of particular programs, short-term forecasting is consistently at the center of the stage in the formulation of overall fiscal policy. The only government forecast that is partially made public is the one underlying fiscal policy. This is the estimate of economic activity agreed upon by the Bureau of the Budget, the Council of Economic Advisers, and the Treasury Department for the President's budget program. In the present Administration, the annual estimates of gross national product, personal income, and corporate profits underlying the budget calculations are stated in the Budget document each January, and this appraisal of the outlook is discussed in some detail by the Council of Economic Advisers in the Economic Report. If a Mid-year Budget Review is published, it contains modified revenue estimates.

The task of assessing the outlook as an internal guide to fiscal policy is, however, a year-round assignment under the present Administration for a working group with representatives of the Bureau of the Budget, the Council of Economic Advisers, and the Treasury Department. The interagency group conducts a monthly review of the economic outlook and the budgetary outlook. A complete set of revised quantitative estimates is prepared each quarter—more often if substantial changes are indicated. Quarterly, rather than annual or monthly data are stressed. Each complete interagency appraisal contains quantitative projections of:

a) The components of national income and product by quarters generally to the end of the current calendar year or fiscal year—whichever ends later. The forecast period thus ranges from two to four quarters. When needed, supplemental, less detailed figures are estimated for an additional few quarters.

b) The unemployment rate, the price level of overall output (the GNP deflator), and an estimate of the discrepancy between actual and potential output, also by quarters over the same period.

c) Federal receipts and expenditures on the national income basis, again by quarters over the same period.

d) Federal receipts and expenditures as measured by the administrative and cash budgets for the current fiscal year and, when it approaches, for the next fiscal year.

The figures are accompanied by an explanation of the forecasts and a brief discussion of assumptions, uncertainties, and contingencies. In the text and tables, as in the formulation of the estimates, the preceding interagency report is the point of departure. Revisions are guided by new evidence on the strength of demand in the private sector, revenue collections by the Treasury, the pace of Federal expenditure programs, and legislative developments affecting the budget plan. While the interagency report on the fiscal outlook does not originate policy recommendations, the working group reviews the impact of alternative policies under discussion in the Administration. In many instances, the group will be asked to make special "add-on" forecasts—estimates of the incremental budgetary and economic effects of possible legislation.

The interagency forecast is first discussed and tentatively formulated by staff economists of the three participating agencies. The estimates are reviewed by policy-making officials and then by the agency heads. The report is finally submitted to the President as a joint memorandum from the Director of the Budget, the Chairman of the Council of Economic Advisers, and the Secretary of the Treasury. The detailed quarterly report is normally discussed in a meeting of the three agency heads with the President.

The following discussion of forecasting techniques applies directly to the work done by the Council of Economic Advisers in its participation in the three-agency group. Nevertheless, much of the methodology also describes other forecasting work in government and indeed a large body of quantitative national income and product forecasting in the private sector. The discussion does not deal specifically with the techniques of estimating Federal revenue collections. These are nevertheless an important part of the work of the three-agency group, and are primarily the responsibility of the Treasury.

2 THE STRATEGY OF THE FORECAST

Assumptions

The forecast of economic activity requires a prediction of the activity of the Federal sector. The Bureau of the Budget takes principal responsibility for a quarterly projection of Federal purchases of goods and services and of other outlays of the Federal government that enter the national income-and-product accounts. One component of Federal expenditures displays significant sensitivity to the level of economic activity in the short-run—namely, benefit payments for unemployment insurance. This item must be regarded as induced and adjusted to the ultimate forecast of GNP and unemployment. But all other parts of Federal outlays can for all practical purposes be regarded as autonomous and predetermined magnitudes.

The budget program is the point of departure for these quarterly projections. But the estimates in the annual budget document are based on legislation proposed and supported by the President—these represent the Administration's best judgment of what Congress *should* do, not its best prediction of what Congress *will* do. The interagency working group must translate from the normative to the predictive. Moreover, during the course of the year, changes in the timing of expenditures lead to revised estimates. The assumptions about Federal revenues take the form of predicting changes in the tax schedules from proposed and pending legislation. The dollar volume of revenues is crucially related to income levels and must be regarded as endogenously determined.

The character of policies affecting future monetary and credit conditions is also specified as an assumption of the forecast. This assumption represents an informed judgment about the attitudes of the monetary authorities. It is not a normative judgment by the three agencies; nor does it rest on any direct statement of intentions by the Board of Governors of the Federal Reserve System.

At times, an assumption about some key uncertainty in the private sector will be specified in the forecast. For example, it may be necessary to predict the outcome of a collective bargaining negotiation if a strike or a large wage and price increase would have marked aggregative effects.

General methodology

The forecast of GNP is derived from eclectic methods, incorporating the specific assumptions outlined above, certain quantified economic relationships, and informed judgments. Like any sensible approach to income-determination, the forecast tries to capture the interdependence of incomes and expenditures and of the various sectors of the economy. Unlike a fully articulated econometric model, it does not have formal and explicit decision-rules for estimating each item from a fixed body of information. Nor do the quantitative relationships it employs have the statistical properties associated with complete econometric models. The Government has not constructed an econometric model of national income and product, but econometric techniques have been used to investigate the various sectors. While opinions differ on the priority that should be attached to such efforts, there is a growing consensus that optimal forecasting requires a blending of applied judgment and formalized statistical knowledge. Even with a fully articulated model, judgment should play an important role. The residuals of econometric equations should not be naively assumed to be zero for future periods; detailed consideration must be given to the recent values of these errors and to evidence that arises from sources that are not explicitly variables in the model. No forecaster should accept the verdicts of a formal model without careful and continuous examination and cross-checking against informed judgment.

On the other hand, forecasting that rests entirely on *ad hoc* judgments cannot take full account of the lessons of history that can be summarized in quantified and formalized economic relationships. Quite apart from accuracy, formal methods have a number of advantages. For example, a complete model is a demonstrably objective predictor; it cannot be accused of coloring the forecast to further its preferred policies or to correspond to the state of its viscera. (This shield can help to supply internal as well as external protection. Many an economic forecaster may have some private moments of doubt as to whether he is maintaining his objectivity and his courage as he prepares his outlook.) Secondly, the more formalized the forecasting method, the more readily it lends itself to systematic post-mortems. The full model reveals its own past errors in stark nakedness. And systematic post-mortems are essential to guide research efforts in refining forecasting.

The CEA forecast of future economic activity is developed against the backdrop of a wealth of data on the current state and recent movements of business conditions. There are monthly series corresponding to most components of GNP and the vast majority are available, at least in preliminary form, by the middle of the succeeding month. Indeed, retail sales and such key production figures as autos and steel are reported on a weekly basis. Much of the forecaster's effort is devoted to interpretation and diagnosis of current data, blending the information on how the economy has been

The United States

moving in the recent past with the projection of how it is likely to move in the near future. When the economic forecaster assesses the future path of the economy, he benefits from reasonably firm knowledge of where it stands currently.

The forecast relies heavily on anticipations data and pre-flow data. Anticipations data are expressions of the intentions or expectations of economic units and are collected by sample survey methods expressly as aids to forecasting. They record, not economic activity, but rather the subjective views of respondents on their future economic actions and experiences. Anticipations series currently cover plant and equipment spending intentions of non-farm businesses, inventory and sales expectations of manufacturers, and expenditure plans of consumers for purchases of major durable goods and homes. Pre-flow data are the orders, contracts, and commitments that precede the actual flow of goods and activity in certain areas. The anticipations and pre-flow series are symptomatic or barometric indicators of future economic activity, rather than causal factors influencing the path of the economy. The use of non-causal variables and their relationships to income-and-product components distinguishes applied forecasting from more basic research efforts to " explain " the dynamics of economic fluctuations. The importance of the non-causal data in the formulation of the forecast will be apparent in the discussion of components below.

In the past few years, prices have been stable and hence the prediction of overall price movements has not been a major source of forecasting error. The interagency forecast has operated recently on the assumption that the GNP deflator would rise by 1.5 per cent a year, and the accuracy of this assumption has been quite satisfactory. Even the movements of relative prices have been predictable, with increases in the GNP deflator stemming principally from the areas of consumer services and government payrolls. The indicated rise in these service prices reflects the characteristics of the price indices as well as the developments in the economy. In view of the stability of prices, the forecast has concentrated on predicting income and expenditure components as undeflated magnitudes; all dollar figures cited in this paper are therefore " current price " undeflated data, unless otherwise noted. At the same time, the forecasters study data on unfilled order backlogs, wage-increases, and sensitive prices, which would be expected to foreshadow any interruption of the record of price stability. If inflationary forces emerged—either from the demand or the cost side—more intensive efforts would be required for forecasting prices. In such a situation, it might be desirable to predict the expenditures of certain sectors initially in constant prices and then to adjust these into current dollars, using the predicted path of the relevant prices.

For many decisions of fiscal policy, the timing of the next cyclical turning-point is a critical issue. The business cycle has remained very much alive in the United States, though it has led a relatively quiet life in the post-war era. While economists who pursue income-and-product forecasting look to their GNP estimates for a diagnosis of the cycle, they also pay attention to the National Bureau of Economic Research techniques of leading indicators. The Bureau of the Census of the Department of Commerce publishes a monthly review of Mitchell-Burns-Moore business cycle indicators which is required reading for government economic forecasters.

Aggregating the outlook

The quantitative GNP forecast is derived from a review of the various components of national expenditure. But the interdependence of the parts of the economy means that no forecast can be a simple sum of the parts. Even for the brief period of one quarter, consumption expenditures and inventory investment are clearly responsive to the overall movement of economic activity and cannot be treated as predetermined.

There are two ways to make the arithmetic reflect the interdependence. One method is iterative: a particular level of GNP is assumed for the quarter in question as a working hypothesis; then each component of demand is estimated for that assumed GNP. The components are then totalled and the resulting GNP is compared with the assumed level; if the two happen to be equal, the working hypothesis is checked out and the forecast may be considered complete. If they differ, a new assumed level is plugged in, and new estimates are made for those components which depend on the GNP of the concurrent quarter. The iterations continue until consistency is obtained. For minor revisions of a previous forecast, the iterative method is quite satisfactory. Because the interagency forecast is frequently revised, the changes are usually minor and the iterative method is often used. But for a new forecast where the assumed level might be far from the mark, the iterative method would be laborious.

A more direct alternative involves simultaneous estimation. At some point, the forecast for a given quarter is specified explicitly as a set of a few linear equations and is readily solved by simple methods of highschool algebra. The summary pieces used to assemble the interagency forecast have taken this form:

a) $G = \bar{G}$.—Government purchases of goods and services—these are considered exogenous and are fixed as dollar magnitudes.

b) $I = \bar{I}$.—Gross private fixed and foreign investment as the sum of (1) business fixed investment, (2) residential construction, and (3) net exports. These items are regarded as predetermined for a quarterly period—depending only on activity of preceding quarters. So long as the forecast is worked through quarter by quarter, they do not require simultaneous estimation.

c) $C = C(Y)$.—Relationship of consumption to GNP derived from (1) the ratio of consumption to personal disposable income, and (2) the relationship of personal disposable income to GNP.

d) $\Delta H = \Delta H(Y)$.—Relationship of inventory investment to GNP.

By substitution of these summary relationships into the accounting identity, $G + I + C + \Delta H = Y$, the level of GNP can be readily determined. The key elements of the forecast can be discussed by looking at the parts outlined here. Even if the arithmetic is carried out by the iterative method, the results will be the same. The logic and the problems of the forecast are more readily outlined in terms of the simultaneous approach.

The United States

3 METHODS OF FORECASTING THE MAIN EXPENDITURE CATEGORIES

Government purchases

Federal. As has been noted above, the quarterly projections of Federal purchases are a translation and modification of the annual budget program. Though they are properly regarded as independent of overall economic activity, these purchases present forecasting problems. The legislative contingencies discussed earlier can be important in looking ahead three or four quarters. But the most significant source of error lies in estimating the specific time of delivery of goods and the pace of construction activity under existing programs. Purchases of goods by the Department of Defense from private business firms constitute more than half of total Federal purchases; they display a significant amount of erratic variation from quarter to quarter. Some of the erratic variation in the very short-run tends to cancel out over a longer period as a quarter of surprisingly low purchases is likely to be followed by a quarter that shows a sharp increase. Detailed data on defense obligations and contracts are compiled; but since the lag between order and delivery is very variable these series have only limited usefulness in forecasting. For the very short-run, the forecaster is aided by the availability of current information on Federal outlays in the Treasury daily and monthly statements.

Payrolls—both military and civilian—are usually rather well-behaved, moving smoothly and predictably. Federal construction activity presents its surprises, but it is a small part of total purchases. Agricultural products, acquired by the Federal government under farm price maintenance programs, are very volatile and, though small in magnitude, are a troublesome element of non-defense purchases.

In looking one quarter ahead, the expected average absolute error in the forecast of Federal purchases might be placed between $\$ 1/2$ and $\$ 3/4$ billion (annual rate) on the basis of recent experience; the corresponding average error for the fourth quarter in the future would be between $1 and $\$ 1 1/2$ billion. But budget programs that call for large changes in total Federal outlays—as in the Korean War—increase the range of error. Moreover, sudden revisions of the budget program—like the added defense effort initiated in July 1961—create larger errors.

State and local. Purchases of goods and services by state and local governments currently amount to about 10 per cent of GNP. They have moved upward strongly along a relatively smooth path throughout the past decade. Annual increases have ranged from 7 to 11 per cent. Early each year in the February issue of the *Survey of Current Business* the Office of Business Economics of the Department of Commerce offers a judgment forecast of this sector for the calendar year. Construction activity (especially highway building) appears to have an unstable seasonal pattern and introduces some erratic variation which can be gauged from monthly data. But employee compensation and other purchases move steadily on their trends. Hence, a naive trend extrapolation (e.g., 2 per cent per quarter) of state and local purchases will hold the average absolute error for a one quarter forecast to about $½ billion (annual rate); and the error for the fourth quarter in the future will average less than $1 billion. The analyst's skill may help to estimate the construction wiggles or to detect changing trends by careful inspection of the most recent quarterly data; but such sophistication can improve only slightly on the results of naive extrapolation.

Business fixed investment

Business fixed investment (producers' durable equipment plus nonresidential construction) is about 9 per cent of GNP. The single most significant piece of information in the prediction of business fixed investment is the government's survey of business investment anticipations, conducted jointly by the Office of Business Economics of the Department of Commerce and the Securities and Exchange Commission. The survey presents the anticipations of nonfarm businessmen concerning their forthcoming plant and equipment outlays. The period of prediction covered by the survey varies from one to three quarters, depending on the time of year. In February, anticipated capital outlays are reported for the full calendar year, as well as explicitly for the first two quarters of the year. Separate figures for each quarter of the year can be inferred from the survey. Thus, intentions data are available early in March that extend more than 3 quarters ahead, covering the full calendar year. But the next two quarterly surveys—in May and August—do not ask for intentions beyond the fourth quarter of the year. The horizon of the survey thus shrinks from 10 to 7 to 4 months. And the November survey delves into only the initial quarter of the next year, again looking only four months ahead. Because capital budgeting (and other types of investment planning by business) are frequently confined to a calendar year period, the survey has adopted this pattern of variable time-coverage. The Commerce-SEC survey is such an important ingredient in the forecast of business fixed investment that the technique of forecasting for quarters not yet reported in the survey is qualitatively different. First, let us summarize the technique applicable to periods for which intentions are recorded.

Even for quarters with survey results, the forecast must consider certain types of capital outlays that are not covered by the Commerce-SEC survey of business plant and equipment expenditures. The omitted areas amount quantitatively to one-fourth of business fixed investment; they include farm fixed investment, construction outlays of religious, educational, medical, and other non-profit institutions, certain capital outlays (such as small tools and some oil-well drilling) which are charged to current expense in business accounts, and autos used for business purposes by the self-employed, salesmen, etc. who do not report in the survey. These items are not very volatile and do not create serious forecasting problems. From the analysis of these uncovered areas, the forecasters make some adjustments of the predicted increases (or decreases) in business fixed investment that apply to the sectors covered by the survey.

On the survey portion, the increases in business fixed investment reported in the business anticipations are themselves a good forecast. For one quarter ahead, the anticipated capital outlays have had an average absolute percentage error of about 2½ per cent over the past decade, equivalent currently to about a $1.3 billion error in business fixed investment. The February forecasts of the full year have done equally well, since erratic quarterly fluctuations tend to be ironed out over the year. But even these relatively small errors can be reduced in magnitude by adjusting the survey results. The differences between actual and anticipated capital outlays are systematically related to movements in economic activity. The historical record shows that the anticipated level of plant and equipment outlays for quarter $(t+1)$, as reported in quarter t, tend to be revised upward when the change in GNP during quarter t exceeds the average (or trend) quarterly increase of GNP. Conversely, less than average increases in GNP usually mean downward revisions of the anticipations.

Another adjustment is applicable to the full year anticipation of capital outlays. Sales expectations for the calendar year for some industries are collected, along with investment plans in the February Commerce-SEC survey. The sales expectations themselves do not have predictive value, but they are useful in adjusting the investment anticipations. For manufacturing industry since 1948, the errors in the sales forecast explain most of the revision in the annual investment plans: for each one per cent excess of actual over expected sales, investment has exceeded anticipations, on the average, by 1.1 per cent. The forecaster can replace the manufacturers' sales forecast by his own and then revise the investment anticipation.

Such refinements help to keep the predicted level of investment responsive to short-run economic developments. In fact, capital outlays do respond significantly in years of marked changes in economic activity; e.g., in 1960, as sales and profits proved disappointing, capital outlays at year-end were about 8 per cent below the figures implied by the February survey. The data indicate that changes in aggregate demand in a given quarter do not significantly affect capital outlays in that same quarter. Thus, plant and equipment outlays are properly treated as predetermined for one quarter ahead, but not for more than a single quarter.

Once the Commerce-SEC full year survey is reported in early March, business fixed investment for the fourth quarter of the year can be predicted with an expected absolute error of perhaps 3 per cent or $1.5 billion. But before the survey results become available, the range of error must be considered about twice as wide. In late 1961, the three-agency forecast overestimated business fixed investment for 1962 by $3 billion and for the fourth quarter of 1962 by $5 billion (annual rate). When the forecaster lacks the guidance of Commerce-SEC results, he is obliged to rely on other survey data; pre-flow data on orders and contracts; and historical relationships of capital outlays to such activity variables as corporate cash flow, profits, capacity utilization, and sales.

    a) Other survey data—McGraw-Hill Publishing Co. makes a serious effort to collect annual investment intentions before the start of the year with a November survey. This preliminary survey is helpful but its record of predictive accuracy shows an average absolute error of more than 5 per cent. The National Industrial Conference Board collects and reports the quarterly capital appropriations of large manufacturing corporations that have formal capital budgeting procedures. The series is difficult to use for aggregate forecasts since the coverage is so narrow and since the lead-time between appropriations and actual expenditure is apparently not stable. Nevertheless, the appropriations data have been accurate qualitatively during the current expansion in pointing to only a modest rise in capital outlays. In view of the recent performance of the NICE appropriations data, the forecast has paid considerable attention to this series in predicting quarters not yet covered by Commerce-SEC.

b) Contracts and orders—There are monthly data covering contract awards for nonresidential construction and new orders (and unfilled orders) for machinery and equipment. These series have been moderately successful as indicators of cyclical turning points. They also offer some assistance in the quantitative investment forecast, especially during the August to February period when the Commerce-SEC horizon is short. Growing backlogs of unfilled orders point to future increases in the production of capital goods. However, efforts to incorporate these series into statistical forecasting methods have not been successful: they do not show a close fit to historical investment data in linear regression equations. Like other pre-flow data, these series are limited in their predictive value by the variability of the time-lag of production behind orders and contracts. Furthermore, the orders data are not a pure investment series; they include an unknown amount of goods ordered for consumer, government, and export use.

c) Relationships between investment and activity variables—A number of investment equations have been fitted to US postwar data. Reasonably good fits are obtained in multiple regression estimates employing such aggregate time-series variables as corporate profits, depreciation allowances, measures of capacity utilization, capital stock, sales, and output. But the equations generally overestimate the capital outlays of 1962. This has spurred new efforts in formulating investment functions, and has especially encouraged the use of a longer sequence of distributed lags. There have also been intensified efforts to improve concepts and data on rates of capacity utilization.

Residential construction

Nonfarm residential building accounts for more than 4 per cent of GNP or about 30 per cent of gross private domestic investment. In the short-run it is volatile and is a key element in the economic outlook. Current and historical data for this sector are particularly unreliable, although improvements of the statistics are getting high priority currently.

Nearly three-fourths of nonfarm residential construction activity represent the building of new housing units. The remaining fourth consists mostly of additions and alterations to existing units; it also includes new units of a nonhousekeeping character. Movements of the portion comprising additions and alterations and nonhousekeeping units are positively related to the fluctuations of activity in new housing units but the smaller component displays a stronger and steadier upward trend and smaller amplitudes of cyclical fluctuation. In forecasting residential construction, attention is focused on new housing units. The positive relationship and the steadier trend of the remaining fourth of activity provide a basis for converting a forecast of activity in new homebuilding into a prediction for total nonfarm residential construction.

Activity on new housing units will reflect changes in value per new unit and in the number of new units. Value per new dwelling unit has shown a consistent rise, reflecting both higher construction prices and a gradual shift in composition toward higher-value housing. While short-run changes in the mix—e.g., as between single-family and multi-unit housing—can produce fluctuations in the aggregate average of value per housing unit, specialists on housing have demonstrated the ability to project value per unit over the next year with reasonable accuracy.

The most significant problem in the housing forecast is thus the prediction of the number of new dwelling units that will be built. Prediction of the number of units and its conversion into an activity forecast are geared to the permits-starts-activity sequence in the statistical data covering new homebuilding. The permits data provide a monthly record of the number of new private housing units authorized by the issuance of local building permits; the permits are legally required in localities which account for about five-sixths of all new homebuilding. The monthly starts data show the number of new dwelling units on which construction activity actually commenced, reflecting both the rate of utilisation of permits and developments in localities not covered by permits.

The recent record emphasizes the significance of the permits data as a symptomatic indicator of the housing market. Most permits are converted into starts within a couple of months and thus the permits have only a short lead; but the permits have helped to clarify the prospects for starts over a longer horizon. For example, starts fell sharply in the winter of 1961-62 and there was concern about a possible surprising collapse in homebuilding. But the permits data were strong—they suggested that building plans were buoyant, that the drop in starts was a retiming of schedules, and a reflection of the different timing pattern of starts on multi-family housing, and that starts would rebound as a result of the growing backlog of unused permits. The diagnosis of the interagency forecast followed the evidence provided by the permits and proved to be correct.

The activity series is a monthly record of the dollar-value of construction put in place on housing units that were started in previous months and in the current month. The activity of a given month reflects most strongly construction on units started 1 to 3 months previously. On the average, 40 per cent of the activity (seasonally adjusted) on new housing units in a given quarter is accounted for by units started within that quarter; 60 per cent is thus predetermined by starts preceding the quarter. This lag offers a safety margin in the activity forecast for the very short-run. An error of 5 per cent in the starts forecast for next quarter means only a 2 per cent error in activity for that quarter. And the permits data help to keep the starts forecast within a reasonable margin of error for the next quarter or two.

The forecaster also has access to several other barometers of the housing market. Not all of these have demonstrable predictive value, however. Vacancy rates have been compiled since the mid-1950's. They have shown a steady increase in vacant housing; and have not displayed a clear relationship to the demand for new units. Similarly, the various time-series on mortgage applications have been a rather erratic gauge of the housing market. The government's sample survey of consumer buying intentions covers plans to purchase homes; it will take another few years before the contribution of this series can be determined. Private surveys of builders' plans have had a measure of success in their forecasts, and some weight is attached to their findings.

Private sources also report on the inventory of unsold new homes in the hands of builders; and such information is useful in appraising dealers' incentives and financial ability to undertake new starts. Data of this type are not available in the government series, since the measures of construction activity do not distinguish inventory-change and final sales of housing. Geographical disaggregation is likely to be needed for a good housing forecast, since housing is an industry with thousands of local markets. The national total of new homebuilding will reflect the gross demands of those local areas which do require added housing. Surpluses of housing in one state will not dampen the market for new homes elsewhere. Specialists on the housing market in the industry and in government provide their judgments of geographical factors influencing aggregate residential construction. Much of this information comes from a national trade association of builders.

Single-family homes are usually owner-occupied and have many of the characteristics of consumer durable goods. Multi-family housing is rental property, largely taking the form of apartment building. In recent years, multi-family units have grown sharply as a fraction of total new dwelling units: they were only 10 per cent of all units in 1956, nearly 20 per cent in 1959, and amounted to nearly a third of the total in 1962. The dramatic change in composition has prompted investigation of the determinants of apartment construction as a distinct component of new homebuilding.

In considering the probable level of starts for the year ahead, the forecaster sometimes begins with an estimate of " physical requirements " for new housing units, as the sum of expected net family formation, demolitions, abandonments, and any initial deficiency in the stock of dwelling units. Such calculations must rely on exceedingly untrustworthy data for the housing stock variables; even the demographic series leave much to be desired on an annual basis. In the past, these calculations have not been successful predictors; for example, housing activity has been stronger in the current expansion than would have been expected from the estimates of physical requirements. In the long run, homebuilding may be dominated by these forces; but, in the short-run, its fluctuations reflect most strongly the interaction of credit and income variables.

While the demand for housing by a family is geared to its long-run income expectations, the time at which it enters the market can be strongly influenced by short-run income changes. A spurt in aggregate disposable income would be expected to stimulate new housing starts, as older units are vacated more rapidly and as families undouble. A levelling off of incomes at higher levels can exert a significant negative accelerator effect on starts; the effect may however be considerably delayed while the housing stock gets adjusted to the level of demand. These income influences would point to strong rises in starts during early phases of expansion, with a levelling off and possible downturn in later expansion, followed by pronounced declines during recession.

Credit factors have amended that pattern somewhat in the postwar era. When monetary conditions tighten, housing credit is rationed—mortgage interest rates are stickier than rates on marketable securities, partly because of regulations on government-insured mortgages; but loan values and the lengths of mortgages are reduced. Such rationing by lenders was widespread in the late stages of each postwar expansion, and it seems to have weakened housing activity in the late expansion. The backlogs of demand caused by tight credit have then strengthened the housing market during recessions when credit eased and terms improved. The periods of greatest strength in housing starts have been in early expansion (1950, 1955, 1959) when credit ease and income gains have reinforced each other in promoting demand. Credit has remained readily available in the current expansion and housing starts have shown more sustained strength than in the corresponding periods of previous postwar expansions.

The qualitative pattern described above can be quantified in a statistical equation employing disposable income, change in disposable income, and a credit factor as independent variables, but the goodness of fit of the statistical formulation leaves much to be desired. The choice of an appropriate credit variable to describe mortgage availability is a particularly knotty problem.

For the one quarter, or even two-quarter, forecast of activity, starts and permits data keep the errors of prediction to fairly modest levels—generally, under $1 billion. In looking farther ahead, the forecaster can assemble a large body of relevant information, but he does not have a tested recipe for a successful prediction. Generally, the homebuilding forecast for three and four quarters ahead contains a liberal sprinkling of subjective judgment. Residential construction is one area where the GNP-forecaster is likely to place his bets close to those of specialists on the industry, respecting their judgments on such arcane matters as the evaluation of local markets and mortgage markets, the relation of the second-hand housing market to new building, and needed information not contained in the official government time-series.

Net exports of goods and services

While the balance of payments is in itself a vital concern for United States economic policy, it does not typically act as a major determinant of aggregate economic activity. Imports are not very volatile, and most of their short-run fluctuations have been induced, rather than autonomous. However, on a few occasions—such as the Suez period and the year from mid-1959 to mid-1960—shifts in the demand for our exports have had a significant expansionary influence on overall business conditions.

For the prediction of exports, the GNP-forecasters rely on the views of government specialists in the field of international trade. The specialists build up their export forecast from a disaggregated analysis of world markets by commodity and by country.

While the specialists are also consulted on the import outlook, standard economic relationships deliver reasonably successful import forecasts. Most of the attention is devoted to nonmilitary imports of merchandise which constitute nearly two-thirds of all imports of goods and services and dominate the short-run movements of the total. The historical relationships suggest the following bases for a short-term forecast of imports:

a) At an unchanging level of privately produced GNP, merchandise imports would decline absolutely through time, at a rate of perhaps 2 per cent per year.

b) At a point in time, imports show an elasticity of about $1\,^1/_2$ with respect to private GNP. The income effect can be safety treated with a lag of one quarter.

c) Inventory change has a particularly strong effect on import demand, again with evidence of a short lag.

Import forecasts following these principles have been quite accurate in recent years.

Personal consumption expenditures

Consumption-disposable income relationship. The strength of consumer demand in relation to income is usually summarized in terms of the ratio of total consumer outlays to personal disposable income (or its complement, the saving ratio). An important step in the forecast is a projection of that ratio over the forthcoming quarters.

In the years since 1950, the consumption ratio has ranged from a low of 92.1 per cent (1958) to a high of 94.0 per cent (1960) and has averaged 92.8 percent. The absolute quarterly changes in the ratio in the post-Korean period have averaged 0.4 per cent; absolute changes over a four quarter interval have averaged 0.7 per cent. These figures indicate a considerable amount of consistency and stability of consumer behaviour. But it is important to note that even small changes in the ratio mean substantial changes in the dollar magnitude of the large consumption component of GNP. At current levels, a decline of half a percentage point in the consumption ratio would mean a direct decline of $2 billion of consumer outlays, and would, in addition, have induced multiplier effects of significant magnitude. Therefore, the forecast cannot afford to treat consumer purchases as purely passive.

The task of forecasting changes in the consumption ratio is exceedingly difficult. The postwar data do not reveal systematic patterns in the movement of the ratio. It does not display a clear cyclical pattern, it does not show any consistent relationship to employment or utilization rates, or to price movements. Nor do the quarterly data offer much support for the hypothesis that consumer outlays lag substantially behind income—at most, there is a slight tendency for the consumption ratio to decline during a quarter in which disposable income rises particularly rapidly. The absence of systematic postwar movements in the consumption ratio contrasts with the record of the 1930's when the consumption ratio was clearly related in a negative direction to the level of economic activity. This pattern pointed to a short-run consumption function with a positive intercept and hence a marginal propensity to consume smaller than the average propensity. But the postwar data suggest that the marginal propensity is nearly equal to the average propensity even for very short periods. Quarter-to-quarter movements of the consumption ratio appear to be primarily random in character.

The absence of a clear cyclical pattern in the overall consumption ratio reflects offsetting movements in the fractions of disposable income spent on nondurable goods and services, on the one hand, and on durable goods, on the other. As a fraction of disposable income in current prices, total outlays for consumers' nondurable goods plus services move inversely with economic activity; also the ratio has displayed a slight upward trend since the mid-1950's. The cyclical pattern (and the trend) primarily reflect the behaviour of expenditures for services. These have grown rapidly and consistently with little sensitivity to short-run fluctuations in income. For example, service outlays increased by an average of $1.7 billion per quarter during the last two recessions; this movement is not very different from the $2.2 billion average increase during quarters of expansion since 1958.

But the ratio of durables outlays to household incomes is positively related to the level of economic activity and to the rate of expansion of activity. A high income elasticity of demand for durables and a dependence on changes in income are consistent with a flexible accelerator (or stock-adjustment) view of the demand for durable goods. Consumer purchases reflect both replacement demand and expansion demand. A rise in income, by expanding the desired stock of durable goods, can generate a much more than proportional increase in the volume of purchases for expansion; on the other hand, a mere levelling off of income levels will tend to reduce the rate of acquisition of new durable goods as the actual stock grows and catches up with the desired stock. But while the observed qualitative pattern checks with theoretical reasoning, there is no reason on *a priori* grounds to expect behavior of the durables-income ratio to net out movements in other consumer outlays as a fraction of income, on the average. Yet, the data point to a standoff as the normal result in the post-Korean era.

Fluctuations around this norm are usually associated with variations in the volatile durables sectors, especially autos. The forecast will predict changes in the overall consumption ratio largely on the basis of judgments about the autonomous strength of demand for durables, i.e., that outlays for durables will grow stronger or weaker relative to their normal relationship with income. The bases for such judgments are not firm, and the forecast has employed a rather conservative strategy, projecting the overall consumption ratio fairly close to its most recent level, and rarely moving it more than 0.2 per cent from one quarter to the next. The changes that are predicted rest on subjective weighting of the following types of evidence:

    a) *Latest developments in consumer markets.* For a forecast of the current quarter, several time-series are inspected to detect straws in the wind. Weekly and monthly data on retail sales and department store sales, and data for 10-day periods on sales of new automobiles help to gauge the latest mood of the consumer. In view of the prime importance of automobile demand, industry specialists are consulted informally and used car prices are inspected as a possible precursor of changes in the demand for new cars. Production schedules reported by automotive producers are a further indication of the industry's own evaluation of the state of demand;

moreover, if the production schedules seem fairly firm for the near future, they may permit a more accurate combined forecast of sales of new cars plus changes in dealers' stocks than would be possible by treating the two components separately.

b) *Consumer survey data.* A quarterly survey of consumer buying plans has been conducted as part of the Federal statistics program since 1960. Buying plans are tabulated for homes, autos, and household appliances and furniture; plans are also classified by the degree of certainty the household attaches to them, and by the number of months between the survey and the respondent's expected time of purchase. Thus, several measures of buying plans for a single item are generated by each survey; this makes it difficult to interpret the results at times. The problem of seasonality in plans adds further to these difficulties. It is not possible to arrive at a verdict on the predictive value of the survey from the performance over its rather short history. But the general qualitative pattern of results suggests that the survey offers a positive contribution to the assessment of markets for consumer durable goods. There are, in addition, a number of privately conducted surveys of consumers—most notably, those of the Survey Research Center of the University of Michigan. Here, data are collected on consumer attitudes toward their financial position and their economic well-being and on consumer expectations about their own incomes and general business conditions, as well as on buying plans. There has been considerable professional discussion about the predictive value of the more " subjective " attitudinal data as compared with the reports of buying intentions. The fact that the government survey concentrates on buying plans reflects the prevailing opinion of government economists on this issue.

c) *Asset and debt variables.* The magnitudes of liquid asset holdings by households and of their consumer debts are generally viewed as permissive factors in the purchase of durable goods. The ease and terms of consumer instalment loans can have important effects on markets for new autos and major appliances. In particular, the supply of consumer credit may set an upper limit on outlays for durables or an upper limit on the duration of a durables boom. Financial variables are less likely to provide a floor or to exert a decisive upward thrust on these markets. While a period of heavy accumulation of liquid assets by households may set the stage for a strengthening of demand for durables, it would be hard to bet on the timing of such a surge. Indeed, high rates of liquid asset accumulation may be symptomatic of consumer disinterest in durable goods.

d) *Structural variables.* Demographic factors, such as family formation, and normal scrappage or replacement demand for autos and major household items are important determinants of the demand for durable goods. But these are slowly changing, persistent forces which are not likely to point toward significant quarterly—or even annual—variations in demand. In the short-term forecast, these structural factors are used primarily to interpret recent levels and movements—they can help to suggest, for example, whether years with sales of 7 million new cars are likely to be unusual and unsustainable peaks of demand or whether they can be typical of expansion periods.

All in all, through careful and detailed consideration of the factors influencing consumer demand, the interagency forecasts of the overall consumption ratio have a rather good record of accuracy for the past few years; they have shown the ability to score a modest improvement over a naive forward projection of the most recent ratio. But the consumer recently has registered only small changes in the allocation of his income, and the forecast has not been put to the acid test of its ability to detect a significant shift in the personal saving ratio.

Disposable income-GNP relationship. The consumption-disposable income ratio must next be linked to GNP by an estimate of the forthcoming movements of personal disposable income in relation to those of GNP. The development of these relations on the income side of the ledger may be viewed through the identity that expresses disposable income in terms of adjustments made to GNP.

Disposable income = GNP—capital consumption allowances—undistributed corporate profits—all taxes + government transfer payments (including subsidies, net interest, etc.)—statistical discrepancy.

The changes in disposable income over time can be linearly related to changes in GNP: $\Delta Y_d = a + b\Delta\text{GNP}$ where the intercept, a, is the sum of the effects that would change disposable income if GNP (in current prices) were constant through time, and the slope b reflects the marginal share of disposable income in incremental GNP at a point in time.

For several reasons, the intercept of such a relationship is positive, and therefore has an upward trend influence on disposable income. Quantitatively most important is the fact that corporate profits would decline if GNP failed to rise over time. Increases in overheads and wage-rates, accompanied by sluggish productivity would produce a substantial decline in corporate profits (before taxes) over a four-quarter interval of stagnant GNP. No appreciable decline in dividend payments would be expected. Hence, nearly all of the decline in profits would be reflected in lower retained earnings and lower profits taxes, placing more of the unchanged GNP into disposable income.

Furthermore, government transfer payments have a significant built-in secular rise, quite apart from discretionary expansion of transfer programs. Transfer payments by States and localities are quantitatively small and expand through time rather smoothly and consistently. Moreover, a constant level of GNP would mean rising unemployment; over a four-quarter interval of constant GNP, unemployment insurance benefits at present benefit rates and coverage would expand by somewhat more than $1 billion. Other transfer payments by the Federal government are predicted with reasonable confidence from the annual budget estimates. All of these forces will add to consumer incomes.

There are two forces offsetting this shift to a certain extent. First, even if GNP were to freeze at current levels, capital consumption allowances would increase through time creating a subtraction from disposable income.

Second, state and local indirect taxes (especially property taxes) would continue to expand even with no rise in GNP.

The predicted magnitude of the intercept of additional disposable income will depend on the outlook for Federal expenditures on transfers, net interest, and subsidies; it can also be affected by tax legislation, e.g., payroll tax rates to finance social insurance programs have risen in five of the last seven years. But the intercept is a substantial positive magnitude, perhaps on the order of $5 billion for a one-year interval.

The slope coefficient relating changes in disposable income and changes in GNP is about .5; each dollar of additional GNP will add about 50 cents to disposable income over and above the increases through time produced by the intercept. The marginal share is thus much lower than the current ratio of disposable income to GNP, 69 per cent. A prime reason for this is the great volatility of corporate profits, in combination with the inertia of corporate dividend payments. Over a one-year interval, for each extra dollar of GNP profits before tax will be higher than otherwise by about 25 to 30 cents. Only about 3 cents of this amount will be returned into disposable income through extra dividend payments. A second key factor lowering the elasticity of disposable income with respect to GNP is government transfer payments, which will, as a result of unemployment compensation, show a negative marginal share of GNP. All in all of the 50 cents of each marginal GNP dollar that do not enter personal disposable income, more than 30 cents go to net Federal receipts (i.e. taxes minus transfers), a little more than 5 cents to state and local receipts and the remainder to gross corporate saving.

The actual movement of the disposable income-GNP ratio over time is thus a function of the rate of GNP increase. The positive a intercept or trend effect means that the ratio would increase from one year to the next if GNP remained constant. But if GNP rises sharply, the influence of the intercept is outweighed by the fact that the b slope is smaller than the existing ratio of disposable income to GNP. Roughly, when Federal tax rates are unchanged, the ratio would be approximately constant through time if GNP rose at an annual rate of 5 per cent; the ratio would fall about one percentage point in a year when GNP rose 10 per cent. Similarly, corporate profits before tax will reflect the combined effect of the change-intercept, which pulls them down through time, and the large 25 to 30 per cent slope at a point in time, which pulls up their share of GNP.

Actually, over a one-quarter interval, a sudden spurt in GNP might add even more than 30 per cent to corporate profits and hence considerably less than 50 per cent to disposable income. The level of profits in any quarter shows a substantial positive dependence on the change in GNP from the preceding quarter, as well as on the level of GNP. The factor payments recorded as corporate costs in a quarter reflect the activity of the last quarter as well as the current one. The reasons for this phenomenon are not entirely clear—the short lag that yields this result may result from such factors as hiring decisions, increases in wage rates, expenditures for maintenance and other costs that have some discretionary aspects, and may lie partly in the accounting record of charges.

The statistical discrepancy in the national accounts is a nuisance element that cannot be ignored in forecasting the relationship between disposable income and GNP. Because there is a degree of independence in estimation

The United States

of the expenditure and income sides of the accounts, the conceptual identity between the two sides is violated in the official historical data. The statistical discrepancy is the excess of GNP (measured officially as an expenditure total) over the income items which should by definition also add to GNP. In its effect on the consumption forecast, a prospective decline (algebraically) of $1 billion in the statistical discrepancy is equivalent to a $1 billion reduction in personal taxes. The statistical discrepancy has been negative in every quarter for the past seven years, ranging from —$0.2 to —$4.5 billion. When the last observed levels of the statistical discrepancy is in the " normal " range—say —$1.5 to —$3.0 billion—the interagency forecast has generally projected it at that level throughout the period of prediction; but when the last observed level has seemed unusual, the statistical discrepancy has been plugged into the forecast at a more normal level. Since the income-side of the accounts in recent historical estimates is no less reliable than the expenditure side, an unusual statistical discrepancy may point toward a future revision of the GNP estimate.

Combining the predicted path of the consumption-disposable income ratio and the disposable income-GNP relationship, we have a predicted consumption-GNP relationship as one principal ingredient of the forecast. At this point, the consumption forecast is still a schedule—dollar amounts for any assumed GNP; the translation into absolute dollar amounts awaits the completion of the inventory forecast.

Inventory investment

The small component of inventory investment is the most troublesome element of the forecast. Inventory swings have been the outstanding feature of postwar economic fluctuations; recessions have been marked by inventory liquidation, and the shift to inventory accumulation has been the major expansionary element in the first year of recoveries. No forecast can hope to capture the pattern of GNP-movements without a successful prediction of inventory investment.

The forecaster benefits from access to a large quantity of monthly inventory data, even though the reliability of these figures leaves much to be desired. The series show stocks (along with sales) for detailed sectors of manufacturing and for wholesale and retail trade. The disaggregations permit inventory-sales relationships to be estimated and studied in considerable detail by sector. The disaggregated data are particularly important for evaluating the significance of special industry situations—e.g., a possible steel strike—that may effect the aggregates. The disaggregation, in general, helps to focus attention on the stocks of durable goods manufacturers. These are, by far, the most volatile portion of inventories and they dominate the movements of the total.

Manufacturers' stocks are also separated by stages of fabrication into purchased materials, goods-in-process, and finished goods. Stocks of finished goods reflect " passive " as well as active investment, as disappointments in the level of sales may temporarily result in unintended accumulation of finished goods stocks. Partly for this reason and partly because it takes time to convert materials into finished products, the finished goods component of stocks tends to lag behind the rest. Hence, it is sometimes possible to detect future trends in aggregate inventory investment from current movements of manufacturers' purchased materials and good-in-process.

One appealing approach in forecasting views inventory investment as an adjustment of actual stocks toward a target level. Then the prediction of stocks involves the estimation of (*a*) the target level (or equivalently the difference between the target and current levels); and (*b*) the rate of movement toward the target. The simplest concept of target stocks would multiply sales by a "normal" inventory-sales ratio. The next refinement would treat target stocks as a linear (but not necessarily proportionate) function of sales. Then, if the speed of adjustment is taken as constant, inventory investment should be linearly related to the level of sales (in a positive direction) and to the level of existing stocks (in a negative direction). Linear regression equations explaining the annual rate of quarterly inventory change yield a coefficient of more than .30 on final sales of goods (as they are recorded in GNP) and about —.75 on the level of stocks at the start of the quarter. The coefficient of correlation is about .65; but the mean absolute error is painfully large, nearly $3 billion (annual rate). When lagged sales and current sales are both used as explanatory variables, the current sales show greater explanatory power. This indicates that inventory investment cannot be treated as predetermined for even one quarter.

The loose fit of this relationship indicates that sales levels alone do not supply an adequate index of target stocks. Orders data can help to augment sales—the change in manufacturers' unfilled orders in the previous quarter has a strong positive influence on inventory investment. Since the change in unfilled orders is simply new orders minus sales, this finding can be interpreted to mean that the desired level of stocks is geared to some average of sales and orders. But orders are no easier to forecast than are inventory changes, so the benefit of the orders variable is limited to the one quarter in which it has a lagged influence.

The Department of Commerce survey of manufacturers' inventory and sales expectations provides information which can be used in estimating the deviation between target and actual stocks. The survey which has been conducted quarterly for about five years collects manufacturers' own forecasts of their expected sales and expected inventories over a horizon of about 4 months. Thus, the analyst is offered a point on the manufacturers' inventory demand-sales relationship. From this information, the current deficiency (or excess) of inventories relative to the target level can be inferred. The performance of the survey to date has been rather encouraging.

Private sources publish several indicators of current inventory conditions: these include reports on buying policies of purchasing agents and on the volume of deliveries delayed by short supplies. *Fortune* magazine specifically asks business executives to state their desired inventory-sales ratios. These data can be helpful, but they hardly eliminate the puzzles of inventory prediction.

At times, it can be inferred that inventories are close to their target levels, and that future movements of stocks therefore will not be strongly influenced by any inherited excess or deficiency. A period of many months when inventory-sales ratios are fairly constant (with no large offsetting movements among sectors) might be adopted as such a benchmark where target stocks can be taken as equal to actual levels.

The forecaster can alternatively ask whether the difference between target and actual stocks is growing wider or narrower without explicitly estimating that difference. If the percentage growth of sales exceeds that of stocks, the inventory deficiency is probably increasing, and inventory investment is likely to accelerate. Conversely, if stocks are outpacing sales (and orders), the rate of inventory investment is expected to decline. The cyclical pattern of inventory investment is consistent with this pattern.

When target minus actual stocks are estimated for the start of a quarter, the data suggest that about one-fourth of the discrepancy will be eliminated within that quarter. Thus, at annual rates, inventory investment approximately equals the deficiency. But the change in sales within the quarter will also affect inventory investment. A reasonable recipe calls for adding to inventory investment about 15 per cent of the increment in final sales of goods predicted for the quarter. Since the service and construction portion of GNP is practically predetermined for the quarter ahead, it is easy to convert the relationship between predicted inventory investment and final sales of goods into a relationship between inventory investment and GNP. But the relationship is not likely to be distinguished for its accuracy; the absolute error for a quarter ahead—even at a known GNP—is likely to average $1½ billion, and it is probably twice that size for four quarters ahead.

4 CONCLUSION

Now the ingredients for a one-quarter forecast have all been assembled. Government purchases, fixed investment components, and net exports have been predicted as numerical magnitudes; consumer outlays and inventory investment have been specified as functions of GNP. The system can be summarized into a single equation involving only one variable—GNP. It can thus be solved for the level of GNP; then consumption and inventory investment can be specified as numerical magnitudes. Next the forecast can proceed on the second quarter in the future, taking the predicted magnitudes for the first quarter as the relevant lagged variables. Thus, quarter by quarter, the predictions emerge.

The prediction of national income and product is studied further by the forecasters for its implications regarding the utilization of capital and labor resources. Increases in private business output (in constant prices) implied by the GNP forecast are compared with the implied growth of the capital stock to determine the future path of excess plant and equipment capacity.

As the Council of Economic Advisers has pointed out in its publications, the post-Korean record indicates that a growth of 3½ per cent per year in GNP (constant prices) has been consistent with constancy of unemployment as a fraction of the civilian labor force. Each extra one per cent of GNP means, on the average, a reduction of 0.3 points in the unemployment rate. These relationships provide a basis for converting a forecast of GNP into a forecast of unemployment; they also permit an estimate of " potential

GNP", the output that would correspond to an unemployment rate of four per cent. In general, the forecast of the unemployment rate has been able to improve somewhat over these statistical relationships. The improvement comes from considering prospective movements in the labor force and from recognizing that the statistical relationships have a cyclical pattern of errors, generally understating unemployment (in relation to GNP) in early expansion and overstating it in late expansion and recession.

The relationship between output and labor input gets a further cross-check from a projection of payroll employment by industry. Here, the predicted GNP is allocated among broad industrial categories and productivity projections are made to derive labor-input requirements. The forecasts of employment by establishment are not conceptually identical with the household survey from which unemployment is estimated but the implications can be checked for consistency. Once average hourly earnings are projected, the forecast of establishment employment can be converted into a prediction of the wage-bill. Since wages and salaries constitute about two-thirds of personal income, this calculation also offers an important cross-check on the disposable income forecast discussed above.

The record of the CEA forecasts prepared in the three-agency working group over the past two years suggests that the one-quarter predicted change of GNP has an average error of about $3 billion. On the one hand, this may not appear as a dramatic improvement over a naive trend forecast, which in the post-Korean period would have displayed an average error of a little less than one per cent of GNP, or about $5 billion at current levels. On the other hand, the one-quarter forecast looks rather good when it is recognized that the first historical estimate by the Department of Commerce after the end of the quarter still shows an average error of about $2 billion when compared with the quarterly changes ultimately shown by revised data. The forecasting record for several quarters ahead in the past two years is blemished by the over-optimism about fixed and inventory investment for 1962 that marked CEA's estimates from the summer of 1961 to the spring of 1962.

During that period, business investment for 1962 was expected to respond to higher utilization rates, sales, and profits much as it had in previous postwar experience. The Commerce-SEC survey of plant and equipment anticipations in March, 1962, and the inventory data for the spring months made it clear that investment would rise more modestly in the current expansion. After five years of continued underutilization, businessmen invested cautiously.

The recent experience would assign top priority to work on the investment sector for an improved forecast of GNP. Hopes and efforts lie in a number of directions: (a) a break through the calendar year barrier in the collection of accurate plant and equipment anticipations; (b) further development of the promising inventory anticipations survey; (c) improved quantitative analysis of the determinants of business fixed and inventory investment; (d) better data on capacity utilization and on orders and contracts for capital goods.

BIBLIOGRAPHY

1 CANADA

Bates, Stewart, " Government Forecasting in Canada, " *The Canadian Journal of Economics and Political Science*, Volume 12, No. 3, August 1946, pp. 361-378.

Beckett, W. A., " Indicators of Cyclical Recessions and Revivals in Canada, " *Business Cycle Indicators*, Volume 1, *Contributions to the Analysis of Current Business Conditions*, Geoffrey H. Moore, Ed., (National Bureau of Economic Research, Princeton University Press, Princeton, 1961), pp. 294-322.

Brewis, T. N., English, H. E., Scott, Anthony and Jewett, Pauline, " Economic Forecasting, " *Canadian Economic Policy*, (The MacMillan Company of Canada Limited, Toronto, 1961), pp. 176-192.

Brown, Merritt T., " A Forecast Determination of National Product, Employment, and Price Level in Canada from an Econometric Model, " *Models of Income Determination*, Studies in Income and Wealth, Volume 28, (National Bureau of Economic Research, Princeton University Press, Princeton, 1964), pp. 59-96.

Canadian Government White Paper, " Employment and Income, With Special Reference to the Initial Period of Reconstruction, " (King's Printer, Ottawa, April 1945).

Firestone, O. J., " Investment Forecasting in Canada, " *Short-term Economic Forecasting*, Studies in Income and Wealth, Volume 17, (National Bureau of Economic Research, Princeton University Press, Princeton, 1955), pp. 113-259.

Grayson, Henry, " Planning and Forecasting Techniques in Canada, " *Economic Planning Under Free Enterprise*, (Public Affairs Press, Washington, 1954), pp. 54-73.

May, Sidney J., *Short-term Forecasting of Non-residential Construction*, Paper presented to the Canadian Political Science Association Conference on Statistics, Quebec, June 8, 1963.

2 FRANCE

Mayer, J., " Réponses à quelques questions sur les Budgets Économiques, " *Études de Comptabilité Nationale n° 2* (Imprimerie Nationale, Paris, 1961).

3 THE NETHERLANDS

Central Planning Bureau, *Central Economic Plan 1961*, (The Hague, August 1961) (especially Annex I, pp. 113-127).

Central Planning Bureau, *Monetary Statement and Monetary Analysis*, Monograph No. 7, (The Hague, 1959).

Central Planning Bureau, *Scope and Methods of the Central Planning Bureau*, (The Hague, 1956) (See also: Appendix VI: Bibliography).

de Wolff, P. and Stevers, Th. A., " State Budget and Planning "; Paper prepared for the Congrès de l'Institut International de Finances Publiques, Warsaw, Poland, September 1-113, 1961.

de Wolff, P. and van den Beld, C. A., " Ten Years of Forecasts and Realizations "; Paper read before the Montreal Congress of the International Statistical Institute, 1963; to be published as a monograph.

Theil, H., *Economic Forecasts and Policy* (North-Holland Publishing Company, Amsterdam, 1958).

Tinbergen, J., *Economic Policy : Principles and Design* (North-Holland Publishing Company, Amsterdam, 1956).

van Eijk, C. J. and Sandee, J., " Quantitative Determination of Optimum Economic Policy "; *Econometrica*, Vol. 27:1, January 1959, pp. 1-13.

Verdoorn, P. J. and van Eijk, C. J., " Experimental Short-term Forecasting Models "; Paper presented to the 20th European meeting of the Econometric Society, Bilbao, September 1958. (Central Planning Bureau, The Hague, 1958).

Verdoorn, P. J. and Post, J. J., " Capacity and Short-term Multipliers "; Paper presented to the sixteenth meeting of the Colston Research Society held in the University of Bristol, April 6th-9th, 1964. *Econometric Analysis for National Economic Planning*, Colston Papers, Vol. XVI, (Butterworths Scientific Publications, London, 1964), pp. 179-198.

Verdoorn, P. J. and Post, J. J., " Short and Long-term Extrapolations with the Dutch Forecasting Model 63.D "; Paper presented to the Centre international d'étude des problèmes humains, Monaco, May 21st-26th, 1964.

Wellisz, S., " Economic Planning in the Netherlands, France and Italy, " *The Journal of Political Economy*, Vol. 68:3, June 1960, pp. 252-283.

4 SWEDEN

Canarp, Curt, " Investment Funds—and How They Can Be Used to Combat Recession and Unemployment," *Skandinaviska Banken Quarterly Review* No. 2, 1963, (Stockholm, 1963), pp. 33-40.

Dahlström, Gösta, " Jämförelser mellan nationalbudgeteringssystem " (" Various Systems of National Budgeting—a Comparison "), *Ekonomisk Tidskrift* (Swedish Economic Journal) 1957, (Stockholm, 1957), pp. 273-281.

Hansen, Bent, " The 'Excess of Purchasing Power' of the Swedish Konjunkturinstitutet " and " A Swedish Estimate of the Excess of Purchasing-Power for 1951, " in *A Study in the Theory of Inflation* (George Allen and Unwin Ltd., London, 1951), pp. 67-72 and 252-256, respectively.

Hansen, Bent, " The Swedish National Institute of Economic Research, " *Skandinaviska Banken* (The Scandinavian Bank, Sweden) *Quarterly Review* No. 3, 1957, (Stockholm 1957), pp. 74-79.

Kragh, Börje, " En grundläggande modell för nationalbudgetering " (" A Basic Model for National Budgeting, " *(Ekonomisk Tidskrift* (Swedish Economic Journal) 1955, (Stockholm, 1955), pp. 165-194. (Also in International Economic Papers, 1957.)

Kragh, Börje, *Konjunkturbedömning* (Economic Forecasting) (The National Institute of Economic Research, Stockholm, 1964).

Lundberg, Erik, " Översikt av inkomst och konsumtionsläget " (Survey of Income and Consumption Development), *Meddelanden från Konjunkturinstitutet* (Report from the National Institute of Economic Research, Series B:3, Stockholm, 1945).

Ministry of Finance, " Utgångspunkt och metoder för investeringsprognosen för 1961 " (The methods of investment forecast for 1961), " Konsumtionsvolymen " (The volume of consumption) (containing an account of the method of consumption forecast), " Produktionen " (Production) (containing an account of the method of production forecast). *Preliminär Nationalbudget för år 1961* (Preliminary National Budget for 1961), (Stockholm, 1961), pp. 55-57, 27-29, and 30-38, respectively.

National Institute of Economic Research, " Foreign Trade " (discussing export forecasting methods), *The Swedish Economy*, October 1962, pp. 17-26. (The National Institute of Economic Research, Stockholm, 1962).

National Institute of Economic Research, " Försörjningsbalans och nationalbudgetutfall 1947-1950 " (Balance of Resources and National Budget Estimates, 1947-1950). *Meddelanden från Konjunkturinstitutet* (Report from the National Institute of Economic Research, Series B:13, Stockholm, 1951), pp. 154-199.

National Institute of Economic Research, "Household Income, Consumption and Savings," *The Swedish Economy*, February 1961. (The National Institute of Economic Research, Stockholm, 1961), pp. 20-27.

National Institute of Economic Research, " Imports, 1961 " (discussing import forecasting methods), *The Swedish Economy*, May 1961, (The National Institute of Economic Research, Stockholm, 1961), pp. 14-20.

National Institute of Economic Research, " Nationalbudgetbegreppet " (The Concept of the National Budget). *Meddelanden från Konjunkturinstitutet* (Report from the National Institute of Economic Research, Series B:10, Stockholm, 1949), pp. 118-127.

National Institute of Economic Research, " The National Budget Forecasts and their Reliability, " *The Swedish Economy*, May 1961, (The National Institute of Economic Research, Stockholm, 1961), pp. 34-44.

National Institute of Economic Research, " The National Budget Forecasts and their Reliability. Addendum, " *The Swedish Economy*, August 1961, (The National Institute of Economic Research, Stockholm, 1961), pp. 38-41.

Nilsson, Thora, " Den internationella konjunkturutvecklingen och svensk export " (The international economic development and Swedish exports) (An attempt to explain the development of Swedish exports in terms of trends in demand abroad), *Konjunkturläget Hösten 1958* (The Economic Situation, Autumn 1958), (Meddelanden från Konjunkturinstitutet) (Report from the National Institute of Economic Research, Series A: 31, Stockholm, 1958), pp. 16-28.

Ohlsson, Ingvar, " Swedish Budget Work, 1947-1952 " *On National Accounting* (National Institute of Economic Research, Stockholm, 1953).

Ohlsson, Ingvar, " The Swedish National Budget, " *Skandinaviska Banken* (The Scandinavian Bank, Sweden) *Quarterly Review* No. 4, 1957 (Stockholm, 1957), pp. 100-107.

Rehn, Gösta, " The National Budget and Economic Policy, " *Skandinaviska Banken* (The Scandinavian Bank, Sweden) *Quarterly Review* No. 2, 1962 (Stockholm, 1962), pp. 39-47.

Svennilson, Ingvar, " Finanspolitik och budgetprognoser " (" Fiscal Policy and Budget Prognosis "), *Ekonomisk Tidskrift* (Swedish Economic Journal) 1950, (Stockholm, 1958), pp. 1-13.

United Nations Economic Commission for Europe, " National Budgets in Western Europe—Post-war experiments in National Income Forecasting in the United Kingdom, the Netherlands and Scandinavia. " *Economic Bulletin for Europe*, Vol. 5, No. 2, July 1953, pp. 63-81.

5 THE UNITED KINGDOM

Brittan, Samuel, *The Treasury under the Tories, 1951-1964* (Penguin, London, 1964).

Dow, J. C. R., *The Management of the British Economy, 1945-60* (National Institute of Economic and Social Research, Cambridge University Press, Cambridge, 1964).

Godley, W. A. H., and Gillion, C., "Measuring National Product," *Economic Review*, February 1964 (National Institute of Economic and Social Research, London).

Godley, W. A. H., and Rowe, D. A., " Retail and Consumer Prices 1955-63," *Economic Review*, November 1964 (National Institute of Economic and Social Research, London).

Godley, W. A. H., and Shepherd, J. R., "Long-term Growth and Short-term Policy," *Economic Review*, August 1964 (National Institute of Economic and Social Research, London).

Klein, L. R., Ball, J. R., Hazlewood, A., and Vandome, P., *An Econometric Model of the United Kingdom* (Blackwell, Oxford, 1961).

Neild, R. R., and Shirley, E. A., " An Assessment of Forecasts 1959-60," *Economic Review*, May 1961 (National Institute of Economic and Social Research, London).

6 THE UNITED STATES

Bassie, V. Lewis, *Economic Forecasting* (McGraw-Hill, New York, 1958).

Bratt, Elmer Clark, *Business Cycles and Forecasting* (R. D. Irwin, Homewood, Illinois, 1953).

Clark, C., " A System of Equations Explaining the United States Trade Cycle: 1921-1941, " *Econometrica*, Vol. 17, pp. 93-124.

De Leeuw, F., " The Demand for Capital Goods by Manufacturers: A Study of Quarterly Time Series, " *Econometrica*, Vol. 30, No. 3, July 1962.

Duesenberry, James S., Eckstein, Otto, and Fromm, Gary, " A Simulation of the U.S. Economy in Recession, " *Econometrica*, Vol. 28, No. 4, October 1960.

Friend, I., and Jones, R., " Short-Run Forecasting Model Incorporating Anticipatory Data," *Models of Income Determination*, Studies in Income and Wealth, Vol. 28, (National Bureau of Economic Research, Princeton University Press, Princeton, 1964).

Fromm, Gary, " Inventories, Business Cycles, and Economic Stabilization, " in Materials Prepared for The Joint Economic Committee, Congress of the United States, *Part IV Supplementary Study Papers*, 87th Congress, 2nd Session. (U.S. Government Printing Office, Washington, D.C., May 1962). Other parts of *Study Papers* also relevant. (See also bibliographies given in *Study Papers*).

Griliches, Z., Maddla, G. S., Lucas, R., and Wallace, N., " Notes on Estimated Aggregate Quarterly Consumption Functions, " *Econometrica*, Vol. 30, No. 3, July 1962.

Klein, L. R., " A Quarterly Model of the American Economy, " Wharton School of Finance and Commerce, University of Pennsylvania, Unpublished, 1961.

Klein, L. R., " The Use of Econometric Models as a Guide to Economic Policy, " *Econometrica*, Vol. 15, No. 2, April 1947.

Klein, L. R., and Borger, H., " A Quarterly Model for the U.S. Economy," *Journal of the American Statistical Association*, 1954.

Klein, L. R., and Goldberger, A. S., *An Econometric Model of the United States, 1929-1952* (North-Holland Publishing Company, Amsterdam, 1955).

Lewis, John P., *Business Conditions Analysis* (McGraw-Hill, New York, 1959).

Lewis, John P., " Short-Term General Business Conditions Forecasting: Some Comments on Method, " *The Journal of Business*, Vol. XXXV, October 1962, pp. 343-356.

Liu, T. C., " A Simple Forecasting Model for the U.S. Economy, " *Staff Papers*, International Monetary Fund, Vol. IV, No. 3 (Washington, D. C., 1955).

Liu, T. C., " An Exploratory Quarterly Econometric Model of Effective Demand in Postwar U.S. Economy, " *Econometrica*, Vol. 31, No. 3, July 1963,

Maisel, Sherman J., *Fluctuations, Growth and Forecasting : The Principles of Dynamic Business Economics* (Wiley, New York, 1957).

Maisel, Sherman J., " Fluctuations in Residential Construction Starts, " *The American Economic Review*, Vol. LIII, No. 3, June 1963.

Malanos, G. J., and Thomassen, H., " An Econometric Model of the United States, 1947-1958, " *Southern Economic Journal*, Vol. XXVII, No. 1, July 1960.

McKinnon, R. I., " Wages, Capital Costs, and Employment in Manufacturing: A Model Applied to 1947-58 U.S. Data, " *Econometrica*, Vol. 30, No. 3, July 1962.

National Bureau of Economic Research, Conference on Research in Income and Wealth, *Short-Term Economic Forecasting* (Princeton University Press, Princeton, 1955).

Okun, Arthur M., " A Review of Some Economic Forecasts for 1955-57, " *The Journal of Business*, Vol. XXXII, July 1959, pp. 199-211.

Okun, Arthur M., " The Predictive Value of Surveys of Business Intentions, " *American Economic Review*, Vol. LII, May 1962, (Papers and Proceedings), pp. 218-225.

Suits, Daniel B., " Forecasting and Analysis with an Econometric Model, " *American Economic Review*, Vol. LII, March 1962, pp. 104-132.

Tunis, W., " First Results of a Quarterly Econometric Analysis of the American Economy, 1952-1959, " (Unpublished, Netherlands Central Planning Bureau, 1961).

U.S. Congress Joint Economic Committee, " Measures of Productive Capacity, " Hearings before the Subcommittee on Economic Statistics, 87th Congress, 2nd Session, (U.S. Government Printing Office, Washington, D.C., 1962).

U.S. Congress Joint Economic Committee, " Inventory Fluctuations and Economic Stabilization, " 87th Congress, 2nd Session, (U.S. Government Printing Office, Washington, D. C., 1962).

Universities-National Bureau Committee for Economic Research, *The Quality and Economic Significance of Anticipations Data* (Princeton University Press, Princeton, 1960).

FROM THE CATALOGUE

METHODS OF INDUSTRIAL DEVELOPMENT
WITH SPECIAL REFERENCE TO LESS DEVELOPED AREAS
Edited by Albert Winsemius and John A. Pincus. Madrid Conference (April 1962)
356 pages (demy 8vo)   30s.   US$ 5.00   F 20.00   Sw.fr. 20.00   DM 16.50

REGIONAL ECONOMIC PLANNING
Techniques of analysis for less developed areas. Edited by Walter Isard and John Cumberland. Bellagion Conference (July 1961)
452 pages (demy 8vo)   37s.6d.   US$ 6.00   F 25.00   Sw.fr. 25.00   DM 21.00

POLICIES FOR ECONOMIC GROWTH
(November 1962)
46 pages (demy 8vo)   5s.   US$ 0.75   F 3.00   Sw.fr. 3.00   DM 2.50

POLICIES FOR PRICE STABILITY
(November 1962)
48 pages (demy 8vo)   5s.   US$ 0.75   F 3.00   Sw.fr. 3.00   DM 2.50

THE PROBLEM OF RISING PRICES
by William Fellner, Milton Gilbert, Bent Hansen, Richard Kahn, Friedrich Lutz and Pieter de Wolff (May 1961)
490 pages (demy 8vo)   21s.   US$ 3.75   F 15.00   Sw.fr. 15.00   DM 12.50

SOURCES OF STATISTICS FOR MARKET RESEARCH
EUROPE AND NORTH AMERICA
Volume 1. Radio Sets (March 1961)
322 pages (crown 4to)   37s.6d.   US$ 6.50   F 25.00   Sw.fr. 25.00   DM 21.30
Volume 2. Footwear (July 1964)
640 pages (crown 4to)   £ 3.3s.   US$ 10.00   F 40.00   Sw.fr. 40.00   DM 33.00
Volume 3. General Statistics (March 1964)
132 pages (crown 4to)   15s.   US$ 2.50   F 10.00   Sw.fr. 10.00   DM 8.30
Volume 4. Household Appliances (February 1963)
362 pages (crown 4to)   37s.6d.   US$ 6.50   F 25.00   Sw.fr. 25.00   DM 21.00
Volume 5. Machine Tools (May 1963)
212 pages (crown 4to)   17s.6d.   US$ 3.00   F 12.00   Sw.fr. 12.00   DM 10.00
Volume 6. Pharmaceuticals (May 1963)
434 pages (crown 4to)   37s.6d.   US$ 6.50   F 25.00   Sw.fr. 25.00   DM 21.00

MARKET RESEARCH BY TRADE ASSOCIATIONS
(September 1964)
98 pages (demy 8vo)   6s.   US$ 1.00   F 4.00   Sw.fr. 4.00   DM 3.30

THE ROLE OF TRADE ASSOCIATIONS IN THE STUDY OF MARKETS
(September 1962)
108 pages (demy 8vo)   9s.   US$ 1.50   F 6.00   Sw.fr. 6.00   DM 5.00

MARKET RESEARCH ON A EUROPEAN SCALE
Paris Conference, 29th June-1st July 1959 (June 1960)
136 pages (demy 8vo)   10s.6d.   US$ 2.00   F 7.50   Sw.fr. 7.50   DM 6.40

MARKET RESEARCH METHODS IN EUROPE
(October 1956)
192 pages (demy 8vo)   9s.   US$ 1.50   F 4.50   Sw.fr. 4.50   DM 3.90

OECD SALES AGENTS
DÉPOSITAIRES DES PUBLICATIONS DE L'OCDE

ARGENTINE - ARGENTINE
Editorial Sudamericana S.A.,
Alsina 500, BUENOS AIRES

AUSTRALIA - AUSTRALIE
B.C.N. Agencies Pty, Ltd.,
178 Collins Street, MELBOURNE, 3000.

AUSTRIA - AUTRICHE
Gerold & Co., Graben 31, WIEN 1
Sub-Agent : GRAZ : Buchhandlung Jos. A. Kienreich, Sackstrasse 6.

BELGIUM - BELGIQUE
Standaard Wetenschappelijke Uitgeverij
Belgiëlei 147, ANVERS.
Librairie des Sciences
76-78, Coudenberg, BRUXELLES 1.

CANADA
Queen's Printer - L'imprimeur de la Reine,
OTTAWA.

DENMARK - DANEMARK
Munksgaard Boghandel, Ltd., Nörregade 6,
KÖBENHAVN K.

FINLAND - FINLANDE
Akateeminen Kirjakauppa, Keskuskatu 2,
HELSINKI.

FORMOSA - FORMOSE
Books and Scientific Supplies Services, Ltd.
P.O.B. 83, TAPEI.
TAIWAN.

FRANCE
Bureau des Publications de l'OCDE
2, rue André-Pascal, 75 PARIS-16e
Principaux sous-dépositaires :
PARIS : Presses Universitaires de France,
49, bd Saint-Michel, 5e
Sciences Politiques (Lib.), 30, rue Saint-Guillaume,7e
13 AIX-EN-PROVENCE : Librairie de l'Université.
38 GRENOBLE : Arthaud
67 STRASBOURG : Berger-Levrault.

GERMANY - ALLEMAGNE
Deutscher Bundes-Verlag G.m.b.H.
Postfach 9380, 53 BONN.
Sub-Agents : BERLIN 62 : Elwert & Meurer.
MUNCHEN : Hueber, HAMBURG : ReuterKlöckner; und in den massgebenden Buchhandlungen Deutschlands.

GREECE - GRÈCE
LibrairieKauffmann,28,rueduStade,ATHÈNES-132.
Librairie Internationale Jean Mihalopoulos
33, rue Sainte-Sophie, THESSALONIKI

ICELAND - ISLANDE
Snæbjörn Jónsson & Co., h.f., Hafnarstræti 9,
P.O. Box 1131, REYKJAVIK.

INDIA - INDE
International Book House Ltd.,
9 Ash Lane, Mahatma Gandhi Road, BOMBAY 1.
Oxford Book and Stationery Co. :
NEW DELHI, Scindia House.
CALCUTTA, 17 Park Street.

IRELAND - IRLANDE
Eason & Son, 40-41 Lower O'Connell Street,
DUBLIN.

ISRAEL
Emanuel Brown,
35 Allenby Road, and 48 Nahlath Benjamin St.,
TEL-AVIV.

ITALY - ITALIE
Libreria Commissionaria Sansoni
Via Lamarmora 45, 50 121 FIRENZE.
Via P. Mercuri 19/B, 00 193 ROMA.
Sous-dépositaires :
Libreria Hoepli, Via Hoepli 5, 20 121 MILANO.
Librera Lattes, Via Garibaldi 3, 10 122 TORINO.
La diffusione delle edizioni OCDE è inoltre assicurata dalle migliori librerie nelle città più importanti.

JAPAN - JAPON
Maruzen Company Ltd.,
6 Tori-Nichome Nihonbashi, TOKYO.

KENYA
New Era Associates Ghale House, Government Road. P.B. 6854.
NAIROBI.

LEBANON - LIBAN
Redico
Immeuble Edison, Rue Bliss, B.P. 5641
BEYROUTH.

LUXEMBOURG
Librairie Paul Bruck, 22, Grand'Rue,
LUXEMBOURG.

MALTA - MALTE
Labour Book Shop, Workers' Memorial Building,
Old Bakery Street, VALLETTA.

MOROCCO - MAROC
Éditions La Porte, *Aux Belles Images*.
281, avenue Mohammed V, RABAT.

THE NETHERLANDS - PAYS-BAS
W.P. Van Stockum & Zoon.
Buitenhof 36, DEN HAAG.
Sub-Agents : AMSTERDAM C : Scheltema & Holkema, N.V., Rokin 74-76. ROTTERDAM : De Wester Boekhandel, Nieuwe Binnenweg 331.

NEW ZEALAND - NOUVELLE-ZÉLANDE
Government Printing Office,
20 Molesworth Street (Private Bag),WELLINGTON
and Government Bookshops at
AUCKLAND (P.O.B. 5344)
CHRISTCHURCH (P.O B. 1721)
DUNEDIN (P.O.B. 1104)

NORWAY - NORVÈGE
A/S Bokhjörnet, Akersgt. 41, OSLO 1.

PAKISTAN
Mirza Book Agency, 65, Shahrah Quaid-E-Azam,
LAHORE 3.

PORTUGAL
Livraria Portugal, Rua do Carmo 70, LISBOA.

SOUTH AFRICA - AFRIQUE DU SUD
Van Schaik's Book Store Ltd.,
Church Street, PRETORIA.

SPAIN - ESPAGNE
Mundi Prensa, Castelló 37, MADRID 1.
Libreria Bastinos de José Bosch, Pelayo 52,
BARCELONA 1.

SWEDEN - SUÈDE
Fritzes, Kungl. Hovbokhandel,
Fredsgatan 2, STOCKHOLM 16.

SWITZERLAND - SUISSE
Librairie Payot, 6, rue Grenus, 1211 GENÈVE, 11
et à LAUSANNE, NEUCHATEL, VEVEY, MONTREUX, BERNE, BALE et ZURICH.

TURKEY - TURQUIE
Librairie Hachette, 469 Istiklal Caddesi, Beyoglu,
ISTANBUL et 12 Ziya Gökalp Caddesi, ANKARA.

UNITED KINGDOM - ROYAUME-UNI
H.M. Stationery Office, P.O. Box 569, LONDON,
S.E. 1.
Branches at : EDINBURGH, BIRMINGHAM,
BRISTOL,MANCHESTER,CARDIFF,BELFAST.

UNITED STATES OF AMERICA
OECD Publications Center, Suite 1305,
1750 Pennsylvania Ave, N. W.
WASHINGTON, D.C. 20006. Tel : (202) 298-8755.

VENEZUELA
Libreria del Este, Avda F. Miranda, 52,
Edificio Galipan, CARACAS.

YUGOSLAVIA - YOUGOSLAVIE
Jugoslovenska Knjiga, Terazije 27, P.O.B. 36,
BEOGRAD.

Les commandes provenant de pays où l'OCDE n'a pas encore désigné de dépositaire
peuvent être adressées à :
OCDE, Bureau des Publications, 2, rue André-Pascal, 75 Paris (16e).
Orders and inquiries from countries where sales agents have not yet been appointed may be sent to
OECD, Publications Office, 2, rue André-Pascal, 75 Paris (16e).

OECD PUBLICATIONS
2, rue André-Pascal, Paris XVIe
No. 18,293

•

PRINTED IN SWITZERLAND